QUEER INDIA NOW

Praise for *Queer India Now*

'This is an anthology of a queer movement coming of age, rather than one about coming out. These essays reflect how far we have come, how far we need to go, and thankfully complicate our notions of what being queer is all about across class, caste, language, geography, living arrangements and many other fault lines with scholarship, empathy and joy as well. Ultimately it messes with the idea of what the well-behaved sanskari queer should aspire to, in modern post-377 India, and thus puts the queer back into queerness.'

Sandip Roy, writer and journalist

'Theoretically complex and richly textured, this volume opens up experiences and reflections on what it is to be queer in India as we enter the second quarter of the twenty-first century. From small towns to metros, from spaces of privilege to the margins. Honest in confronting difficult internal differences, imaginative in thinking through new ways of loving and living and changing the world. Moving beyond queer as related exclusively to sex or gender, the collection aims to leave the reader with "an abiding sense of queer as a practice of radical empathy." To quote the concluding words of one of the essays—imagine that.'

Nivedita Menon, feminist scholar and writer

'*Queer India Now* is a remarkable amalgamation. As if its expansive mapping of queer diversity were not enough, the book goes further—bringing together narratives and visuals as diverse as queer lives themselves, spanning past and present, marginalisations and movements. These stories are woven with care, gently grounding us in the histories we inherit and the ground we stand on today, without the weight or ostentation of opaque academic language. This is a book for queer individuals, and for all human beings in their frailty and courage. It deserves a place in our bags and on our bookshelves—to be read, carried and gifted.'

Maya Sharma, feminist activist and writer

'What work can queer do in a world and a state riven by caste-based structural inequality and economic injustices? *Queer India Now* speaks to this question with hope and heartache. Both poetic and polemical, this urgent anthology explores what it means to be queer in India today with essays and first-person vignettes that cover a wide scope from language, law, governance and healthcare to polyamory, fashion, cinema and kink. We learn of queer experiences from new vantage points, like a small town mall and a historic Delhi safe house. The anthology grounds its inheritance in a varied and complex history but also casts itself forward into previously unimaginable directions. This necessary and beautiful book holds both these realities and inspires otherwise futures.'

Naisargi N. Davé, academic and writer

QUEER INDIA NOW

EDITED BY
DHAMINI RATNAM
DHRUBO JYOTI

First published by Westland Books, a division of Nasadiya Technologies Private Limited, in 2026

No. 269/2B, First Floor, 'Irai Arul', Vimalraj Street, Nethaji Nagar, Alapakkam Main Road, Maduravoyal, Chennai 600095

Westland and the Westland logo are the trademarks of Nasadiya Technologies Private Limited, or its affiliates.

ISBN: 9789371976121

10 9 8 7 6 5 4 3 2 1

Typeset by Jojy Philip
Printed at Parksons Graphics Pvt. Ltd

CONTENTS

A Note from the Series Editor ix

Introduction xi

Where You Weren't Looking: Tales from Small-Town India 1
Dhrubo Jyoti and Dhiren Borisa

Our Place in Democracy 25
Dr B. Kiran Nayak

Amar Katha: My Life in Garbagan 32
Sintu Bagui

Straight Outta Bolangir 37
Rabi Raj

Love Mattre 43
Vijeta Kumar

Someday, I Will Be an Old Woman 52
Vqueeram Aditya Sahai

A Song of the Outcast Goddess and Her Jogati:
Manjamma, and Her Practice as Archive 58
Siddarth Shanthala Ganesh

Walk Your Own Ramp 79
Kenny Awomi

A House Where Every Child Can Be 82
Dit Thoudam

Silence, Faith and (In)Visibility 86
Dr Aijaz Ahmad Bund

Is That Any Way to Treat Someone?: A Conversation on Healing 91
Dr Aqsa Shaikh and Aryan Somaiya

The Medical Landscape of Transition: A Personal History 106
Dr Sameera Jahagirdar

Subspace 121
Written by Ammel Sharon
Illustrated by Sharanya Ravi

The 11th Direction Aka Disha Pinky Shaikh 124
Written and illustrated by Priya Dali

The Forest 132
Written and illustrated by Payal Rathva

Surviving Homelessness and a Life of Crime 137
L Ramakrishnan, Randhoni Lairikyengbam, Swetha Shri, Khush Pahuja, Amit Bisoi, Rahmathulla, Sharmista Das and Biswa Bhusan Pattanayak

Your Name, their Rules 140
Kavish Kaushik

On the Force 143
Ronit Jha

Queering the Law: An Advocate's Tale 147
Amritananda Chakravorty

What a Drag!: Reflections on Queer Joy, Euphoria, Transgression and Performance 160
Vikram Phukan

The Trans You See, and The Trans I See (And Show You) 178
Bonita Rajpurohit

Neither Monk, Nor Nun 184
Tashi Choedup

Now It all Makes Sense 187
Oviya V.

Bedrooms 194
Vasavi Kalluru

Some Things I Learnt on Bad Dates 198
Ankur Tangade

In Our Own Image: Sex in the Age of Apps 201
Prathyush Parasuraman

Begumpura 214
Shripad Sinnakaar

The Hardest Part is Letting Go of Hope 217
Susan Dias

Queering the Family, Choosing Your Kin 223
Dhamini Ratnam

About the Contributors 235

Acknowledgements 242

A NOTE FROM THE SERIES EDITOR

Welcome to Queer Directions, a collaboration between Westland and the Godrej DEI Lab.

Under this label, we hope to offer a space for new kinds of books and writing that prioritises pride, progress, imagination and joy for queer people. Westland has supported queer writing under different formats for many years, and this imprint cements its commitment to breaking barriers through writing and publishing narratives that describe, as well as reshape, our present and future. The Godrej DEI Lab (including its previous avatar, the Godrej India Culture Lab) has worked to advance inclusion for LGBTQIA+ people and other historically excluded groups within and outside the workplace for more than a decade.

I serve as the hyphen between both these organisations—a Westland author who outlined and described the contours of a queer-inclusive India in my book *Queeristan*, and also as the head of the Godrej DEI Lab. Over many conversations with Karthika, Publisher at Westland, we decided to join forces to create this imprint in 2025 to serve as a meeting ground where contemporary and future queer writing could gather.

Queer Directions recognises and builds on decades of work by publishers, both independent and corporate, and will publish work by LGBTQIA+ writers from the Indian subcontinent and diaspora, as well as work about queer South Asia that matters to readers from these groups. We seek to be as plural as possible. We believe that the truly queer direction is forward, into the future.

Join us, collaborate with us and reach out to us, as writers, readers, allies. We're here to build a bridge, not a border—a bridge to a more beautiful, inclusive and queer-friendly world.

PARMESH SHAHANI

INTRODUCTION

Queer India Now!

What does it mean to be queer today? Or, put another way, what does it mean to be queer today compared to 165 years ago? Or, even fifteen years ago?

The answer is layered and complex. Some possess legal recognition for their right to live, but lack real, ground-up entitlements that are needed to actually live a life of dignity. Some find their rights rendered brittle by the vicissitudes of structural oppression. And still others find themselves erased from the imagination of the state, or criminalised and hounded.

The Transgender Persons (Protection of Rights) Amendment Act, 2026, passed in March, systematically disempowers many self-perceived gender identities—gender queer, non-binary, trans men as well as a clutch of socio-cultural ones—making their access to critical healthcare and accurate documentation even more precarious. It inserts layers of bureaucracy into life-affirming care and threatens to criminalise every queer person and ally with vague but punitive language, cloaking colonial anxieties about the unfamiliar in modern, but regressive, attire.

To be queer today, therefore, is to have a love that finally dares to speak its name,[1] but no real legal protection or sanction to realise it. That's not for the lack of trying, though.

Over the last three decades, the Lesbian, Gay, Bisexual, Transgender, Queer, Intersex, Asexual (LGBTQIA+) communities have made ground-breaking strides towards their hope of leading a life of dignity and respect. This includes the 2009 Delhi high court verdict that first decriminalised homosexuality,[2] the Supreme Court's 2014 *NALSA vs. Union of India* judgment,[3] the 2018 Navtej Johar verdict of the Supreme Court that led to the decriminalisation of consensual same-sex relationships,[4] the Transgender Persons (Protection of Rights) Act, 2019 [5], and a bouquet of court rulings that upheld our rights to life, liberty, non-discrimination and equality. These steps have often been polyphonous—for instance, the recent amendments sparked nationwide protests and multiple legal challenges—but the singular desire for rights and recognition is unmistakable.

Young people use courage and irreverence in smashing fossilised ideas of how one should look, feel, act, run, behave and live. Small-town India stares down social censure in starting Pride parades. Section 377 is read down. Conversations on gender, sexuality and equitable relationships are everywhere. Apps glow with possibility in the darkness of bedrooms and parks, airports and colleges. Cafes and bookstores, pubs and dance floors pulse with joy, curated families are chosen and cherished. Cinema now, finally, occasionally, whispers our stories on screen. We have literature, art and activism that refuse erasure and affirm that we are here as we have always been.

Yet, the egregious changes to a law, ostensibly meant to protect trans persons, show how brittle our victories can be. As a hurricane of anti-queer/trans bigotry sweeps up momentum across the globe, those left most vulnerable by this wrecking ball are those wedged between social censure and state apathy—think of the large swathes of people left out of the purview of the reconfigured definition of transgender, and the predicament of those offering support and community, who now fear being brought under the lens of penal scrutiny. Those who do fall within the narrow definition offered by the law must offer up their bodies to medical and state examination for certification and further necessary documentation. The demand by transgender people for horizontal reservation and dignified medical care hangs in the air. Shelter homes, or Garima Grehas, born of a 2020 government scheme, face financial difficulties, police ignorance and violence from birth families of its residents. The top court's denial of marriage equality still stings [6]; the police continue to lodge false cases to separate same-sex partners; queer people are still forced to undergo spurious and harmful medical practices such as so-called conversion therapy and electroshock therapy. We have no legal recognition of our partnerships, families or children. We cannot make medical decisions for the person who knows our heartbeat better than their own. Offices and classrooms continue to penalise those who they think of as 'shameful'. Many of us face ignominies for being from the margins. For hundreds of millions of our fellow citizens, queerness remains unspeakable, a shame to be buried deep. And with constitutional morality—that foundational concept that illustrated the promise made by the republic to its citizens, of a life of dignity—under attack, people of various expressions and identities might reasonably believe the road to a fulfilling life is narrowing.

So, what does it truly mean to be queer today? If it feels difficult to pin down, it is probably because we live suspended between two worlds that refuse to reconcile: Holding someone's hand and deleting an insulting message on the bio-family WhatsApp group with the other. It is the electric thrill of dancing at a Pride parade, confetti in your hair, and then the unbearable silence of the public bathroom where you change into someone you don't recognise, editing yourself at the workplace sentence by sentence until you become a translation of a person. It is both, feeling pride and conviction in your truth, but also suppressing gurgling bubbles of fear about the future in an increasingly hostile world.

To be sure and then not, happy and then not, foot leaden, unable to move forward for no fault of your own.

This anthology won't attempt an answer. Instead, we will present you with a mosaic of snapshots of what it is to be queer today. These pieces hold up a mirror in which, we hope, the reader will be able to view not only themselves, but also the backdrop that forms the landscape of our collective lives.

When we began our careers in the 2000s, the word 'gay' was a shorthand for an entire set of identities. Words such as 'transvestite' and 'transsexual', or acronyms such as 'FTM' or 'MTF' (that is, female-to-male or male-to-female)—now dead terms—were used as synonyms of 'transgender'. Gender affirmative surgeries were referred to as sexual reassignment surgeries. 'Lesbian' was sometimes considered a pejorative; 'gender-queer' and 'non-binary' were in limited circulation. Then, in the mid-to-late 2000s, activists associated with the legal struggle against Section 377 began to formulate and/or excavate words in Hindi in their effort to create literature on gender and sexuality;[7] others produced pamphlets to train media across vernacular and English-language publications and television channels.

To be sure, the fight for recognition and the right to name one's desires long precedes the decriminalisation of homosexuality. Within women's movements, lesbians, who had been denied the space to speak of matters like sexual desire, spoke up at the annual autonomous women's conference held in 1994 in Tirupati, and argued that they were done hiding under the garb of single women, and deserved a space of their own to discuss their issues within the conference. This led to a showdown and anti-lesbian protests by feminist activists.[8] The question of dignity—which would go on to become the central theme of the LGBTQIA+ movements—was pioneered and foregrounded by people dreaming of a future free from the stench of caste for 200 years.

Social movements around language changed how we imagine queer-trans lives, whether through the self-respect efforts, building on vocabulary like Thirunangai/Thirunambi, or the magical lifeworld of Ulti or Farsi, or other tongues used by trans persons within their communities. The words in circulation today have also come from more recent sources: from reclaimed pejoratives to terms formulated by international non-governmental organisations and the World Health Organisation around HIV/AIDS prevention, such as MSM (men who have sex with men), now a commonly used identity term.

These shifts are epochal. For us, as editors, the complexity of putting this selection together lay in comprehending what queer means, especially in our contemporary times marked by rapid cultural shifts in lexicon, policy and culture. How does queerness fit into the cataclysmic changes that took place in the country post-liberalisation? How did it converse with people's movements both young and old? Whether it is the rise of the so-called middle class, collectives such as India Against Corruption that claimed to espouse non-political causes (but held an anti-reservation, meritist mindset close to its chest), the blizzard of street agitations on causes ranging from the 2012 Delhi gang rape protests to Armed Forces Special Powers Act (AFSPA) and the atrocities in Kashmir or Manipur, the tsunami of electoral support for the right-wing, the subsequent churn in universities or the prolonged detention of political prisoners, queer movements have been moulded by the same forces that have shaped modern India. Queerness today (as always) reflects the fault lines of society, whether they are on questions of politics and ideology, caste and food practices or how we dress and present ourselves. Disagreements have led to splinters in the movements and even multiple Pride events in the same city. Right-wing ideologies and faith-based assertion are now commonplace among sections of the community—as in the rest of the country—whether in people aligned with the government or those leading religious 'akhadas' or deriving pride in religion and caste. By using their personal stories of devotion, or arguing for inclusion using the same language of faith as those in power, many of these new religious leaders have gained popularity among ordinary people, while also triggering deep divisions. The deification of the trans body—seen among the thousands who seek blessings in kinnar akharas during the Kumbh Mela, as well as in the speeches of ruling party lawmakers who reference mythological characters to speak of the regard that must accrue to transgender persons—can be juxtaposed against the vociferous demands from trans persons to first be counted as human, offering a stinging indictment of state and institutional apathy towards them.

These fractures are not unique to India. Queer people the world over grapple with similar questions of identity, politics, discrimination, war, occupation and race. Movements only reflect the society they spring from—no worse, but certainly, no better. Moreover, the sheer ease with which we have available to us information that is potentially biased or false, but is algorithmically supplied to us to fit our worldviews, means that how we experience queerness today is vastly different from even a decade ago.

In 1884, an unusual case came up before the colonial Allahabad High Court. For months, the police had been tailing a person named Khairati on the suspicion that they were a 'eunuch' after being tipped off that on a visit to their ancestral village, they were found dancing and singing 'dressed as a woman'. A scandalous trial ensued. The British Raj hauled Khairati before its surgeons and magistrates, turning their anatomy into evidence. 'He is shown to have the characteristic mark of a habitual catamite—the distortion of the orifice of the anus into the shape of a trumpet... which distinctly points to unnatural intercourse within the last few months,' noted the judgement by the ironically (or aptly) named Justice Straight. The case was eventually dismissed because the paperwork was sloppy and the indictment forgot to name when or where or with whom this supposed crime occurred. But the judge took pains to commend the police for stomping on such 'disgusting practices'.

Queen Empress vs. Khairati [9] is considered to be when Section 377 first drew blood, in the sense that a body that wore the wrong garments and desired the wrong intimacies received stiff legal opprobrium. Over the next 150 years, the law blurred the lines between moral policing and justice, mapped identities that were most vulnerable to its bite, forcing us to confront the question of whether the provision was meant to criminalise the act of sodomy—or the people who appeared likely to commit this offence? Was there any difference?

If Khairati etched one epoch in tortured colonial understandings of gender and sexuality, Bhoorah marked the other. A guru within the discipleship lineage of the Hijra community, Bhoorah lived with her two chelas, Dullah and Mathee, in Mainpuri town. Her other companion was her lover Ali Buksh, before she left him for another man. On August 17, 1852, Ali Buksh forced Bhoorah to return to him. Neighbours saw the couple arguing in the street before entering their house. Hours later, Bhoorah's disciple Dullah ran out into the street, shouting that Ali Buksh had murdered Bhoorah. The Mainpuri Sessions Court, and subsequently the Nizamat Adalat — the highest provincial court at the time — tried Ali Buksh and Dullah. Ali Buksh was convicted of murder after the judges declared that he killed Bhoorah due to the 'severance' of their 'infamous connexion'. But something more sinister was afoot.

As Jessica Hinchy noted in *Governing Gender and Sexuality in Colonial India*, the judges were alarmed at the presence of transgender people, variously describing them as 'beggars' and 'unnatural prostitutes', seen as an 'opprobrium' and a 'reproach' to the British government. 'The sickening details of this case involve the disgusting exposure of an abominable trade of unnatural prostitution regularly carried on by eunuchs dressed as women,' said Unwin, the sessions court judge.

Over the next decade, the flood of anxiety unlocked by Bhoorah's murder calcified into a policy for the regulation and ultimately extermination of the transgender community–Part II of the Criminal Tribes Act (CTA), which mandated police registers of'eunuchs', expanded surveillance of these communities, banned 'men' from wearing women's clothing or performing in public, and asked authorities to remove children in transgender-populated households. CTA was repealed after independence, but as the new trans law has shown, the kernel of bias continues to thrive 174 years later.

Go further back in time to 1835, and you find Thomas Babbington Macaulay, the then president of the Indian Law Commission, calling homosexuality 'an odious class of offences'. 'So revolting' was the subject, he wrote, that 'the injury which would be done to the morals of the community by such discussion would far more than compensate for any benefits which might be derived from legislative measures framed with the greatest precision'. And yet, in 1861, he went on to codify a law in the Indian Penal Code which not only conflated bestiality with homosexuality, but also negated the very thing that forms the bedrock of sexual relationships between adults: consent. Section 377 made homosexual sex synonymous to rape and equated homosexuality with sexual perversity.

Sodomy, a biblical abhorrence, was already to be associated with a certain type of 'oriental vice' by the time Macaulay was tasked with developing the penal code.[10] He merely wrote and codified laws as part of a racialised imperial project[11] that gained supremacy through the engines of science (Charles Darwin's theory of evolution), institutionalised religion (Christian missionary projects) and commerce (English East India Company).

This is what Section 377 stated: 'Whoever voluntarily has carnal intercourse against the order of nature with any man, woman or animal shall be punished with imprisonment for life, or with imprisonment of either description for a term which may extend to ten years, and shall be liable to fine. Explanation: Penetration is sufficient to constitute the carnal intercourse necessary to the offence described in this section.'

Of course, this connection between communities and criminality, personhood and pollution is not alien to us. The ritual dehumanisation of some groups already formed the social bedrock of India far before Macaulay; neither homophobia nor colonialism birthed it. The geometry of caste turned water into a boundary between human and less-than-human, codified cruelty into law and condemned some bodies into supposed carriers of pollution. No wonder that this habitual denial of dignity ossified into sociolegal logic, rendering impossible even the imagination that those whose shadows you abhorred, whom you forced to scrape off refuse, could possess interiority, ambition, heartbreak and humanity. Dr Bhimrao Ramji Ambedkar's [12] revolution—whether it be in smashing the barrier around access to a water tank in 1927 or laying down a new playbook for the annihilation of caste in 1936—repeatedly underlined this simple truth; that prejudice cannot flourish on fallow soil. The complex interplay of social attitudes and cultural practices in which dehumanisation was de rigueur made sexuality and gender sites for the enactment of caste privilege long before colonialism added its own peculiar brand of racial prejudice and misogyny to the mix.[13]

Fast forward to a little over a century and a half later, in 1987, when two policewomen in Madhya Pradesh became famous overnight. Leela Namdeo and Urmila Srivastava met on the job and fell for each other. One winter afternoon in Sagar, accompanied by a few trusted friends, they entered a temple, exchanged vows and placed flower garlands around each other's necks in a quiet gandharva ceremony. They even posed for a studio wedding portrait before returning to their posts.

But the photo leaked and society reacted with fury. Branded a 'bad influence', they were dismissed and briefly jailed, but drew a curious reaction from some neighbours. In *Love's Rite: Same Sex Marriage in India and the West* (Penguin Random House, 2005), author Ruth Vanita recounted a local woman asking, 'After all, what is marriage? It is a wedding of two souls. Where in the scriptures is it said that it has to be between a man and a woman?' Such implicit acceptance co-existed with the varied nuanced feminist positions that the autonomous women's movement came to formulate over the 'lesbian marriage', including one that opposed all discussion on it.[14]

Over 35 years on, supporters and detractors of the recent marriage equality petitions reiterate the need to recognise the viability of a same-sex relationship, on the one hand, and of the larger structural inequalities that beset queer individuals even today, on the other.

In what way has the social life of the law, which ensured that Khairati's behaviour marked them as a criminal and Bhoorah's murder criminalised no one but their own community, changed? After all, it doesn't take a law to inscribe deviance onto the bodies of people who look, or talk, or walk differently; prejudice is enough. Who among us can claim respectability and remain unaffected by the social side of the law? Who can do without struggling for broader civil rights? Who enters the room and who sits at the table? What does the shift towards demanding personal rights (marriage, adoption, tax benefits) over public ones (education, employment, health) mean? What does progress mean when the State can erase every painstaking stride with callousness? Whose comfort is privileged over whose survival?

The writers of these pieces bring up these questions, and offer, by way of answers, their own experiences. We hope that you will also find it remarkable how far we've come even if sometimes it doesn't seem like we have covered much distance at all.

Part of the collection are essays that frame the concerns of contemporary queer India: on dating and sex; language; relational networks; performance (whether as drag or as dance, rooted in local cultures); on the chasm between small-town India and its megapolises; on the pathologisation of the trans body, especially now, in light of the new Act; on why a dialogue between physical and mental health practitioners is vital; and finally, without full legal equality, what being queer might really mean.

We begin in the small towns, where the crevices of normativity house green shoots of queerness. 'Where You Weren't Looking' presents four snapshots of the delicious melee that queerness is when you go outside the metropolis. 'Our Place in Democracy' spotlights the disability rights movement as an adivasi trans man. 'Amar Katha' resists the social censure on sex work and workers. 'Straight Outta Bolangir' details the painstaking work of building a rural queer collective. 'Love Mattre' talks about using the malleability of language to challenge masculinity, prying open a little space for homosociality and, dare we say it, queerness.

We then move to art, aging, desire and longing—even when battling hostility. 'Someday I Will Be an Old Woman' explores aging, queerness, longing and love. 'A Song of the Outcast Goddess and Her Jogati' uses conversations with Padma Shri laureate B. Manjamma Jogathi to illustrate the extraordinary life of an artist who transformed the Yellammanāṭa artform in to the theatrical spectacle it is today. 'Walk Your Own Ramp' is a practical guide for young queer people in fashion. 'A House Where Every Child Can Be' narrates the experience of an intersex person managing a shelter home. 'Silence, Faith and (In)visibility' underlines the many contradictions in the life of a queer Kashmiri person.

Across the works of three artists, we see a kaleidoscope of queerness. 'Subspace' spotlights a liberatory experience of kink and aftercare. In a Warli dreamscape, 'The Forest' imagines a queer person escaping their home prison. 'The 11th Direction' illustrates the extraordinary journey of politician Disha Pinky Shaikh.

But what has been achieved? Tangible strides forward are interspersed with official apathy and patchy responses. A conversation titled 'Is That Any Way to Treat Someone?' discusses healthcare for trans and queer people, the relationship between mental and physical healthcare, and what care for queer people should look like, even when legislatures don't offer the sort of support or protection they are meant to. 'A Personal History of the Medical Landscape of Transition' is about coming to terms with trans identities, and undergoing surgery at a time when there were no protocols around how to conduct such surgeries and long before the 2019 law. 'Surviving Homelessness and a Life of Crime' talks about vulnerable young people and their struggle with government attitudes. 'Your Name, Their Rules' details the travails of negotiating the bureaucracy gatekeeping trans identities in rural Haryana. 'On the Force' describes the various real and proverbial hoops trans men have to jump through in a police recruitment exam.

Queerness today envelops a diverse gamut of experiences. 'Queering the Law: An Advocate's Tale' talks about the social life of the law in the courtrooms and its corridors, and why, despite constitutional morality, unfamiliar bodies and genders are still treated with judicial indifference. 'What a Drag!' shines a spotlight on drag performances and queer parties that are reminders of not just the fragility of queer visibility and expression but also of the sheer irrepressible nature of joy. 'The Trans You See, and the Trans I See (And Show You)' talks about the call of the camera. 'Now It All Makes Sense' speaks of the experience of an ace person seeking love and friendship. 'Bedrooms' draws tender circles around caste, mental health and gender. 'Some Things I Learnt on Bad Dates' cracks a joke or two at our expense. 'In Our Own Image' delves into the changing nature of sex against the backdrop of the new sexual economy of dating apps, where the denizen is not all body, but mostly image. 'The 11th Direction' illustrates the extraordinary journey of politician Disha Pinky Shaikh. 'Begumpura' stitches together experiences of the city and caste. 'The Hardest Part is Letting Go of Hope' explains the daily struggles of a queer couple in the absence of real entitlements, and what it's like to carry on with everyday life after being told that marriage is not a fundamental right. And 'Queering the Family, Choosing Your Kin' shows how chosen family networks can provide care but also emotional, financial or medical support in the absence of legal and natal family recognition, even when their own existence is fragile.

These pieces do not purport to offer a definitive queer experience, because there cannot be one. An incident that took place shortly before the Supreme Court began hearing the Navtej Johar petitions, in May 2018, reflected the fissures. A group of people associated with the fight against Section 377 had gathered at the Constitution Club in New Delhi. Seated across a large rectangular glass table, a young Dalit gay man quietly said that he felt he had nothing in common with the community, whose upper-caste politics he deplored. Another activist stated that the bigger battle was against the rising tide of Hindutva politics in the country.

Referring to another person sitting in the same room—whose political ideologies were understood to lean right—he said that the fight against Section 377 was the only reason they would ever share space.

In drawing rooms and Pride parades, Sulabh cubbyholes and hostel rooms, ideologies have diverged. Many Dalit queer people showed that sexuality meant little more than a performance of caste,[15] and that alienation and hurt inflicted by caste didn't make a distinction between homosexual and heterosexual. Some ask, how much work can queer do?[16] Does it mean anything to be queer in a society where touch was once regulated by the accident of birth and desire,[17] and still is? Can you be queer when no one will rent you a home, not just because of your sexuality but because of their excavation of your last name, because of the imagined odours of your kitchen or the food in your fridge? Some believe the movement has been gatekept from younger people who don't hail from big cities, don't speak English, or don't have money to go to the parties. Others bemoan the lack of unity necessary to fight for full citizenship and the rights that could make everyone's lives better. Some think we aren't being practical enough, or making enough allies; others want to focus on a more equitable, if somewhat unattainable goal; some feel frustrated by strategies that privilege the legal and the individual, and others believe bridging fissures in the face of an existential threat should take precedence.

At the same time, queer mobilisation has also meant thousands of hours of nameless, faceless toil such as late-night crisis calls, traffic management of pride parades, tense negotiations with the police for protest permissions, phone calls to friendly doctors, professors, therapists and lawyers to help other members of the community out. It has offered a scaffolding to countless in their moments of utter alienation, and an ideological hook from which to critique the orthodoxies of even progressive and liberal politics. In the interstices of disagreements reside pockets of air that let people from the margins breathe. It can take the form of a scream from a protest stage or tears quietly streaming down one masked face in the crowd. Neatness is not always a friend of democracy.

Why did a movement come into being in the first place? Sometime in the late 1980s, as the Human Immunodeficiency Virus (HIV), that led to the deadly Acquired Immunodeficiency Syndrome (AIDS), became a global pandemic, the law—and the lack of justice—became a site of contestation, as evidenced by a booklet published in 1991. Brought out by the AIDS Bhedbhav Virodhi Andolan (ABVA), the seventy-pager, with a pink cover, titled 'Less Than Gay: A Citizen's Report on the Status of Homosexuality in India', was a first-of-its-kind document which broke the silence around queer lives. 'Many people deny that homosexuality exists in India ... Others label it a disease ... The present report has been prepared to show how none of these views can stand the test of empirical reality or plain and simple common sense,' it stated boldly. One of its main authors, Siddharth Gautam, who died shortly before the booklet was published, inspired many queer feminist activists who went on to memorialise him by starting what is widely considered to be the first film festival on queer issues, in 1993.

The death of Dominic D'Souza, a young HIV/AIDS rights activist, often referred to as Goa's Patient Zero, also galvanised a young human rights lawyer, Anand Grover, to work in the field of HIV legislation. A decade later, it was Grover who represented Naz Foundation India[18] in its petition against Section 377.

Socially, too, things were changing. In 1990, Ashok Row Kavi—who had come out as a gay man in an interview to *Savvy* in 1986—founded *Bombay Dost*, India's first openly queer magazine. Around the same time, Delhi activist Giti Thadani created Sakhi, a postal network for lesbian women. Advertised in *Bombay Dost* Sakhi soon received letters from big cities and small towns alike.

In Tamil Nadu, the Koovagam festival, where trans persons ritually marry Aravan, one of the sons of Arjuna, and then mourn his death, was already drawing crowds from beyond the state. And trans communities continued to pave the way for the rest with their courage and braving of social and state violence—like they've done since forever, without support or attention.

Through the 1990s, informal support circles blossomed into community spaces. From Kolkata (then Calcutta), Lucknow, Patna, Delhi, Bhopal, to Mumbai (then Bombay), Pune, and Bengaluru (then Bangalore), queer people formed groups to meet in safety, and set up systems for connection and help during crises, like PO box numbers or telephone hotlines to assist those facing mental and physical assault. Delhi's Jagori nurtured networks of single women; Mumbai's Women to Women began in 1995, after years of correspondence between strangers; and letters poured into pen-pal organisations like Kolkata's Counsel Club, in 1993. Some of the voices were heartbreakingly direct. In 1991, Anuja wrote to a PO Box number from Allahabad: 'We are very few lesbians here ... Please let me have some addresses of lesbian sisters.' Another, an anonymous voice from Jammu, said: 'You are my only hope.'[19]

As Pawan Dhall noted in 'Out of Line and Offline: Queer Movements in 90s Eastern India', yellowing envelopes and inland letters became 'a repository of the desires, doubts and aspirations' of queer India. A crucial cog of this network was *Trikone Magazine*, started in January 1986 in the Bay Area by Arvind Kumar and Suvir Das, as well as the Deepa Mehta film *Fire*, and the right-wing protests in 1998 against the depiction of lesbianism in it. In local magazines, pen pal columns became conduits of desire and friendship, morphing a decade later, into the heady internet chatrooms where anonymity and pleasure formed a volatile cocktail.

The road towards decriminalisation of homosexuality was arduous, and included two attempts at striking down the law—one, a public interest litigation by ABVA filed in 1994 that languished and was ultimately dismissed, and another, a petition by Naz Foundation that snaked its way through the Delhi High Court for nearly a decade, was chucked out, brought back, sent to the back of the row, retrieved, and finally, found success in 2009.

While the Supreme Court decided to shut the closet door in 2013 by reversing the Delhi High Court's judgment, the four-year period had exposed contemporary society to the 'normalcy' of something that had been considered deviant and perverse for more than a century. What's more, such exposure also allowed other conversations around gender and sexuality to flourish: the community found allies in common people: school teachers, college professors, doctors, businesses, human resource departments of multinational corporations, politicians, journalists and even religious leaders. Many nights and days were spent locked in consultations, picnics, parties and dinners that melted into breakfasts pulling apart the minutiae of language, rights, the law and community demands—what it meant to go to the court, to think of oneself as a queer citizen, to ask for rights, to live in India, to be a queer Indian.

Of course, there were detractors. Astrologer Suresh Kumar Koushal, the most notorious among them, challenged the Delhi High Court's verdict. No one has still forgotten the scars of 2001, when activists in Lucknow were arrested by the police, thrashed and humiliated—all for the crime of distributing condoms and possessing literature of safe sex and HIV/AIDS.[20] Yet, the voices that grew in support only multiplied, made louder by social media platforms and media. When two judges taunted the communities as a 'minuscule minority', Global Day of Rage protests across the world roared back against the unbearable wrong of Koushal. Among them was a young teenager who had travelled alone all the way from Udaipur to Delhi for the judgement, had changed in the bus into his best shirt, shouting the loudest slogans at the back, fire in his heart. 'This is the first time in my life I have met anyone else who is gay. I know you all are sad, but you don't know what this means to me,' he told one of us.

The next year, we were back before the same altar. The Supreme Court, in *National Legal Services Authority vs. Union of India*, marked a landmark in Indian constitutional law, recognising transgender persons as a 'third gender' and affirming their fundamental rights, holding that gender identity is integral to constitutional dignity and autonomy. It famously declared that gender identity is 'an innate perception of one's gender,' and cannot be reduced to biological criteria. Justices K.S. Radhakrishnan and A.K. Sikri recognised that fundamental rights apply to 'all persons,' thereby including transgender individuals within the scope of equality and freedom protections. 'We, therefore, declare that transgender persons have the right to decide their self-identified gender and the Centre and State Governments are directed to grant legal recognition of their gender identity such as male, female or as third gender,' the court declared. Its declarations remain at the heart of the protests against the new trans rights law.

By the time a crop of lawyers[21] brought petitions from the LGBTQIA+ community to the top court between 2016 and 2018, the world in which people openly spoke of their identities and the society that understood these identities was vastly different from that of 1835, 1861, 1949, 2009 and even 2013.[22]

On 6 September, 2018, a five-judge bench ruled favourably on a batch of petitions filed by thirty-four individual petitioners as well as interventions filed by Naz, parents of queer persons and Voices Against 377, a collective of human rights groups, among others. Justice Indu Malhotra, the lone woman judge of the Constitution bench, was particularly effusive. 'History owes an apology to the members of this community and their families, for the delay in providing redressal for the ignominy and ostracism that they have suffered through the centuries.'

Queer lives have always flitted in and out of the shadows long before the current crop of identity terms came into existence, in laundebazi, masti, mitr, saheli, in the delicious uncertainty of aadat, rangeen, shauk, marz or lat, and in the puzzling mundanity of 'they were always roommates' or 'lifelong bachelor'. Film and books have captured nuances of our lives, right from when Pandey Bechan Sharma 'Ugra' was describing beautiful boys in 'Chocolate' in the 1920s, to the rustle of Ismat Chugtai's 'Lihaaf' in 1944 to the arm squeezes and longing looks between a truck driver and the younger man whom he takes under his wing in Prem Kapoor's *Badnaam Basti* (1971) and the electric triangle of Bapu, Mitra and Nama of Vijay Tendulkar's *Mitrachi Goshta* in 1981.

Maya Sharma, a queer and feminist activist, who has worked for decades in Gujarat, has written about the practice of 'Maitri Karar', a contractual agreement that indicated a financial arrangement between two people. Though employed by heterosexual men to validate their relationships with women who are not married to them, Sharma found that Maitri Karar was often used by same-sex couples too.[23] Scholars Saleem Kidwai and Ruth Vanita trace the arc of same-sex desire in various literary texts across languages, from the religious to the contemporary.[24] Hijra characters have been appearing (though often caricaturised) in movies since at least the 1940s.

In 1999, when the first anthology of lesbian writings from India came out—edited by Ashwini Sukthankar, it was titled *Facing the Mirror*—many writers included in that voluminous book wrote under pen names, but the issues they wrote about held up a mirror to their times. Other anthologies and memoirs followed. In 2000, poet Hoshang Merchant released an edited volume of gay writing termed *Yaarana*. The following year, Ruth Vanita and Saleem Kidwai chronicled the journey of queer literature in India. In Delhi, *Myself Mona Ahmad* opened a new kind of visual and textual storytelling around an extraordinary life. In 2002, Manju Kapoor released *A Married Woman* and the next year, R. Raj Rao burst on to the literary scene with his searing *The Boyfriend*. *Because I Have a Voice*, *Cobalt Blue* and *Gay Bombay* all came out in quick succession, changing the face of queer publishing in India. Whether it be the autobiographies of A. Revathi, Living Smile Vidya or Santa Khurai, children's books by Suniti Namjoshi and Shals Mahajan, fiction by Firdaus Kanga and Parvati Sharma or the blizzard of small magazines, zines by groups such as Tarshi, Varta and Sappho for Equality, writings on queer lives and/or by queer writers proliferate. More recently, *The World that Belongs to Us* (HarperCollins, 2020), an anthology of poems, offered us a grounding in our present.

As we put our anthology together, we found that queer means many things. It is the steel in the spine and the fire in the heart that young people, running away from their biological families, suddenly find. It is the culture that takes root when students colour Pride parades blue, and shout slogans that stretch the rainbow across the sky, and when strangers sit on chairs next to each other for hours, making pamphlets, writing petitions and debating terms. It is groups of trans folks zigzagging across the country to meet politicians to lobby for their rights, all because they dream of building a better world for everyone. It is the friendships between people who love each other more tenderly than any bloodline could guarantee, dispelling the dark clouds of loneliness and aging. It is people holding each other in doubt and despair one afternoon at Delhi's Jantar Mantar, the sun searing overhead, assuring each other of a better life, even if their elected representatives won't imagine it.

We hope that this book helps situate queer as more than sexual orientation, gender identity and sex characteristics, and that our readers are left with an abiding sense of queer as a practice of radical empathy; a lens with which to view intersecting marginalisations; a prod to one's psyche to acknowledge, and humanise, the other; a multidirectional view of the past and multiple futures. Queer is, after all, hope, forever evolving.

Notes

1. The line comes from the 1892 poem, *Two Loves*, by Lord Alfred Douglas, the lover of poet Oscar Wilde, and was used to describe homosexual love.
2. On 2 July 2009, a two-judge bench of the Delhi high court comprising the then Chief Justice A.P. Shah and Justice S. Muralidhar found Section 377 of the erstwhile Indian Penal Code (IPC) to be unconstitutional and ruled that it should apply only to non-consensual penile non-vaginal sex and penile non-vaginal sex involving minors. Since the high court is a constitutional court, its judgement applied to all states. The judgement came after years of community mobilisation against Section 377. In 2013, a two-judge bench of the Supreme Court comprising Justices G.S. Singhvi and S.J. Mukhopadhaya heard several petitions challenging the Delhi High Court verdict, and ruled to reinstate Section 377 in what came to be called the Suresh Kumar Koushal case, named after the main petitioner. The bench found that the number of people affected by the law was a 'miniscule minority'.
3. On 15 April 2014, a two-judge bench of the Supreme Court comprising Justices A.K. Sikri and K.S. Radhakrishnan declared that transgender persons have the right to self-identify their gender, and directed the Centre and states to grant them legal recognition under a third gender category. The judgement was hailed as path-breaking because it not only ascribed agency to the trans person, but also because it did not seek validation of gender identity from any medical institution. The

verdict was called NALSA after the original petitioner, the National Legal Services Authority which challenged the Union of India in the matter of discrimination towards transgender persons.

4. *Navtej Johar and Others vs. the Union of India*, referred also as the Navtej Johar case, refers to the 6 September 2018 verdict that decriminalised consensual adult same sex relationships. A five-judge constitutional bench of the Supreme Court read down the colonial law after hearing a fresh set of petitions challenging it, including one brought by Bharatnayam dancer Navtej Johar, his partner Sunil Mehra, chef Ritu Dalmia, hotelier Aman Nath and Ayesha Kapur. Soon, other petitioners also joined the case, including activist Arif Jafar, who was jailed in 2001 under Section 377 for distributing condoms and possessing literature on male sexual health. Jafar ran Naz Foundation International, a non-governmental organisation that worked in the field of HIV/AIDS awareness.
5. In December 2019, the Transgender Persons (Protection of Rights) Act was passed after several rounds of agitation, protests and community consultations on previous iterations. The act upheld the NALSA judgement by recognising self-perceived gender identity, and laid down a procedure for legal identification that involved medical and state certification. It promised measures to ensure trans persons are not denied their rights and entitlements such as to education and employment, but stayed silent on significant issues like adoption, marriage and discrimination. It also offered a lowered punishment to perpetrators of crimes against trans persons. Over the years the government came up with directives to state governments on gender reassignment surgeries as well as shelter homes, and even made provisions for a national council on transgender affairs. However, in March 2026, the Union Social Justice and Welfare minister introduced a bill with amendments to the Transgender Persons Act, which narrowed the definition of transgender, wrongly conflated it to persons with intersex variations and differences in sexual development, and introduced stringent penalty clauses for persons found to 'allure' or 'force' someone into gender affirmation surgeries, among other things. The bill was passed despite strong debates within the Parliament, and

several protests and public hearings conducted by transgender activists across the country.

6. In 2023, the Supreme Court of India denied fifty-two petitions (*Supriyo@Supriya Chakraborty & Anr. vs. Union of India*) seeking changes in the various secular and religious marriage laws, dashing the hopes of many seeking marriage equality. The petitions brought up a host of issues like ease of adoption, joint bank accounts, tax concessions, insurance benefits and end-of-life decisions, among other things that partners in same-sex relationships simply did not enjoy on account of not being considered each other's spouses.
7. Delhi-based Nirantar Trust, which worked in the area of gender and sexuality education, particularly among girls and women in urban and rural areas, produced booklets called 'Khulti Parte, Yaunikta aur Hum' in 2011. Even before that, the Nirantar Trust was part of a group of NGOs working in the field of children's rights, human rights, health, law and gender and sexuality, which called themselves Voices Against 377. The group produced a Hindi booklet titled 'Adhikaar Ho Sabke Liye: Dhara 377 Ke Tahit Yaunikta Aadhaarit Bhedbhav Ko Khatam Karne Ki Aur' in 2005, in which a detailed socio-legal argument against the colonial law was presented.
8. The first meeting of women who love women which can be traced back to 1990, during the Calicut Conference of autonomous women's movement. It was organised by women's groups like Jagori who were working on single women's issues. At that time the language of sexuality was missing and what was used instead was something on the lines of—women loving other women, women outside the family structure, etc. In 1994, at the conference, this time in Tirupati, a group of same-sex desiring women met on the sidelines of the women's conference, and faced a great deal of resistance from 'antilesbian protestors'. 'This inaugural gathering of lesbians and bisexuals within the auspices of the national women's movement created a chasm between heterosexual and non-heterosexual feminists—a distinction that I do not believe had previously existed at the national movement level.' Read more here: https://nazariyaqfrg.wordpress.com/2020/09/11/our-lives-our-tales-documenting-early-queer-activism in-india/ and in Naisargi

Dave's book, *Queer Activism in India: A Study in the Anthropology of Ethics*.

9. Read Alok Gupta, 'Section 377 and the Dignity of Indian Homosexuals', *Economic and Political Weekly*, 18 November 2006, https://www.iglhrc.org/sites/default/files/15-1.pdf
10. Alok Gupta, 'Section 377 and the Dignity of Indian Homosexuals', *Economic and Political Weekly*, 18 November, 2006. The piece examined how the proscription of 'carnal intercourse against the order of nature' under Section 377 of the Indian Penal Code, 1860 makes criminals out of homosexuals.
11. *Colonial Desire: Hybridity in Theory, Culture and Race* (1995) by Robert Young offers a deeper dive on how race became the common principle of academic knowledge in the nineteenth century.
12. *The Annihilation of Caste*, Dr Bhimrao Ramji Ambedkar, the architect of the Indian Constitution and the first law minister of independent India, 1936.
13. Dr B.R. Ambedkar, who headed the drafting committee of the constituent assembly tasked to come up with the Constitution of independent India, wrote in the 1930s that caste was not simply 'a division of labour' as its supporters claimed, but a 'division of labourers'. In 'The Annihilation of Caste'—written first as a speech for the annual lecture of a Hindu reformist group, the Jat-Pat Todak Mandal, but which remained undelivered as the members found its contents 'unbearable'—Ambedkar offered an impeccably logical take down of the chaturvarnya (the fourcaste structure), which, he pointed out astutely, also offered no clarity on what happens to women in such a system.
14. Leela and Urmila's wedding resulted in sharp debates among different groups of the autonomous women's movement. Some, like the Forum Against the Oppression of Women (FAOW, formerly Forum Against Rape) declared their marriage to be a viable alternative to heterosexual matrimony, while feminists in Delhi, from organisations like Jagori, were troubled by the identification of this marriage within the ambit of lesbian politics, especially since both Leela and Urmila had rejected the term 'lesbian' for themselves in an interview to a journalist. Other feminist groups opposed discussions on lesbian identity all together.

15. *Reflections of a Queer Dalit*, Sumit Baudh, 2007.
16. *Dalit Queer Project*, Aroh Akunth.
17. *To be upper caste/to be a victim*, Akhil Kang, 2024.
18. A Delhi-based non-governmental organisation run by Anjali Gopalan, working in the field of rights of men who have sex with men (MSM) and other HIV-vulnerable populations. At one point, it also ran a support group of LGBT people, as well as a helpline/crisis centre.
19. *Queer Activism in India: A Story in the Anthropology of Ethics*, Naisargi Dave, 2012.
20. Arif Jafar, who led Naz Foundation based in Lucknow (not the same as Naz Foundation India), was imprisoned for forty-seven days and while Section 377 was eventually dropped, other sections like Abetment to Crime and Criminal Conspiracy, remained part of the charges against him. The case dragged on till Jafar petitioned the Supreme Court to decriminalise homosexuality in 2018.
21. Including Menaka Guruswamy, Arundhati Katju, Anand Grover, Jayna Kothari, Saurabh Kirpal, Arvind Datar, Mukul Rohatgi, Chander Uday Singh, Shyam Divan, Krishnan Venugopal, Ashok Desai, Mihir Samson and Amritananda Chakravorty
22. The first petition was filed by Navtej Singh Johar, a Sangeet Natak Akademi awardee, his partner and journalist Sunil Mehra, chef and restaurateur Ritu Dalmia, hotelier Aman Nath and Ayesha Kapur. Following them, a clutch of six petitions were filed, which included petitioners Akkai Padmashali, a trans rights activist, hotelier Keshav Suri, activists Arif Jafar and Ashok Row Kavi, as well as a group of IITians from an all-India alumni group, Pravritti.
23. *Loving Women: Being Lesbian in Unprivileged India* (2006) and *Footprints of a Queer History: Life Stories from Gujarat* (2022).
24. *Same Sex Love in India: A Literary History* (2000, later revised in 2008).

WHERE YOU WEREN'T LOOKING

TALES FROM SMALL-TOWN INDIA

Dhrubo Jyoti and Dhiren Borisa

Small-town India is a bewildering bouquet. Here, a woman unfurls her heart in a string of staccato phone calls with a reporter, a student confronts the big city, a young man in a festive town struggles with the arrival of a stranger and a college hopeful walks the tightrope between aspiration and despair.

Telephone

The phone rings.

'Hello, hello ...'

'Haan, kaun?'

'Hello, is this Rani-ji?'

'Haan, I am Rani. Who is this?'

'Ma'am, I'm a reporter. About your case ...'

'Oh, phir se case. What's the point now?'

'No, no, ma'am—'

The line goes dead.

'Hello, Rani-ji, sorry I am disturbing you.'

'Arey bhaiyya, again you've called about the case?'

'Haan ma'am, it was a historic case.'

'Kya historic? It is gone now.'

'Ma'am, I need just five minutes. Your story—'

'My story? What story? There is no story anymore.'

'Ma'am, please. Only five minutes.'

'Okay, bhaiyya. Call in the evening.'

'Hello ma'am, thank you for giving us time.'

'No problem. Sorry, I get tired after working the whole day. There's no break also for talking on the phone.'

'Not at all, ma'am. Please tell us about your case.'

'My case. It seems so far in the distance. *Jitna yaad hai, bata dungi*, whatever I remember, if that will help you.'

'Yes, of course, ma'am.'

'I was born in a small village and raised like girls are. I went to school, helped Maa with housework, cooked and cleaned the vessels. Babuji had a job that paid little, stayed away most of the time. Maa managed our household. When she fell sick, I would make the rotis. I was enrolled in the village school, and went as often as I could—maybe a few days a week, if housework allowed me. There, my benchmate was Urmi. My friend, saheli. *Do gali peeche rehti thi lekin mohallo me ana jana nahi tha*. Her house was two lanes down, but there was no thoroughfare. We'd only meet in school. *Phir kya, bas mujhe pasand thi*. I liked spending time with her. Slowly, slowly, our ties deepened. We'd *chup chaap se* meet after school. It got tougher after I dropped out, *ghar ki halat theek nahi thi*. But even then, I'd make sure to meet Urmi, sometimes at the park, sometimes near the river, at least once every seven or ten days.'

'Then ma'am, how did you decide to get married?'

'That was in 2018. Urmi and I watched a video where a reporter was saying that the court had freed people like us. Now, even two women could live together. We thought we should also take a chance. There's a mandir outside the village; one afternoon, we quietly slipped out of our homes and tiptoed down there. It was desolate. The sun was searing. We got married, put garlands around each other, held hands and came back. We didn't whisper a word to anyone. *Darr tha*. We didn't even get a photograph clicked. But believe me, it was no less than your marriage. And it meant no less to us. No one forced us. *Humari hi marzi thi, bas*.'

'But why did you file a case?'

'We don't know how but our families found out. Urmi *ko kamre me bandh kar diya*. She was locked up. Her relatives started threatening to thrash both of us. Both our parents, my two brothers and a boy from her neighbourhood Rakesh threatened us with murder. We went to the police station also but they didn't listen to us. When Urmi tried to register a complaint against Rakesh, his father shamed her and sent her home.'

'But the court backed you.'

'We were two girls from the village. We knew no one, but *hamari jati ke ek* lawyer helped us. We told the court that we didn't want to be with any man, we were happy in each other's company. Urmi *toh* turned out to be a big *dabangg*. She told the judge sahab that we were not influenced by anyone, that no one can separate us and that we could adopt a child in the future too. The judge sahab helped us and told the police that we had the right to stay together.'

'That's wonderful, ma'am. So you live together now?'

'*Kahan, sahab*. After the court's verdict, Urmi's family locked her up again. I thought two or three times that I'd go to the police station, but you know people from our samaj are scared of the police. By then, the whole village knew of us. They would abuse us, spit at us on the road. Urmi's family spread a rumour that I had led their daughter astray, that I had a male lover on the side whom I wanted to run away with. Rakesh even confronted me *ek ya do baar* on the road, threatening to beat me. I just escaped.'

'But why didn't you go back to the court or police?'

'*Kaun jayga*, sir? Who will go? Who has the money, or the time? *Waise ghar se nahi aate hum*, sir. We don't come from that kind of household. I work at a construction site, I lift mounds of earth. When the contractor calls, I have to be there. If I miss a day, I might not get called the next day. Can I keep circling the police station? How will my house run? How will I fill my stomach? It's been a while since I have seen Urmi. Sometimes, I linger near her house, hoping to catch a glimpse. But even that seems *mushkil* now. I've heard her marriage has been fixed. I don't feel angry, how could I be angry with her? She showed a lot of courage. *Lekin woh bhi majboor thi*. She was helpless. We both were.

'This ... is our life. My memories fail me sometimes. I go to the site, I come back in the evening. *Akelapan mitne laga hai*. The bite of loneliness is not as sharp anymore. I try not to think about what was. Maybe she'll leave the village after the wedding. I'll meet her once, *chup chaap*. Slip her a card. That's all I think about. Nothing more. Sorry... maybe this doesn't make for much of a story. *Maaf karna*, sir. The power's out again and my phone's running low. The contractor's called me early tomorrow. Hope your work is done. *Rakhti hu*.'

Terrace

The first time I came here, it was with you, on the back of your motorbike. Seelampur pressed in like a clenched fist. Life thrummed within. Lives were vertical—sleep on the roof, cook on the landing, bathe by a shared tap that wept all day. I felt I could lose myself here, in you, in these lanes where every inch was spoken for.

It had been three years since I moved to Delhi for college. Papa worked as a scientist in a public sector company. We lived in a one-storey government quarter, its mesh doors and slanted dapples of evening light reminding us that we were well-to-do, but not enough to stop feeling middle-class. Only twice, Mumma never tired of reminding us loudly, had we splurged—once in class seven, when Papa bought a car, and in class ten, when a Windows computer was installed 'for studies', the same computer that was used to drown my cries for a scooty two years later. I missed missed missed the breathless cycling up the hill to my friend Teja's house where we'd take math tuitions, then the dizzying rush downhill to the CD shop that charged ₹25 a week. Between four friends, there was only one scooty and endless weekend plans to the river that was once just outside town but now took a twenty-minute ride. Two Sundays we missed our CD payment, having been caught riding helmetless and fined. The CD bhaiyya threatened to tell our parents, and I became the official treasurer of our pocket money. I missed the Saturday jaunts to the main market road and malai kofta lunches with Papa and the Bhima Hotel that sprinkled red chilli powder on veg noodles when Mumma was tired of cooking at home.

You pulled me off the conveyor belt of teenage nostalgia, dull PG dinners and canteen lunches. Our eyes met outside an infamous toilet many layers underground. I had skipped a double physics lab to take the metro. In an internet chatroom, I was told about the toilet, the lurking strangers, the fingers dancing on flies, the furtive glances, the grip, the gasp. My pulse raced. It took me a few minutes to find the right landing, after the metro spat me out on the platform. I had never been so far into the city before. I didn't even look up when walking in, fearful that the Sulabh attendant would read my eyes and know who I was, why I was there. But you stood confidently by the basin. The acrid stench didn't seem to affect you. You had a faint whiff of the gym, hair cropped short like a real man. Your eyes followed me around the toilet and then out. Turned out I was a coward and flinched at the first hand on my thigh. I scurried out. You followed me to the escalators. Waited till I calmed down. Held out a hand—confident and furtive at once. We exchanged phone numbers. You told me you were thirty-five. You didn't tell me you were married and had two children. I didn't ask.

On restless nights at the PG, I texted you on WhatsApp. Twice, I even tried to text on TrueCaller. No response. A drunken video call was abruptly cut. Six months passed. Now in the second year, I was less terrified of people finding out. A few dates around the arts faculty lawns and one jaunt around the ridge had me even thinking of going to the queer club meeting soon. And then, one day, your message landed with a thud.

That was the second time we met; I wasn't sure why you had messaged me. It was again Dr Khanna's double physics lab. I leaned against the relentless escalator, scanning the traffic on the radial of Connaught Place. I was twenty minutes late. Astride a black Splendor, you were next to the green Palika board, your black shirt sticking to your back. Without saying a word, I sat behind you.

You asked if we could drink together. This was the farthest I had strayed from my north campus PG, but I nodded. As you rode, you told me you lived in Seelampur. I imbued you with all the things I wanted to be—carefree, masculine, romantic. You asked me if I would like to accompany you home. Still scarred from the helmet fines, I said, 'But we don't have two helmets.'

'It won't be a problem,' you roared, slapping me on the back.

As we rode past the old ITO bridge over the Yamuna, the topography changed. The grey expanse of waste and buildings stretched out beyond the river. The stench was back. There were bikes and bikes. What was this even? My PG stood on a crowded road but the college was quiet and green. Questions buzzed in my mind. Are we going too fast? Am I sitting too girly? I tried to ask you if this was still Delhi. You laughed again.

You told me you work as a safai karamchari. *Hum jis side rehte hai*, UP, Bihar, Haryana *wale bhare pade hain*. There, shanties huddle together like gossiping elders, packed with people from Uttar Pradesh, Bihar and Haryana, you said, as we stopped at a red light. *Roti ke chakkar me shehr aa gaye, ek ek kamre me teen khandan thusse rehte hain majdoor*. Families jostle in a single flat rented out to labourers. The men sleep on terraces, you explained, as we took a left from under the flyover, a giant concrete '8' hovering over my head. By then, the buzz in my head was dulling, my fingers had formed a web around your waist. You told me you were also not from here, and how you were building a life in a city that didn't want people like you. *Bas sar par chhat mil jai*. I listened, my head resting against your arched back as you sped past trucks.

Near the Seelampur metro station, you screeched to a stop, saying you wanted to buy some vodka. We rode past a garbage dump as streets turned into ribbons, procuring chicken fry, ice and soda. Outside one gaunt building, you asked me to get off the bike carefully, hissing that everybody knows you here. You darted anxious glances around before shoving me up the stairs. The stairs were just stacks of bricks with dabs of cement slapped on them. Why were we going up? Just to drink? Only? Why weren't we going to your home? *Andhere me peene ka mazaa hi kuch aur hai*, you said. But you never asked me, I thought, as I clambered onto the roof. Maybe this is how dates began. I could see that the terraces nearby were full of men smoking, drinking, gambling. There were also a few dirty toilets I spied. We stationed ourselves in one of the corners and started drinking. You told me that politicians came to the terrace to bribe locals for votes and that ₹500 had been the rate for the municipal elections four months before.

After two pegs, I was tipsy. I swayed a little. You held me at the waist. You pointed out that all the terraces were knotted together, folks jumped from one to another all the time. Anybody could go anywhere. We hopped from one to another, laughing, falling into each other. You told me how you brought 'many girlfriends' to these rooftops 'and sometimes, boys as pretty as you'. Under the water tank; behind a stack of bricks, no no no, the stairwell, next to the motor, the nook near the door where the bulb was perennially sick. Your hands on my hands, my nails in your flesh, breathlessly untucking the shirt, slipping one finger in, then two. You held me close to your chest, a low growl escaping. The terrace, and even more, the terrace in the late evening. Darkness made so many things possible.

The next time I went back to Seelampur, you took me to your home. I didn't expect it. You knew my PG by then, and my college. When you picked me up, I wondered if we were going to the same terrace again. But the sun was blazing overhead and you didn't take the right under the flyover. Won't we kiss this time? Why did I even come? I was disappointed but I'd be lying if I wasn't curious to see your home. No no no, I said again, and you held my hand and dragged me in. It was a little better than a shanty, its entrances marked by undulating sheets of tin stapled together in a facsimile of a gate. Corrugated metal sheets and weathered tarpaulins formed a patchwork roof, its blue clashing against the depressing geometric disorder of poverty.

We sat on the bed in the only full room. I could see your two boys playing in the corner. You walked in and picked one of them up—*kya ho raha hai, shaitan*? I don't think I had heard you laugh so fully before. But later, after you had laid them down and barked at your wife to make tea, you became cold again. My yaar from school, you said, waving in my direction. He knows English and works in a college, you said. She quietly made pakoras for me, telling me about her hamlet in Mahoba. *Ab toh yaad nahi kuch ghar ka*. Oh, my grandfather is from there, I offered weakly. You were on the bed already, scowling, maybe tired. I felt pity for her.

Kya pata, shayad hum kabhi behne ho, I joked, maybe sisters from another birth. She didn't say anything and turned to the gas. Bhai behen, you grunted. I flinched.

You told me you seldom bring people you meet back home. I wondered if I was special. You said your wife should not know. Did she not? You told me about the time you had sex with a boy in the house when your wife was cooking outside. There wasn't much privacy. There was no room for it. I dragged my leaden feet outside, us three aliens in this metropolis of 20 million people. You offered to drop me back to the metro station. From the door of your house, I saw you both, at a distance from each other, eyeing me with both suspicion and longing. I no longer knew who suspected and who longed.

I smiled. 'No, it's okay.'

Two

Dada wasn't happy when I was born. An imposing man, he was disappointed that his grandson was a bundle of cough and hair. Largely out of bravado, my mother later assured me, he told the neighbours to not go by the baby's size. *Akhir u hamar pota hai, ham uske bagh banai deb*. He's my grandson, I'll make him a tiger, he said.

Far from it. He died long before I got strong. In those years, he petrified me into respecting our family's honour. All the afternoons after (bunked!) classes were filled with stories of how our crumbling house was once the site of great pride, how the tallest of leaders made a beeline for our courtyard in recognition of his contribution in bringing down the dhancha, structure. He would lie astride our broken maalish chair while dadi kneaded his unseemly muscles with mustard oil.

Across the courtyard that flooded every monsoon from the nullah outside home, were rooms open like mouths mid-yawn, revealing the insides in reluctant confession. His prize was our baithak. Dada had it painted pink because he thought that went best with the photographs he had framed—one with him with that dhancha in the background on that fateful day, another with him and the village chief when you could still call it a village and a third of him outside the new temple.

'*Ab ke jaṛiyan uttani ṭhanī naahin rahin jaise tab rahin*,' he would say. The cold has lost its bite.

'*Kyu, Dada*?' I would say with practised astonishment. '*Kaisa tha tab*?'

Spitting at my lack of language prowess, he would continue, '*Hamar sab galiyaan se march karat rahen. Aisan lagat rahaa jaise poora sansaar wahin rahaa. Ek pukaar bhais rahaa, aur hiyan ke sab jawan log uska jawab diyein. Duri se police bhi dekhat rahen ki u log bandook uthaye rahen. Lekin hamka Bhagwan ke kaam pura karna rahaa*.'

His hands would find sudden life to paint that morning when young men poured out of their homes to fill the streets, marching with lathis, determined zealots. One cry was enough to gather a crowd that even the police were wary to confront. They'd watch from afar, their guns raised but Dada wasn't afraid, nor were his friends. They were fulfilling a millennia-old mission, to rescue the birthplace of god.

It was here that his voice would trail off, and finding a moment to slip away, I would run to Harish's house for his new DVD player that only his elder brother was allowed to operate. Once a month, Bhaiyya would come down from Kanpur with pendrives bursting with movies, both the blockbusters and the other kind that made our teenage bodies shudder.

Drrrp! The sharp trill of the app shatters my reverie. Who is messaging me now?

'Sir, veg or non-veg?'

The smooth drone of the steward breaks my stupor. Falling asleep before early morning flights got off the ground is my personal superpower. But this is a short trip, and the harsh white light has come back on too quickly. Mechanically, I reach out for the red-stickered box and regret it immediately—two flavourless folds of egg trying their best to hide undercooked, overdressed wedges of potato. I slump back into my seat again, its anaemic cushion trying valiantly to cosplay comfort.

The flight is electric with the vague animosity characteristic of Indians in closed spaces, but everyone appears to be heading towards the same destination, to see the grand temple that has just opened after decades of tension, to fulfil an old promise. I, of course, am going for work, to see and write about them. I drift off to sleep as my middle and aisle neighbours discuss loudly their plans to squelch up maximum punya in the holy city.

Spirituality rewards glacially. A swarm of rented cars jostle outside the airport. From here, it is a couple of hours to my destination. As we swerve off the highway and the temple looms into view, I flip through the information book—reams of mythmaking on the millennia-old city and its position as the sacred heart of India, also making the point that this is a vegetarian-only town. No Zomato, no Blinkit. Definitely no Grindr. The grid looks desolate, behind the yellow mask icon, an army of shadowy faceless silhouettes stares back at me. Thankfully, accommodation presents no such dilemma. The mass of similar sounding holy-appendaged hotels on the apps had confused me but the very wise Sanjeev-ji in Lucknow warned me that the only liveable (for you iPhone walas, he had added) hotel was also the only place in town with 'Italian pizza' which, like all small-town fares, effortlessly conjoined divinity with 'intercontinental' appetisers.

Unfortunately, Sanjeev-ji had no similar hack for the gridlock of cars, bikes and rickshaws streaming in from more directions than four. It is late evening before we reach the hotel. *'Sahab, aaj toh bahar nahi jana hai*? Anyway, the temple is now closed,' my driver says, hoping that whatever is left of the day, he won't have to spend with me. I nod.

From the lone window in the room, the city opens itself to me. The guttural rumble of earth movers forms a background hum to the chants wafting out of loudspeakers. Along a single wide stretch of road, buildings are awash in the glow of trident-shaped streetlights.

It is not yet past eight but the phone rings in my room. 'Sir, room service? Dinner?' The voice on the other side asks before rattling off a host of options that all seem to begin with paneer and end with masala. The TV toggles between disembodied heads shouting at each other and men and women with little pouches round their shoulders playing house under cameras. Even talking to the provincial silhouettes is better. But what to send? Will they know English? Maybe 'hey' is better, a kind of dipping your toe in this world. I turn my attention to the paneer when my phone lights up.

It is a busy evening. Harish and I are lounging at our spot on Gajendra Chowk, a mesh of wires drooping like tired limbs overhead. We offer tours for between ₹500 and ₹2,000, fusing fact and fiction depending on the required level of reverence. The basic package has a quickfire tour of five temples, two where we have a setting with the pujari who smears kumkum and chandan on the tourists' face amidst chanting; a mid-level package where we add a ghat where the Mother Goddess bathed and a maidan where we say the queen's elephants were kept; and the top-tier, full-blown Ramayana tour package involving four ghats, four palaces and six temples, with seating guaranteed at an evening arati and 'pure' veg prasad.

It's not been that good a day. Not a single Ramayana tour. Harish is restless. I obscure the glow of my new phone, and peer into the screen.

'Hey.'

English! My skin tingles. So probably not from here. A local who works in Delhi? But why would they use English when here. So, a Delhi guy? Maybe NRI? I quickly open the profile. Waah, face photos and so many of them. I swipe through quickly—a kurta, a leather jacket, though a bit bland. Hair and beard aren't styled at all, and bhai is showing some greys?!

A message pops up on my screen. 'Any photos to share?'

I frown. 'No. Mute video call?'

I wait, shuffling away from Harish every time my phone buzzes. But there is no response. No answer. I send a question mark. Nothing. I suspect something is wrong but I am restless too. '*Nikalta hu yaar*,' I shout in Harish's direction before slinging onto my bike. Ten minutes later, I am outside the biggest hotel in the city. The 'hey' emanated from here, I am certain. It's the Delhi–Bombay hotel. *Thoda unsure toh lag raha hai* but what can go wrong? I gym. I look good. I can take him. Plus, this is my town.

'*Neeche aakar dekh lo*.'

A mound of glistening naans in front of me, my phone lights up again. It's irritating enough for these small town types to refuse to share their face but he appears to have shown up here. How did he know where I was? God. I check my phone. Another day more, a visit to the temple, some conversation with the locals and I'll be back in Delhi.

But he IS downstairs. I try to peer from the window but it's dark outside, the newly installed street lights extinguished. Should I go? Warnings from friends loop in my head—*be careful, it's a conservative city, don't get trapped, you know these guys blackmail, don't go out randomly with someone.* Yet my feet are already traipsing down the stairs.

There is a clot outside the hotel but my eyes don't miss him. Uff! Leaning against a red Pulsar, his t-shirt tight across his chest, wrists threaded in red and the faint smear of something orange across his forehead. The fade I hate on most people looks good on him, his jawline helping rescue the severe sharp lines of the small-town beard arrangement. I hold out a hand.

'Hi, wow, you showed up here. What's up? You're from around here?'

'Yes, myself native of this town. And yourself?'

'I'm from Delhi, yaar, but here for a couple of days on work. Just trying to get to know your town.'

'I can show you?'

The words of caution still ringing in my head, I slide behind him on the bike. No helmet, our hair are kites in the wind. Not since college have I been out like this, I fumble with my hands—maybe hold on to the side of the seat? But that's a bit unseemly. I want to look sexy. Maybe an arm on his shoulder? Waist is out of the question, of course. I struggle to keep up with the facts about the city that he's spouting—we're taking a left from the chowk named after a god's son apparently and then onwards to a ghat where another god opted for water burial, and then for a quick nip to the palace that a third god gifted to the reigning queen. Nothing is less than a thousand years old, apparently. Is this guy for real? But it's kinda cute also that he's really into showing me the city. Charming, even if a bit of a charlatan. I nod along vigorously, pretending to gobble up all this holy information. I look impressed. I ask questions, I say things like, 'Oh this looks more than a thousand years old.' (It doesn't.)

In spite of myself, I am enjoying this. Enjoying him. He swerves between buffaloes and bikes, often at the last minute. I gasp and my traitorous arm is yanked from the seat rest to his shoulder. Shit! Is he trying to impress me? Am I getting impressed?

'What can we eat? The food at the hotel wasn't good.'

He looks surprised. 'Not good? But they have pizza *joh bahar toh nahi milega*.'

'That's fine, that's fine,' I assure him.

'You must be non-veg, but we have a great kachori–sabzi place,' he says.

The place is a cart with its paint peeling off. But it really is good. We eat, he smirks when the green chutney is too spicy for me. We don't pay but he chats with the old man who smashed our kachoris into a puddle of aloo. Old friend, kaka, he says. Okay, he's definitely trying to impress me. It's a bit cringe though. I try to look suitably impressed.

We're back on the bike and he's motoring off again—he's some kind of a tour guide, his school friend is the seed money and they're doing very, very well. They have clients from Mumbai and Delhi and NRIs also. Most believable. 'You know, we have a water park better than Delhi,' he claims.

'Show me.' My second hand is now creeping around his waist.

It is dark already and the park is closing but we slip past the cordon. A nearby temple is lit up with diyas; as we walk silently, in the water below, the reflection trembles like a liquid mirage of fire and stone.

He speaks and speaks—something about how the friends would vault over the wall and bunk classes every Friday afternoon, and run to Alka Cinema that was half off for matinees; he believes in god and prays every day but is also kind of scared and worried his life is not going in the right direction; he worries he's done something wrong and is not pious enough; apparently, his grandfather was strict and he both hated and loved him at the same time and is anxious that he's not becoming the man his grandfather wanted him to become; guilty that his dream of starting a business in Dubai will take him further away from piety; how he wants to consult someone from Delhi about his business plans.

I nod at every turn. I am not listening. Every time he runs his fingers through his neatly cropped hair, along the edge of the water ... I can scarcely believe my luck—here is a sweet guy, earnest, hot, out with me on a night jaunt. No blackmail, no coercion, no catfishing. I almost don't notice when he shifts from *aap* to *tum*.

'*Tumhare paas latest iPhone hoga na?*'

The reverie breaks. I laugh, shake my head. '*Khud hi dekh lo.*'

'*Acha jo bhi hai, jaldi jaldi mera vlog subscribe karo.*'

He fumbles with my phone in his hand, tapping on the bell icon. This is my chance. I tug at his hand firmly, he turns and our lips brush—and suddenly, it is as if a siren splits the stillness inside my chest. I hold him briefly, before he pulls away and stands half a heart away, looking at me. Why, why, why? I can feel the wheels turning in his head. What is he thinking? Was this a mistake? Is the night over?

And then he smiles. 'Do you want to see my mohalla?'

❦

We are two charged ions that night. This Delhi man, this man who spurts English like a faucet, likes me! Kissed me! Praised my blog. Offered to help me. I've never spoken to anyone about my dreams of Dubai before. Okay, maybe to Harish but he had laughed and slapped me on the back saying, '*Chal hatt saale.*' As I ride, I feel his hands now wrapped around my waist. I run through my mental list of the things that impressed him—the bike, definitely, maybe the kachori and obviously the water park.

Why am I taking him home? I know you think you know what's happening next, but *sach mein*, I don't know myself. I've never really given myself time to think about what it means to like boys and anyway, it's not like I know what to do with girls either. Harish or I have barely spoken to a couple of them. I only know that meeting with guys has to be kept quiet, that I need to be manly with them and then block them after or if they ask for photos of my face. I haven't even heard of this term he keeps using to talk about his Delhi friends—'kwiyar'? Maybe it means rich.

Maybe this is my chance, this is what people talked about, *ek mauka*. We are cursed to stay here. *Na upar, na neeche, beech me fase.* Papa likes to say, squeezed by both sides. He doesn't share Dada's gusto. Kadua (bitter), as everyone calls him, is always mumbling furiously—'The big guys have forgotten us, they've forgotten the sacrifices Babuji made to bring the dhancha down, not the MLA, not the block president, not even the councillor. They don't call us anywhere, no allowance, no invitation to a programme, none of those new shop allotments. Nothing, nothing for all this *gaurav*.'

I know Papa is home. But I have a plan. Our house has a prize, ramshackle as it may be. I know it'll impress him. It impresses everyone. I screech to a brake outside my house. Thankfully, the *nala* is dry. 'Our family is a very old family and very famous here. We helped bring down that dhancha,' I tell him.

His face is blank. That's how writers must be, I think. Maybe he's not believing me.

'You want proof?'

I whisk out my phone and scroll through the camera roll.

'There, very clear.' I point.

'A brick?'

'Yes, it's from that day, from the dhancha we brought down. You're a writer, na? You want to see it? It's inside the house. I can show you.'

I can't believe it. This is what he is? He thinks this will impress me? This is the guy I liked? I was ready to spend the night with, get to know, help even?

I get off the bike, my ears burning. I can feel my fists balled, my smile vanished, my lips curled downward, tense. I try to arrange my face into nonchalance. I think he has noticed too. Taking an imperceptible step back, waiting for my reaction.

'Can you please drop me back?'

He gulps and nods.

The ride back is quiet. His hands are by his side, and the bike feels like a boat and us on its two edges. The street lights are now molten halos; the cows also seem to have gone. There are no sharp curves.

Outside his hotel in fifteen minutes, he slips off the backseat. Papa's curse is true, I see, this mauka is slipping. The words won't come out of my mouth but I don't want to watch him walk in without a try. I coax the words out, now with my dreams at stake, dreams that this night has shown are not impossible. 'Will you?' I whisper. 'Will you teach me English?'

Thirst

Dhiraj had not slept all night. The morning was soft. A breeze blew damp relief into the house, the sky above his hill town slowly inked by light. A calm stupor dulled the usual tourist cacophony into silence.

But Dhiraj couldn't be calm. In two hours, his fate was to be decided. Like millions of other young men in middle India, Dhiraj had slogged through the two final years of school, hoping for a foothold on the ladder out of the small town morass. What if it wasn't enough?

It wasn't easy. Dhiraj's grandmother would wave her hand dismissively each time he mentioned his plans to go to Delhi. Our boys never come back alive from the big city, she'd whisper conspiratorially. His father wasn't as disapproving but he was a timid man, aware that his son was studying with kids from families at stations far above his own. Run by Catholic priests, the English-medium school's gothic arches were as removed from Dhiraj's cramped dwelling as its expansive verdant grounds. The classrooms with their tall ceilings had shaped lawyers and judges, administrators and politicians. Destinies were determined by lineages. And money, old and new.

Dhiraj's father had neither. A server at a restaurant, he encouraged his children to dream, but not dangerously. In the school that Dhiraj was never supposed to attend but found himself acing, he had a sprinkling of friends, most who fit neatly, almost seamlessly, into those invisible cloaks of hierarchy that adorn adolescents.

And then there was Abhishek.

The mossy-haired boy was perfect. Sprezzatura. His mother was a college lecturer and his father a government officer. Sometimes, he'd wear jeans to Founder's Day or the inter-school debate. He even knew how to ride a bike. Each time he rode his elder brother's Hero Honda through his colony, he precipitated minor heartbreaks.

The two had grown close. But under this closeness was a kind of transaction which is part of school life. They both had something to give each other. Dhiraj basked in the glow of the attention of someone like Abhishek, and Abhishek used the more studious boy as a go-between for his girlfriend in the same section as Dhiraj.

So far, so good. But something else was afoot. Because under that ordinary transaction, that minor schooltime symbiosis, lay a little bomb: Dhiraj had fallen headlong into a crush. He had known nothing like it before. It was like someone had taken out all his organs and stuffed his skin back with this crushiness, this mushiness, this inability to keep himself from staring at Abhishek. The boy was gone. There was no way it could be kept under wraps. Dhiraj never thought of keeping it under wraps. In any case, crowded classrooms aren't the best to hide furtive glances, and poor brooding Dhiraj's were particularly filled with longing. Blink. Stare. Blink. Stare. Stare. Stare some more. One afternoon when the teacher had better things to do than watch over a bunch of unruly teenagers, Abhishek took Dhiraj aside. '*Abbe, tere jaiso ko bohot dekha hua hai.* I know people like you. *Yeh sab aadat badal sakta hai, badal de.* You know you can convert your desires back, right?'

Dhiraj was perplexed. But somewhere deep down, he was also relieved. Was it that? Could he call it relief? Because all the time Dhiraj spent staring at Abhishek, niggling eye floaters of doubt always crossed his vision. You stare and you stare and yet, something says beware. No one said it out loud. It was just there. Now Abhishek spoke of 'people like him' and the possibility to 'go back'! He did a minor somersault in his head. He was right. So much would make sense if he could switch his desires back.

'Come home after school,' Abhishek announced, as if to a crowd.

Little beads of sweat rolled down Dhiraj's back. People like him didn't go to Abhishek Joshi's house. That was not the rule of this town. It was on no notice board. No *daroga* was keeping you from doing it. But still. After alternatively digging his nails into his palms and thighs during the last two periods of school, he made up his mind.

The school bell rang. He knew what he had to do. He walked the longest five hundred meters of his life to Abhishek's house, and then, before his fingers could reconsider it, he rang the bell.

Abhishek swept him inside. They played games and talked about school and friends and Delhi, where his family spent their holidays. It was as if Abhishek had completely forgotten why they had met.

It was hours before the bell rang again. 'Quick, go hide in the bathroom,' hissed Abhishek, but seemed to dither a minute later. 'Actually, no, stay.' The door flew open, and Mr Joshi was standing there, expressionless, before walking away. 'Phew,' Abhishek said. 'I knew I could bring you home, you don't look like the others. Papa has told me not to talk to the *maali* types.'

Dhiraj returned home quietly. The sky above him was unduly crunched.

The next time, it was Abhishek who came over. By then, the two were jumping over the fence to climb the water tank, cosplaying as army brats to get past the defence club guards, spending languid afternoons being close, too close.

There was no longer any talk of converting anything. Dhiraj somehow forgot that sentence in this breathlessness of climbing and jumping and playing.

But the skies don't forget what people under them choose to let go. The skies remember. Cosplaying army brats is one thing, cosplaying reality is another matter. In front of Abhishek, Dhiraj wanted to hide his parents' professions. A stiff performance ensued. The only real conversation was when Abhishek accidentally ran into Dadi; he was talking about the waffles of Connaught Place when the shrivelled lady repeated her warning, 'Our boys die in these cities.'

'No, no aunty, I'll take care of him,' Abhishek said.

Underneath her edentulous cackle, was there a sigh of relief? Did Dhiraj hear it? Worse, did Abhishek hear it? If you're not a part of us, maybe you can protect us, was her hint. Dhiraj wanted to climb out of the sound and exit the room.

These memories pirouetted around Dhiraj's mind as he walked to the local cyber cafe and then back that morning, waiting in vain for the board's portal to refresh—10.00 a.m., then 11.00 a.m. Finally, shortly after noon, the grainy blue background gave way to two terrifying boxes – one to enter names and another roll numbers. One click, then another, then the hourglass tilting on itself, before loading a table with the scores. The marks he had scored would be enough for any college in any city. Dhiraj leapt into the air.

The next month sped by. Before he knew it, his train had hissed and honked into the New Delhi railway station, and a cold steel snake metro had picked him up and deposited him outside Abhishek's home. Dhiraj was to crash here. That heady first week was filled with hours and hours of walking with Abhishek, from India Gate to Daryaganj and then to Matia Mahal for grub, spinning cold fingers into webs, walking in Lodhi Garden, sitting on lawns in Humayun's Tomb or being lurched back and forth by the swells of Lajpat Nagar, and finally returning to the room they shared. They watched cricket and tennis on the big television, hunched up on the big sofa with packets of chips before falling asleep on each other. The unspoken happened repeatedly. The unspoken also hung in the air and in the fat pillow that partitioned their bed. But the capital's rhythm pulsated in his heart. It felt like an embrace.

The second week ushered in reality. Dhiraj had made a mistake. He'd left behind a crucial certificate. The college bureaucracy had made it clear, his future hinged on this smudged piece of paper. 'What's the fuss?' asked Abhishek. The older-by-only-a-few-months boy had not begun (or found a) college yet. 'Dad is coming to Delhi tomorrow, he can carry it.' He squeezed Dhiraj's shoulder playfully. 'Did you hear that, Papa,' Dhiraj beamed in the evening call.

The father wasn't sure. 'I know you trust him, *beta*, but *woh bade log hain*,' his voice trailed off.

It was close to midnight when the phone rang again. 'Papa?' Dhiraj asked, hearing stifled sobs on the other end. Abhishek's father hadn't taken well to being asked to carry the paper. '*Sala chamar ka naukar samajh rakha hai kya*?' he had barked before slamming the phone down.

A streak of white hot anger coursed through Dhiraj's spine, but only for a second. The embrace was loosened. He was alien to this city, with nowhere to go, and now staring at college disqualification.

Heartbreak had to wait.

Dhiraj drifted off to fitful sleep, Abhishek next to him but very far away, the pillow now a wall.

The next morning, the phone rang again. It was his father. Dhiraj tiptoed into the bathroom.

'Beta, do you remember Rohit? Seems you met him in Delhi?'

Oh yes, the other boy in school who came from the same *basti*. He hadn't thought of him in a long time till he'd run into him recently. Dhiraj's eyes had always been trained upward. Outside the 'residence' of the college that accepted Dhiraj and spat out Rohit, the two met briefly. The admissions list was out and Dhiraj was first. 'Arre, didn't you give English speeches on stage?' Rohit had asked. Dhiraj nodded but had walked away before Rohit could open his mouth again. Abhishek was waiting inside.

'Beta, I ran into Rohit and Rajesh-ji yesterday. Maybe I was looking *pareshan*. He asked me what was wrong. I explained the issue, but before I could finish, Rohit jumped in and said, "Uncle, *mein de dunga*. You don't worry, I'll go to Delhi." How come you never told me you were friends?'

Dhiraj disconnected the phone to a dim ping of a text. 'Don't worry, yaar, booking *nahi tha* but I got on the train. Even found a place to sit by the toilets. Will reach tomorrow with your certificate. *Kahan* ...'

The rest of the text was obscured by mist.

OUR PLACE IN DEMOCRACY

Kiran Nayak

I was three years old when polio attacked my legs. I was twelve when I learnt my sister was being married off and that I was next in line. In the small adivasi settlement of Hanumanthanda in what is now Telangana (then part of Andhra Pradesh), my community of Lambada people were governed by a mesh of strict culture, customary rules and deep-seated traditions.

I was told I must not go to school; I must not move freely. I hated that. And I hated more the plan my family was bent on—that I should be given away in marriage because that's the tradition of the village. I did not want that future, though I didn't yet have the words to express why. I didn't have the language for it then. I didn't know the word 'trans man' until I was twenty-two. All I knew was that I felt uncomfortable in women's clothes, that something fundamental about how the world saw me was wrong.

A teacher named Krishnamurthy changed the trajectory of my life. He arrived on his Bajaj bike when I was nine and began picking me up for school. For years, he was my only bridge to education. By the time I reached Class 10, that bridge was crumbling. The women's hostel in Warangal town, forty kilometers away, had no wheelchair access or first floor accommodation. Forty-fifty girls staring at someone who didn't fit. I lasted one day. How could I wear a girl's uniform and not feel uncomfortable? When I returned to my village, people called it inevitable. When has a disabled person, let alone a disabled Lambada, ever belonged anywhere?

So I completed Class 10 in my village. It seemed the only option. The hostel walls, the separate rooms, the gender division made visible what I already knew: I did not fit. Soon after, I met Sarita, a friend with a disability too. She became my anchor. Our conversations gave me glimpses of something I didn't yet understand.

At eighteen, my mother began taking me to MGM Hospital once a month for disability certificate processing. We would sleep on the platform outside the hospital. No bedsheet. No wheelchair access—my mother carrying me up the floors, through mosquitoes and mosquitoes, the doctor saying, 'Come tomorrow' at the last minute.

We did this for four years.

I learnt then that every right is a fight. Every certificate, every document, every acknowledgement of existence must be wrested from a system designed to ignore us. I learnt to be loud. To sit without water all day because there were no accessible washrooms, because drinking water meant needing to go to the bathroom, and needing to go to the bathroom meant confronting my body in a world built for other bodies. Even today, I have a water allergy and kidney stones.

My first dream was simple: a wheelchair. When I was sixteen, an organisation in Anantapur gave me a bicycle operated by hand. Not a real wheelchair, but for the first time, I could move independently. Five hundred kilometres from home, one month of struggling without money to bring the bicycle back, and I was happier than I had ever been. Later, I would dream of a bike. Then a car. Each vehicle was a small revolution against immobility.

In my college, the classes were on the first floor with no ramp and no lift. I asked the principal each time for accommodation, begging for access. Disability access was treated like charity. No official ever had time to meet us. Our reach was limited to the watchman.

I founded the Pratibha Disabled Foundation when I was eighteen, after a rally on World Disability Day. We hadn't even secured police permission. I had sent postcards to 300 disabled people because we wanted data, recognition, proof that we existed in numbers large enough to matter. The MLA thought we were cutting a cake. He called the press. By evening, we had an organisation.

But as my activism grew, so did my isolation around gender. I had learnt to fight for ramps and health camps and disability certificates. I did not yet know how to fight for my own name, my own expression. In temple after temple, I stood outside—steps were barriers, no ramps, no way in. I fought with police in Puri for being denied access. The priest said: 'You're not allowed. The ramp is only for VIPs.' They'd ask us to remove our shirts. I was not comfortable. Even today, that uneasiness lingers.

Love came in the form of Sarita's younger sister, Kavya. When she proposed, I thought she wasn't serious. I thought about all the reasons we couldn't be together. No money. Societal judgement. Familial rejection. But when her family began arranging her marriage in 2008, we ran away. We found a free mass marriage ceremony in Tirupati, and travelled in the disabled bogie of a train with Rs 280 between us. On 9 March 2008, we married. Kavya left a note for her father: 'Leaving with Kiran.'

Her father filed a kidnapping case. The media descended. 'Girl marries girl,' they shouted. Police tracked us across Andhra. We were easy to identify—one of us in a wheelchair, the other walking beside. The thought of suicide crossed my mind more than once. Then Sangama, a Bangalore-based organisation, reached out. Manohar from Sangama called us to Hyderabad, where I met transgender people for the first time. A crisis team took us to Bangalore. I learnt the words: FTM. MTF. Trans man. It was 17 March 2008—nine days after our wedding. I was twenty-two, and I finally had language for who I was.

But language doesn't erase violence. When I moved to Chikkaballapur to work on disability and transgender issues, I discovered a new form of administrative cruelty. My Scheduled Tribe status in Telangana had vanished in Karnataka. My disability pension couldn't transfer across state lines. Ration cards, voter IDs, housing—all required documents that required other documents. It took me months to fight for my caste certificate alone.

I founded Karnataka Vikalachetanara Sanghatane (KVS) and the Society for Trans Men Action and Rights (STAR) to address the specific erasure at the intersection of disability and transgender identity. The organisation now serves over 8,600 members with various disabilities. Every day, I receive calls from people asking about food, shelter, suicide prevention. The phones ring at 1.00 a.m., 2.00 a.m. If I don't answer within five minutes, I fear someone might die.

For trans men, the invisibility hasn't been dispelled. Trans men face the problem of talking. For a long time, I hesitated to express myself in the open—what will we tell the landlord? The neighbours? What if people ask who's the husband and who's the wife? I only came out in 2015-16, after many trans men were found dead, some by suicide, some killed, some killing themselves by hanging. I couldn't understand why it was happening and how to stop it. I thought maybe if I spoke openly, it could help someone.

I slowly realised that the double invisibility was the point. Disability organisations don't address gender. Transgender organisations don't address disability. When Karnataka gave me a social award in 2016, they also gave me a choice: disability pension (₹1,400) or transgender pension (₹600). Pick one. You cannot be both. If I chose disability, they would delete my name from the transgender registry and I would cease to exist as a trans man in their data, even though my body required hormones and surgeries they would never subsidise.

In 2020, the National Centre for Promotion of Employment for Disabled People honoured me with the Helen Keller Award for building networks and increasing access to healthcare for transgender people with disabilities. But awards don't change the fact that I spent months fighting for my gender dysphoria certification. Awards don't stop doctors from asking, 'Are you male or female?' before they touch you. Awards don't prevent the kidney problems I developed from holding my urine because there are no gender-neutral washrooms I can access.

I underwent top surgery in 2019. I now live with a fifteen millimeter kidney stone, arthritis and orthopedic disabilities that compound daily. Each day feels urgent because I don't know what comes next. At thirty-nine, I'm planning to enter politics. It's a challenge. Activism from outside the system has limits. We need disabled transgender people in gram panchayats, in MLA offices, in the rooms where decisions are made.

I think often about temples. Bhadrakali temple in Warangal, where people looked at me with pity, as though my body was a tragedy requiring their sympathy. But I don't need sympathy. I need ramps. I need hormones covered by insurance. I need trans men recognised as a distinct category, not collapsed into 'transgender', which the government assumes means trans women. I need intersectionality acknowledged in policy, not just in theory.

My wife Kavya has been beside me for seventeen years. She takes care of me when the work becomes too heavy, when the midnight calls threaten to drown me. She makes chicken biryani.

We eat rice three times a day. I watch cricket, especially Virat Kohli, and allow myself one beer per month.

My favourite leader is Dr B.R. Ambedkar. I've visited Deekshabhoomi in Nagpur because I understand that without the Constitution, I wouldn't be here. We are starting life in Ambedkar's vision, even as we fight daily to make that vision real for those of us who exist at multiple margins.

I'm building second-generation leadership now because trans men keep dying. Young people hang themselves because there's no education, no shelter, no language for who they are. Rural areas remain the hardest. In cities, you can find community, language or at least the fiction of progressive politics. In villages, everything is at risk. Blackmail. Violence. The threat of being killed for being visible. I operate from a single rented room in Chikkaballapur, the same room for the past thirteen years. I haven't changed it. I haven't returned to my village in three years. My community has no framework for understanding gender diversity. It would take three to four years to change each mind, one conversation at a time. I don't have that kind of time.

Today, we are again fighting a new battle—against a new law that erases us and hurts us. We are struggling for a safe life where our identities will not be questioned, our rights will not be at the mercy of someone else and our existence won't constantly be under pressure. Who will take responsibility for causing us pain? Who will ensure this does not happen again? How many more lives must be pushed to the brink?

We are human. We deserve respect, recognition and protection. To my people, I want to say, don't be scared. We have the NALSA judgement. Now is the time to come together with all our strength, to change social bias and challenge this law. We have to be strong. Our voices, our unity and our resistance matter now more than ever.

OUR PLACE IN DEMOCRACY

My name is Kiran Nayak. I am a trans man, disabled by polio, tribal by birth and an activist. My dream is a shelter home for disabled transgender people, where people can call and know they'll have food, safety, a bed ... It's such a small dream. It shouldn't be revolutionary to imagine disabled trans people having shelter. But here we are.

AMAR KATHA

MY LIFE IN GARBAGAN

SINTU BAGUI

If you ever find yourself at the Howrah station, take a local train for about half an hour to come to my town of Sheoraphuli. There, I have lived since childhood in the neighbourhood of Garbagan—roughly a five-minute walk away from the station. I was born on 12 October 1991. In a building we shared with fifteen other renters, my childhood unfolded between the municipal school where I learnt my alphabet, the kachha brick roads of my locality, my friends and their mothers and my parents. I still stay in the same crumbling building, though many of those friends have now moved away.

My address has never changed, yet for the longest time, I hid it from everyone I knew. It began at school, and then followed me around even when I had grown up and applied for a passport. Why? Because Garbagan was a red-light area, and my mother a sex worker. Even when I was a child, nine years old, I knew there was stigma attached to my home—a brothel. No one knew about it. There was no awareness.

I would wonder why I could never mention my para. Why did I have to hide my address? Why would I be harassed or made fun of for my address? My friends had to surreptitiously visit to my house then. Now they're older and so am I. Now they come to the home openly.

Our red-light area in this part of Hoogly district is roughly 300 years old. I was born here and grew up here. My mother died thirteen years ago, but I still live here. My childhood was filled with friends and laughter at the local school barely 100 metres from our house. My mother, father and dida took care of my two sisters and me at home.

In 2003, when I was in Class 7, I dropped out of school. Mom had fallen sick and dad didn't have much work either. I started working in a local shop for ₹400 a month. It wasn't much but the burden of the house was on me. Plus, the abuse and ridicule at school was also mounting—I was effeminate, so high school boys would call me 'chakka', 'boudi'.... I was never comfortable wearing the half shirt-half pant uniform. But I didn't have the language to explain why. I'd just absorb the abuses and simmer within.

Looking back, we were drowning. At the time, I didn't understand much. Every Durga Puja, whatever shirt-pant combo mom gave, we wore happily. If there was alu sheddo bhat for dinner, we'd happily gobble it down. Mom was sick all the time, and the doctor uncle would come give her medicines. She'd mortgage her gold, but never let us feel the struggle. It was not like now, where children demand mobile phones. Sometimes, I'd quietly realise there was no rice at home that day, but whatever would be made, we'd eat. We had little but we were happy.

At the shop, things were bad. The owners liked me and took pity. But the salary was too low. My clothes were tattered. Stitches and patches held together my trousers and shoes. Telebhaja costing ₹10 was all we had for dinner for the four of us on some days. For mom, when a vaccine was required and it was only available in Srirampur town, I walked seven kilometres to get it because I couldn't afford the bus.

The next few years were a blur. In 2005, I started working at a plywood factory that paid ₹70 for twelve hours of labour. After one-and-a-half years, I came back to the shop for an increased salary of ₹1,200. Then I went to work for a marble tiles unit in Uttarpara. Every morning, I'd take the 7.25 Bandel local to Uttarpara, walk three kilometres to the contractor's site and get to work. Harassment was daily, we'd not be fed or allowed to sit the whole day. We'd have to climb five or six floors with tiles. After I went back to the plywood factory for a night shift duty, I got paid ₹100 for twelve hours. Men would cat call, grope, abuse me. Every morning I'd return home, clean it and get to cooking before feeding mom.

In the middle of this, activism was seeping into my life. I loved going to protests and meetings called by Durbar even before I had joined school. Now of course, that intensity is not there. We don't see that many andolans on the streets anymore. In 2009, I joined Durbar. But I had started thinking about transgender activism years before, when I worked in the shop. I wanted to learn to dance, keep my hair long and grow my nails out. Mom thrashed me and so did dad. They chopped my hair off. You know what? For all us trans people, the battle begins at home. Even when I started doing advocacy work, parents beat me up. At the time, I worked with a troupe that toured UP and Bihar and put up mythological plays. But they also objected to my hair and nails, so I left the troupe. Why would I suppress my identity? If I can't express myself, why would I come here? My nails or hair are not your performance. I am your performance.

But that cut off a source of income. There was no organisation, no mental support, no talk of rights. But I was certain—even if I got paid ₹500, I wanted to do activism.

It's now been many years. I became a Lok Adalat judge, made a film with others, toured the world. I have seen sex worker rights become a full movement, hit the streets, worked with food, labour, feminist, labour activists. But now, there is a lull. I live in a brothel, but I cannot see the impact of the movement as much. How are we helping old sex workers? How are we fighting for basic necessities—food, clothes, a home? I am not sure. My dream is to build an old-age home where sex workers of all genders and expressions can share a roof over their head.

Sex worker rights is important because sex work is work. We are not forcing anyone to come to us. Our brothel is 300 years old. So this work is not new, but some people are bent on denying them rights. You've heard of Noti Bindini? The famous Bengali theatre actor from the early twentieth century? There are thousands like her. Why can't millions of sex workers and their families get rights? They vote, pay taxes. Why shouldn't they have rights? If we go to a doctor or barber and feel satisfied, we go back. Isn't the same true for sex workers? It isn't immoral, it doesn't hurt society.

Trans identities and sex worker movements have been linked for a long time. They're both part of a larger battle. Unfortunately, many sex workers are transphobic. The reverse is also true. But it's our *peter lorai.* The LGBTQIA+ community has to fight for sex worker rights, we have to know people from other movements, understand them. We say we are marginalised, so do they. Every person's struggle has to be understood and respected by others. Only then can we move forward. It was true earlier. People fought and shared struggles. But now, andolans are slowly disengaging. We cannot let that happen.

Life isn't easy for most of us. Thousands of women still live in this red-light locality, but the customers have dwindled since the lockdown. Most sex work has gone online. Our girls sit night after night, hoping to earn a living. During the four nights of the pujo, many bit back tears as no one came.

The locality has changed too. The brick lane has given way to a concrete road. There are now streetlights. But the mentality hasn't changed much. People still ridicule, still hold biases. But that doesn't mean things aren't changing. When we were children, pujas were often spent wearing a single new shirt. Now, many organisations come to donate clothes and food to the children and women. It is lovely. But these actions shouldn't come from a place of sympathy. *Aha re, you're suffering*—this mindset has to change. We don't want that. We want empathy instead. We want to work and earn our bread. Just like anyone else.

STRAIGHT OUTTA BOLANGIR

Rabi Raj

I grew up in a small village in Odisha, in the district of Bolangir, ringed by forests. The dense forests kept out roads and visitors, but couldn't ward off the stench of caste. Many of the 8,000 villagers came from Dalit and tribal backgrounds. Us Dalits were largely labourers. In school, we would be made to sit separately from the upper castes. The mid-day meal was served to us after others were done with eating. It stung but that is how things were. Untouchability was a part of our life. We were used to some people interacting with us from a distance, giving and exchanging things from afar. We'd be addressed not by our names, but as 'gana', our colloquial caste name. Abusive language was common, especially of the *maa, behen* variety, as were slurs. They were much more dominant than us so the question of pushing back didn't arise.

We were poor. If we didn't work for a day, there wouldn't be anything to eat at home. From this morass, the promise of a government job appeared to be the only way out. It carried prestige and stability. But our station was so low that a year or two of fixed salaries and relative stability would make little difference.

My childhood was spent in destitution. Two trousers were all I had. I wore the same clothes everywhere. Our meals comprised dry lumps of rice and some *ambula* on good days. Food could be sparse at home so I studied in a school meant for scheduled caste and scheduled tribe students where mid-day meals were guaranteed.

It was only during graduation—and also when I felt the first stirrings of attraction towards other men—that I fully understood the extent of the crisis engulfing our home. I felt isolated and depressed because of my queerness—friends in my village had stopped talking to me for two years after I told them of my attraction towards men—as well as disturbed. I dropped out and worked as a labourer for some months, before sitting for a government teachers' recruitment exam.

Things are somewhat better since I started my job at a primary school. The people who had stopped talking to me, those who would gossip behind my back, those who would boycott me, have started talking to me again.

Caste still lurks, its bite somewhat blunted. When I first joined this school, the students openly talked about my caste—*this sir comes from the gana caste, look, look, don't touch him by mistake*. They wouldn't say it to my face, but would make jokes among themselves. The cook discriminated, though not openly. Economically, I'm better placed but they tried their best to not touch me. But at least we have good food twice a day now.

When I first started feeling I was different, I didn't have a name to put to what I was feeling. Was I the only one in the village like this? The only one in the universe? I googled and opened an account on Facebook to talk to men from different states. In one of the groups, I realised that—okay, maybe I'm like this. But the suffocation of not having anyone in the real world was very real. It drove me to the brink of suicide. My friends in college would talk about girls they liked. I would act and try to play along with the banter. I couldn't tell them the real thing—that I liked them. Maybe it is wrong, I thought. I wondered what my future would be, how I would show my face to my family, to society.

But when I got selected for the job, I came out to my family. I started going to a queer gathering in Bhubaneswar. I met people, got confidence and thought, okay, it's not such a big deal. When I came out on Facebook, I was flooded with messages from anonymous accounts—'We are also queer; we are also from your region, your district, your village; we feel good when we see your post.' I came from the same place, status and situation as them.

But this journey was not smooth. In a queer WhatsApp group, I once shared a viral photo with the caption, 'Smash Brahmanical Patriarchy'. Many started complaining that I was denigrating Brahmins. There was no support from anyone. On Ambedkar Jayanti, I shared a photo of Babasaheb. Almost instantly, the admin of the group called and said, 'You already posted one photo that created many problems. Will you delete this photo?' I asked, 'What's the problem with Ambedkar's photo? He wrote the Constitution and because of him, we got our rights and got rid of Section 377, so what's the problem?' He said, 'Yes I understand, but it's a problem.' He asked me again to delete it. That was the moment I realised this was not our place.

With a few friends and ₹1000, we started a group of people affected not just by queerphobia, but also by poverty and caste. Local queer people started coming. We felt good, talked about what bothered us, what made us happy. It helped stave off our loneliness. I had never seen Odia posts about queerness, but we started putting up poems and writing on *samalingi mahila* (queer women), *samalingi purush* (queer men), *vishamlingi* (heterosexual), *ubhaylingi (bisexual)*.

We have started going to colleges for sensitisation and hosting events for Transgender Day of Remembrance and Pride month. The first goal of our meeting is to help people who feel isolated.

We connect with many people over social media. If we speak to someone, we ask them, where would you feel safe to meet? In the village? Somewhere outside? We show them our work. We talk about our feelings. We also give travel allowance to those who come from distant villages. Maybe some people come for the money. But whoever comes even once, always returns.

Mu jane nari bina yonira,
Dimbasaya o garbhasaya bina mu jane nari.
Tume jadi mora sharirika gathanaku dekhi
Mora linga nirupana kara,
Tebe huet mu tumara stri-purusha bigyanare khapa khai napare,
Kintu mo hrudayare thiba bhabana
Kaunasi narira bhabanathu alaga nuhen.

Matebi sajei hebaku bhal lagé,
Bhal lagé mate makeup o lipstick lageiba.
Mo chehera upare samanya badhithiba dadhi huet tuma akhire dekha jaithiba,
Kintu tumaku mora labanya dekha jau nathiba.

Tume sabu kahipara je,
E sabu kariba mate narire paribartana karipariba nahi,
Kahinaki na, tume mo jangha duiti majhire kana achhi dekhibaku chahuncha,
Bujhibaku chahuna mora hrudayara bhabanaku,
Tume khali dekhu cha charma–mansa–hadaku.

Kebe jadi ichha kara nischaya dekhhipariba,
E rakta–mansa–hada ra gadha sharira bhitare jane nariku.
Nischaya bujhipariba,
E sharira bhitare thiba jane narira manara bhabanaku.
Nischaya bujhiba mu jane nari,
Mu jane nari.

[I am a woman without a vagina,
Without ovaries or a womb, yet I am a woman.
If you look at my body
And decide my gender,
Perhaps I do not fit
Into your science of male and female.
But the feelings within my heart
Are no different from any woman's.

I too love to adorn myself,
I love wearing makeup and lipstick.
You might see a faint beard on my face,
But you fail to see
The grace within me.

You may say
That doing all this cannot make me a woman,
Because you wish to see
What lies between my legs,
Yet you never wish to understand
The feelings of my heart.
You only see skin, flesh and bone.

But if you ever wish to truly see,
You will find within this body,
Made of blood, flesh and bone, a woman.
You will surely understand
The emotions of a woman's soul.
You will realise,
I am a woman,
I am a woman.]

Establishing trust is a difficult process, as is logistics—sometimes we send the travel money before and tell the people to rent an auto or bike to the main highway, from where they can take a bus. The smallest of things make a difference. In events, we always tell them, earn money, be stable, ensure that people can't hurt you financially. That's also my personal goal—I want to earn lots of money. Yes, I want love, I want a partner. Yes, I want marriage equality. But money is a big problem for us, as is caste. But before that, I hope caste discrimination ends. We need that more than marriage equality.

LOVE MATTRE

Vijeta Kumar

My brother was four years old when he arrived at some form of a hetero logic through which to see the world. It puzzled him that gods had wives, goddesses had husbands and that they often appeared together, standing side by side, except for Buddha who was always single. At home, there were two small idols of Buddha—one green, one golden and both in different corners of the showcase. He made them sit next to each other one day, and called them Buddha and Buddhi.

'It makes sense because Appa plus Amma equals Buddha plus Buddhi,' he later said. The world was clearer, no one was alone, boy had girl and all was well.

Looking back, I am more intrigued that my four-year-old brother was paying attention to things in the showcase and giving them spouses, and less by the fact that he'd marked the more feminine-looking golden Buddha as Buddhi. I probably would've done the same. Singledom was neither an option nor desirable. And beautiful golden things were (are?) more feminine than stony stern ones.

The urge to give an *ii* to an *aa* was fulfilling. We weren't anywhere close to seeing the tragedy in this yet. As children often left to fend for ourselves at boring functions that elders dragged us to, we kept busy with their chappals left outside. We matched ladies' chappals to the corresponding gentlemen's, and when errors were made, they were quickly remedied.

As children, even in our child minds, adultery was as easy and tempting to commit as it was to leave the wrong set of chappals next to someone else's. We had a big responsibility on our hands and we weren't about to commit adultery by matching the wrong chappals, lest it happen in real life. That chappals came in pairs carried the beautiful arrangement of coupledom in marriages, and by being able to play with them, this small coupledom became ours for those twenty minutes. The game became more layered when a cousin had the ingenious idea of putting a child's footwear on top of her parents'.

What we were probably also toying with was the idea of ourselves as married adults. We sometimes took turns wearing these large chappals, barely able to walk but head held high, shoulders bent, mimicking responsibility.

All the other games we played mimicked similarly laid hetero traps. When we played *Raja Rani Kalla Police,* it was cool to have a girl play either the kalla or police. Her playing the raja or him playing the rani wasn't in the picture because we took cues from adults, as well as mostly from each other.

Even when we hid from adults to play FLAMES, a uniquely designed, full time pass game where people's names were put together and a few added numbers revealed the relationship they had—Friendship, Love, Affection, Marriage, Enemies, Siblings—we were careful about not taking risks. We stayed within the boundaries of propriety, using only firmly established, strongly married names, cackling when they showed up as enemies or siblings but didn't dare pair people married to others. And the matter of pairing boy–boy or girl–girl names never arose because it seemed neither risky to entirely avoid nor too tempting to invite us.

The moderately interesting letter in FLAMES was and remains S because it changed depending on where we were. It is meant to be 'siblings' and within the peripheries of proper English spoken at school, it was. But at home, the word was too foreign and didn't make it anywhere near our circle, so for us, the 'S' meant sister, the other overtly safe hetero word.

Like many other words, 'sister', when it entered South India, stopped being English and became all other languages. Another English word that comes to mind for losing its Englishness isn't Mother but 'matter', which is full of a deeply vivacious South Indianness. Matter became 'mattrr'. Several other words feature prominently in this special category — enjoy, feeling, feels, love, love mattrr, half, one-and-a-half, dead end and sincere.

In Philip Roth's *The Human Stain,* Coleman Brutus Silk is born to a man who assigns the middle names of each of his children based on characters from Shakespeare's works. As a Black man, speaking English in a white country wasn't enough—he had to *be* Shakespeare in order to be respected or, in this case, forgotten enough to be left alive.

English has the capacity for this—it keeps people alive, fosters respect for people who weren't previously respected, gives them jobs and brings them love. It's not very different from what English did here in India. In South India though, the English language was able to do more than it came here to do.

In Kannada and Tamizh languages particularly, the word 'love' has been surgically removed from any sensation or context of English. Kannada language heroes from the 1990s to the late 2000s, whether Vishnu Vardhan or Golden Star Ganesh, have professed undying commitment to their heroines by using the phrase, 'Nan nimmana sincere aagi lou maadta idini' or 'I am loving you sincerely.'

The word 'sincerely', exhausted from being overused far too formally in official and personal letter-writing (whether for leave or addressed to a friend or the government), appears to have been rescued single-handedly by the hetero heroes of Kannada cinema.

What the hero is essentially saying to the heroine when he says he loves her is also that he is hers—sincerely. He is proposing to her but really, it's a letter he is writing. There seems to be no difference in the way he proposes and the way boys in my school talked about asking a girl out for coffee—hold your breath—sincerely. Rest assured if the word 'sincerely' is mentioned, it means longevity.

Kannada and Tamizh are languages that have equal parts *rasa* and play. Apart from the most significant takeaway from any Indian language—which is the fulfilment it must offer its speaker while swearing—there are other functions of a vibrant language. Its capacity for romance, for instance, and its potential for what is called 'Amma sentiment'—that bulbous, expansive, brimming-with-emotion relationship between mother and son—as also its ability to be of use to those in love and to those grieving its loss.

Here, I'd like to propose the flawed albeit amusing notion that English's lesser-noted contribution to Kannada and Tamizh languages is in making them less frigid, possibly less masculine and a little queerer. Not to say that these languages were otherwise straight or masculine, but when English mixes with Kannada or Tamizh and submits to them, there's great potential in these languages to foster homosociality when it cannot openly foster queerness.

Homosociality is explained in sociology as a tool that enables solidarity among men, making it easier to uphold patriarchy. Its identity also possibly comes from a shared homophobia that allows men to remain intimate with each other socially while secretly also nourishing a deep fear of the possibility of the sexual.

The work of caste in producing or changing homosociality isn't as studied though, which leaves a lot to be desired. That homosociality might work differently among Dalit and Bahujan peoples is yet to be fully understood. The entry of the English language into a group such as this makes this complication more layered. One of the ways in which the malleability of the English and the regional become visible is through cinema.

Area Bois (2022) is a short film directed by Mahishaa, a Kannada filmmaker and founder of Neelavarana media, an Ambedkarite production house. The film opens to a Bengaluru playground which is, in and of itself, a thing of fascination for its endless capacity to allow 'mixing'. Three friends—Aashith, Kashif and Sachin—meet here with an intention to play cricket and then proceed to do everything else except play cricket. From the playground, they go to eat at Baba Ka Dhaba, a familiar, local joint, where Kashif hasn't paid the bill in three months but enquires availability of 'the big one', i.e., beef. We are given the sense that they sit here for hours talking about love, affection and good looks. But today, they are here specifically to discuss Aashith's plans to propose to a girl that evening.

Shot primarily in areas that are not typically represented in the great Bengaluru metropolitan, *Area Bois* takes us beyond MG Road, Church Street, Indiranagar to a Bengaluru we know of but rarely see in present-day cinema—the Ambedkar colonies in Mathikere, its parks, roads and footpaths too.

In English, *Area Bois* means what it sounds like—boys of the area. In Kannada it means 'street boys', not the backstreet style boys, but in a more demeaning third-class roguish kind of way, which the boys in the film are anything but.

At the beginning of the film, just when Aashith is talking about proposing to this girl, Sachin pulls him out of the playground to smoke and talk about it over chai. The route often taken by homosociality to build intimacy is in talking about love constantly, particularly hetero love. Love also becomes an opportunity to be there for your hetero friend because the impossibility of that love is what keeps this friendship alive. Spending time with him, eating and drinking with him, sharing feelings as they say. Even within the remarkable confines of a 'soup boy', referring to boys who are depressed because of 'love failure', male friendship requires the impossibility of hetero love to sustain itself.

A little later in the film, Aashith approaches the girl he loves with adorable timidity and is almost apologetic for having interrupted her walk. For the first time on screen, I am witnessing a moment that I don't quite know what to do with. He tells the girl that he has been seeing her 'sincerely' for three years, that he has not even looked at another girl and that he will take good care of her. He says all this with mild discomfort, feeling insincere himself, fidgeting a lot, not knowing what to do with his hands. She gives him a simple response: 'If you'd told me this three years ago, I'd have said no then only.'

Still not knowing what to do with his hands, he sadly walks back to his friends and together they sit in a park and laugh. It takes Aashith a while but before we know it, he's laughing too.

Aashith, an area boi, avoids being a soup boy because of a very specific kind of homosociality. For all practical purposes, the three of them are area bois but very unlike ones we have seen before. After screening the film in class one day, the students and I talked about whether the film offers us an opportunity to see masculinity differently than the ones we'd been seeing post Arjun Reddy and Kabir Singh. One student responded with a word that defined the core energy of the film. These boys are 'awkward', he said. He also added that he rarely sees this awkwardness being represented on screen, perhaps also because these boys are not your typical upper-caste boys of the city. Rather, these are boys of the area, the local sort. Male, yes, but not Savarna.

Their limitation with money and other kinds of capital guides their intimacy with each other, as also with the city and how much and how frequently they are able to engage with it. Money, social capital and caste are often uncomfortable to talk about in friendships, but these are the very things that define how intimate we are able to be with a city or in a relationship.

Something about the coming together of the words 'area' and 'bois' allows for some sense of play to occur not just in the film but also in their friendship with one another. Sure, they have leisure time, and they are men, so they are able to hang out in public, smoke, walk about lazily, leisurely and chill in Bengaluru. In so doing, they are bois all right, but not the area bois that we have been warned about. They seem more interested in the idea of love, not girls. They keep to themselves, don't get into trouble and give us the sense that they have each been rejected before, have heard 'no' before. In some way, they've seen enough life to fear consequences. The girl wasn't as rattled by Aashith as he was by her.

This kind of homosociality is found across the city, and aided in part by the privilege of being male, upper class, upper caste. But what the film shows us is a maleness that is neither nourished by caste nor class. This is maleness that is aware of its smallness, in part by being powerless in caste and class, and in part also by the desire to not want to bother anyone.

After decades of speculating over Indian masculinity, as if it's one giant collective homogenous toxic pot, as if Arjun Reddy were its sole and sturdy representation, it was a relief to watch *Area Bois* that gave us unsureness, uncertainty, intimacy, awkwardness, and three boys who just chill with one another and rag each other. Being jilted or rejected in love didn't cause the boy to do anything except return to his friends to *maalish* his broken heart back to life. A pleasant detour from the depressing machismo of the Bengali devdas or even the Tamizh soup boy.

Which brings us to a key moment from the 2013 Tamizh film, *Idharkuthane Aasaipattai Balakumara* that illustrates the effect of language on homosociality and masculinity. In most Tamizh films depicting 'love failure', the relationship between love and English is the same as alcohol and English. If Kannada heroes can only love sincerely, Tamizh heroes feel less inhibited to converse in English only after downing alcohol. After a 'heartbreak moment', Vijay Sethupathi's character, Sumaar Moonji Kumar (average-looking Kumar) heads over to a friend who is himself not sober, in the hopes of drinking and talking about his heartbreak.

It's after midnight and all the shops are closed. Together, they ride all over the city looking for a place that can give them alcohol. Sumaar Moonji Kumar directs his friend to plead with the owners using these exact ten words: '*Friendeh, love mattreh, feel aitapla, half saapta cool aiduvapla*,' six of which are in English. I could translate it but it would be unnecessary. Drunk Tamizh lovers don't have to be translated, especially when they are nursing heartbreak because they are mostly speaking in English.

Even so, the sober translation would be, 'My friend is dealing with a love matter, he is feeling quite sad, if he can have half a bottle of liquor, he will become cool [fine].'

Eventually, Sumaar Moonji Kumar and his friend find a fellow broken-hearted man who promises them a lot of alcohol in exchange that one request be accommodated—he would like these lines to be repeated as many times as possible because they are honey to his ears: '*Friendeh, love mattreh, feel aitapla, half saapta cool aiduvapla*.'

Mattreh fresh, he observes because love is fresh.

In English, the word 'matter' is understood as a noun in the following ways:

- Subject or affair: A subject, issue or situation that is being considered, dealt with or concerns someone.
- Importance: The significance or consequence of something.

—And as a verb in the following ways:

- To be important: To be of consequence or have an important effect on someone or something.

In Tamizh, 'matter' expands to produce each of these meanings and possibly more, at the same time.

Dhanush who plays Raghuvaran, an unemployed engineer in the 2014 comedy film *VIP*, switches from Tamizh to English when he gets drunk. His mother waits for him to begin speaking in English to assess how drunk he is.

It is challenging to speak about maleness without mentioning caste in each of the homosocial instances mentioned so far. In these cases, homosociality is rendered out of a resistance against visible and invisible caste structures.

I find it hard to wholeheartedly agree with the stance that homosociality is a kind of homophobia at work because of a hopscotch of several moments splattered across popular culture in South India, particularly in cinema.

There is an amusing scene moments after Sumaar Moonji Kumar's friend recites the 'love mattre' line. The man promising them alcohol brings his mouth close to the friend's, lips touch, and wetness exchanged—and acknowledged. The friend calls attention to this unusual closeness, only to be ignored. 'We can wipe the saliva later,' the other man says.

More recently, in Girish A.D.'s *Premalu*, best friends Sachin and Amal Davis share a sensational kiss after delivering a cutting homily against posh CBSE graduates and how state board kids aren't some sorry figures. That kiss caused several young Malayali men and women to stand up and cheer in the theatre, a student (who also cheered in the same theatre), tells me.

I am left wondering then if the intimacy in homosociality shown willingly is coming from an inability to acknowledge queerness, much less permit it.

SOMEDAY, I WILL BE AN OLD WOMAN

Vqueeram Aditya Sahai

1

my favourite sight in the city
is old women
in a market, taking a taxi,
idling in a balcony,
crossing the road,
going along, all alone.
someday, i will be an old woman
a sign that life can be cut only one way
and i didn't.
survival of the weakest, and still.
someday, i will be an old woman,
seen by a boy of twenty-nine, wistfully,
he will believe
that grief comes in a silk saree
with roses in her hair,
that the only threads let loose
are the ones we keep open or drape,

and to live till eighty
is a matter we choose.

2

it must have been one. i was on my way home when i saw an old woman, held by someone younger, leading her, from *Nai Sadak* into an alley that slumped into a small darkness. some decades from now, time would have flown. my sarees would inch every year, till eventually, they scrape my calves, so i don't have to lift them to walk. my bones would break, not of wisdom, but of stubbornness. my hair would be thinner than the finger i would point to the direction i want to go. promise then to hold my hand when i need to cross the road. and i would cross it back. just to hold your hand.

3

the yellow light turns white
a boy twenty years younger
puts cold steel
on crushed paper skin, says,
your heart is going strong.
do i have my teeth? i forget
but i smile and believe him.
he wants more blood
than my body has.
i give it to him.
he informs, doesn't ask,
when he undoes my salwar
to press here and there.
three diseases he throws at me.
where did they find the room?

what are they gnawing at?
why don't they knock?
i'm so lonely all the time.
we could talk.

at fifty-five,
then seventy,
now eighty-two,
these are halls i come
to be reminded how to live.
i have sold my gold
for a little pride.
the doctor takes that too from me
as he asks his helper
to lay me into the wheelchair
without tying everything back together.
the kurta hides
what no one wants to see
and the boy looks away
just in time.

i hear my mother teach me,
at four years old, how to make the rabbit go
through the hole in my shoe laces.
and like a child,
slowly, clumsily, with fingers
that don't stop shivering,
follow my mother to a T.
(god bless her soul!)
the helper wheels me through the wet floor
of people without shadows,
buys me my medicines
no, i don't want the expensive ones.

just the antibiotic and the multivitamin.
finds me an auto,
asks, if it's okay,
i nod and bless him
with blessings he can take.
i return to my house
make a cup of tea
and while it boils red
sit in prayer for this boy
who got me out of that concrete
smelling of pus, urine, vulnerability.
all my own.
i take my new meds
with two Marie biscuits.
(i have become my grandmother.)
i hear my heart beat
(so loud!)
in a house all walls.

i fear i will live to see the doctor again,
now that the boy gave me
the only smile in weeks.
my salwar scraping the last off the floor.
he saved me that most terrible suffering.
when he looked away,
i felt seen.

4

love is liquid,
it rushes,
fills gaps in our bones
made by hurt.

but bones
and their gaps
are calcium,
hard ebony
thriving in the sun.
this is why
hurt people
refuse the love
that comes.
this isn't the opposite
of healing
but radical acceptance—
the past isn't a story
in need of edits,
it is a poem—
spaces between words,
awkward line
breaks
that hide when we read aloud
almost no punctuation
or, sometimes, too much.
the past poem
addresses someone
but not the lover.
that's too easy.
love is too easy.
ash turns to bone
under strange temperatures
in unlikely places
at glacial paces.
to refuse love in healing
is to say
my memory is fine.

SOMEDAY, I WILL BE AN OLD WOMAN

i was living
when i was hurt.
i can live
in all times.
i'm not broken.
look!
this gap in my bone
is how it moves,
arches, folds.
my fingers hold
this poem in my skin.
this other gap
is how i bend.
and this small one,
is how i unhinge
my jaw
to laugh.
all my broken bones
is how i dance.

A SONG OF THE OUTCAST GODDESS AND HER JOGATI

MANJAMMA, AND HER PRACTICE AS ARCHIVE

SIDDARTH SHANTHALA GANESH

The echoing ululation of the chowḍki[1] plucks at the ears. The edgy almost human-voice-like sound is tempered by the single stringed śruti, joined with the clapping brass of the tāḷa and announces the beginning of the story of the Goddess Yellamma.[2]

Dressed in a mehndi green Ilkal sari, bordered in red and yellow, Manjamma Jogathi stands at the centre of the stage. Three horizontal lines of vibhūti are drawn across her forehead with a large kuŋkuma circle at the centre, under which the bhanḍāra colours a pale yellow.[3] Her wavy hair is gathered into a low loose bun encircled with strings of mallige and kanakāmbra. Around her neck is the necklace of white and red beads, the muttu, which symbolises her being dedicated to the goddess. Green glass bangles are stacked high on each arm, and with every shift of her feet, the brass ankle bells chime.

At her right, to the side of the stage is seated her troupe of nine people. Eight of them are jogatis dressed similarly to her. Ramavva Jogati on the chowḍki will lead the instruments. The ninth is a man, in dhoti-kurta-turban, playing a ḍholak. Behind her, on a table to the back of the stage are five medium-sized brass bindige[4] adorned with peacock tail feathers on which are affixed silver mukhvaḍa of Yellamma. The faces are framed by garlands of pale jasmine and fiery kanakambra. Their gaze is palpable, seeming to stand in witness.

Manjamma turns to her troupe and they begin their performance of the Yellammanāta, singing:

'*Satyi nï kēḷamma, Rēṇuka da Yellamma, Jana bārada Yellamma* ...' Listen to this true account of events, of Rēṇuka Yellamma's life, Yellamma unknown to the people ...

Yellammanāṭa is an ancient folk-art, lasting from sunset to sunrise. It is the ritual narration of the chronicle of Goddess Rēṇuka-Yellamma, wife of sage Jamadagni, parents of Paraśurāma, the sixth of the Daśāvatāra of Viṣṇu. The artform is sustained by sects of Yellamma worshippers who are dedicated to the Goddess—jogammas, jogatis and jogappas.[5] The collection of stories that compose the Yellammanāṭa have been passed down orally from performer to performer for centuries.

Two paradigm shifts characterise the history of the Yellammanāṭa: the first, Manjamma Jogathi and her guru, the late Kāḷavva Jogati transformed this artform, from the original narrative singing accompanied only by the chowḍki and the śruti, to the theatrical spectacle it is today. The second, are the measures being taken by Manjamma and her troupe in recent years when faced with the threat of the artform being forgotten, no longer practised by a majority of the communities who birthed it. This work is thus an assay at understanding how a queer artform evolved with the lives of two of its major proponents. Through their story, we are further challenged to re-examine our relationship with queer archives.

Kāḷavva became a jogati when they were already married and their wife was three months pregnant with their second child. While out begging in Chornur, they met Chowḍki Yellappa (from a family of jogappas that maintained a chowḍki) who was narrating the Yellammanāṭa. When they expressed interest in learning, they were told that they had 'a throat meant for the stage'. Chilagodu Fakiramma, a jogati who played the harmonium, joined them too. They started visiting different villages to narrate Yellamma's story for subsistence.

When Kāḷavva met the much older Gajapura Ningamma Jogati, who played the śruti, they along with Fakiramma left Yellappa to start a new troupe with her. The three of them started undertaking night-long performances. Soon, they were joined by Basalingamma Jogati (who had been a Lingayat).[6] They thought to enliven the format of their performance—narrate in the traditional manner until the birth of Paraśurāma, and then stage the story like a piece of theatre with different roles. Basalingamma was cast as Paraśurāma, Kāḷavva became Yellamma. Bannikallu Ramavva soon joined the troupe and provided comic relief on stage and Somavva Jogati interpreted some of the other male roles.

Decades later, when Manjamma joined the troupe, dancing had been incorporated into the format. Like the twin instruments which define the Yellammanāṭa, the artform itself has a sister counterpart—the Jogati Nritya. Performed to appease the goddess, the jogatis dance with a decorated bindige balanced on their head to the music of chowḍki pada.[7] It had remained a personal artform of the jogatis until Kāḷavva merged it with the theatricised Yellammanāṭa.

By the time Manjamma met Kāḷavva, she had already learnt Jogati Nritya. Manjamma started living in Davangere at the age of twenty-eight when her family disowned her soon after she attempted to end her life. One day, while she was out begging in the city, she happened across Basappa playing the śruti for his son Paraśurāma who danced the Jogati Nritya at a bus stop. They lived in extreme poverty, eking out each day from performance to performance. What Manjamma saw was a transgender person bold enough to dance in public while wearing a saree—she yearned to learn. Basappa took her under his wing, and initially trained her by teaching her how to dance with a small chombu on her head. She began accompanying the father–son duo on their performances, but she never got paid. She spent a year with them. 'He would not let me eat with them. If they sat to eat inside their hut, I would be asked to sit outside. This reminded me of how in our village, we would not let the lower castes use our wells. If they needed water, we would draw it for them, but they could not touch our well. While I was learning the Nritya from a lower-caste teacher, he treated me with that same disdain. Life can be bizarre—nothing is permanent,' she told me during a pensive conversation over the phone.

She moved to Chilakanahatti soon after. She wanted to make a livelihood for herself; she wanted to stop begging. She started making and selling idlis every day—she made around five kilos of idlis with chutney every morning and sold four idlis for a rupee. She used to tutor the neighbourhood children in the evenings. During this time, her family started to make amends with her. They started visiting her occasionally and she even returned home.

At night, she performed the Yellammanāṭa with Somavva Jogati. Somavva told Kāḷavva, who was around fifty at the time, about Manjamma. Kāḷavva's troupe was scheduled to perform at the Haravanahaḷḷi jātre [village fair]. They came to Chilakanahatti a few days prior to meet and invite Manjamma, who initially refused, saying she didn't know how to perform a play. However, Kāḷavva insisted and reassured her that they would take care of her. Manjamma agreed. On the day, Basalingamma did her makeup—she mixed pigments with oil to create the face paint, and then used kajal and powder. She got dressed in a langa–dāvaṇi. As Kāḷavva sang, Manjamma danced. She did not get paid for it, nor was she paid when she was called to perform with them the next time, but she did not mind, she was obsessed with dancing. When she asked to be paid, she was initially hired for four to eight annas, or a rupee. Over the months, she slowly learnt the different roles in the play. She became quite famous for her acting, singing and dancing. This became her main livelihood. In the early years, all members of the troupe got paid a total of ₹100–150 for a whole night's performance.

Manjamma transformed the Yellammanāṭa even further by making the entire narration into a play. She herself began to interpret seven different roles (five female and two male), and she added the ḍholak and tabla to the accompanying instruments. The troupe started making more money for their night-long plays.

In 2005, Kāḷavva's death made the troupe Manjamma's responsibility, and she inherited the role of Yellamma. Ramavva, Anjinamma, Bhagyamma, Gowri and other jogatis who had joined after Manjamma were all taught multiple roles in the play.

She also tried to bring more tolerance in her circles. When Manjamma lived in Mariyammanahaḷḷi, she enjoyed getting her eyebrows and hair done. But the generation of jogatis older than Kāḷavva used to fight with her, saying this was to be looked down upon. Body modifications of any kind were thought to diminish the sanctity of jogatis. Even though some jogatis did undergo castration/surgery, they were treated as pariahs—when Kāḷavva had poojes at home, the ones who had had surgery would sit outside, and would not be allowed inside until the non-transitioned jogatis had finished eating and washed their hands. Manjamma started changing this after Kāḷavva's death. Everybody is now welcomed inside: 'I think all of us are equal, the same.'

'This is how it all began, the story of my art. Initially, I did not like to learn it. But my guru held my hand and told me they would teach me. When they put make-up on me, and I saw myself in the mirror for the first time, my artform captivated me, invited me to learn it. I accepted wholeheartedly,' she said.

In 2021, Manjamma received the fourth highest civilian award conferred by the state from the President of India. After she walked up to receive the award, she performed an elaborate gesture before the then President Ram Nath Kovind, to ward off the evil eye. 'You have been here for three days, so many people have met you. I want to remove the evil eye on you,' she told him in Hindi.

Manjamma was born in 1957 into a family that had twenty-one children and was assigned male at birth. She recognised her inner feelings as feminine when she was in her fifth grade, she recalls.

At a discussion, where I was her interpreter, she shared in Kannada with the audience: 'In the seventh grade, in a school play I was given the role of Paramēśvara, a role for all of one scene. After that, Basavarajappa, my teacher, asked if I could be dressed in a blouse and skirt to dance. It was exactly what I wanted. I used to dance; I was known for my grace and feminine manner. For my first dance, my classmate Leela lent me a dress. The music played on a gramophone with a record the size of a dinner plate. I don't remember which movie it is from, but this is how the song went: '*Atta itta nōḍibande, avanu sigalillā, yatta hodno yēnu gotilla. Mogginante idda jīva … ha … mogginanate idda jīva araḷi hūvāgide, adara tumba jēnu tumbi dāri kādide …*' [I looked here and there, but couldn't find him, have no clue where he went. Life was like a flower bud ... ha ... life was like a flower bud and has now bloomed into a flower, which is filled with nectar and waits along the path]. I loved dancing to it, and everybody clapped loudly for me. After that, I started dressing up in a sari and making myself up like a woman, walking around all feminine.'

Her father, Hanumantaiah, discovered this and blamed her mother, Jayalakshmi, for encouraging her. She defended her: 'He alone helps me around the house, let him be however he wants to be.' In the tenth grade, Manjamma had stopped socialising with the boys in her class and wished to spend her time only with the girls. But: 'I was rejected by both boys and girls in school, nobody wanted to be associated with me. Despite this discrimination, I continued to study but failed my Secondary School Leaving Certificate. Father removed me from school then, saying tenth grade was enough education for our community.' She was forcibly sent to live with her uncle and elder brother in Kallukamba where she worked as a pigmy collector for Nandi Finance which was 'the only time in my life I wore pants. Otherwise, I used to wear lungi or knickers.'

However, she never relinquished her femininity. She wore saris at home. Sometimes, feeling possessed by a goddess, she would go to people's houses to act as a seer. The people around her began to assume she was a jogati. But her kith and kin detested this. 'Enraged, my family members said: "This is not for our community, it is beneath us! Yellamma is a Śūdra Devi, she does not come to us Shettys! She's bringing dishonour to the family by behaving like a woman. She's doing this because she doesn't want to work!" My older brother in particular was physically abusive,' she said.

She was taken to Kampli to live with her maternal uncle, Gandhi Shetty, who was also a jogati. When Gandhi Shetty became a jogati, she was kicked out of home and never welcomed back. 'I hoped that I would be treated better because we were both alike, I hoped that my feelings might finally be understood. But my māva [uncle] started hitting me even more, saying, 'I have already suffered so much at the hands of society and family. Why do you want to experience the same? Don't don the sari. Don't become dedicated.' So, I was sent to work in rice fields, or in banana orchards,' Manjamma recalled.

One day, when Gandhi Shetty had gone to the next village, Manjamma used the respite to go watch *Apoorva Sangama* in the nearby Bharath Talkies. 'I used to love the cinema, still do. Rajkumar is one of my all-time favourites. I got dressed up in lungi, shirt, towel, earring, meṇa [lipstick] and made my bed to seem like somebody was sleeping in it. The ticket was for ₹2. I was sitting in a balcony seat. My māva returned unexpectedly and, having been informed by the neighbours, came looking for me, stick in hand. I ran back home but I was still beaten up very badly, and screamed for my life. The neighbours intervened saying, "If you can't raise her with kindness, take her back to her parents."' Gandhi Shetty took her back to her parents.

Her father took her to a doctor in Davangere who declared her mentally sound and instructed her father to let her live as she wanted. Hanumantaiah then took her to Reṇukāchārya, who recognised a divine energy in her. He tied a rudrākṣi around her throat and told her father to let her be. After consulting with other community members, he decided that it was time Manjamma was dedicated to the goddess. 'Sixteen of my twenty-one children have already died, I will consider this son of mine dead as well, my father must have thought,' Manjamma said.

She was taken on a May morning in 1985 to the Huligemma Temple, at Huligi near Hospet, to receive the jogati dīkshe. Gathered on the banks of the Tungabhadra nearby, five jogatis bathed her and gave her a new sari to wear. For someone assigned male at birth to become a jogati, the first ceremony is the cutting of the uḍḍāra.[8] 'Only an elder jogati is accorded this privilege and is henceforth considered their new mother. Gandhi Shetty came there that day to cut my uḍḍāra,' said Manjamma.

'Thus far he was your son, but henceforth she is our daughter,' they announce while cutting it.

'My mother began to wail, beating her chest in mourning. The loss of my masculinity was for her the death of her son. I was ecstatic, but my mother cursed the goddess: "Did I raise a son so he could become yours like this? You destroyed my family. May your shrine be overgrown with thorns! May it become deserted and filled with rocks!" Manjamma's eyes overflow, her chest heaves with sobs, her voice catches. A kerchief is fished out. Every time I see her tell this story, in person or in videos online, she is engulfed by emotion. 'Back then, I only thought of my own happiness, but today, I understand her pain. When I remember this today, I cannot stop crying.'

'Dressed in the new sari, I was then led to the temple, where the priest tied the red and white beads around my neck. These are the muttu of the muttukaṭṭuva ceremony, the pearl-tying ceremony, which marks a jogati as being dedicated to the service of Yellamma.' Next, she was given a tāḷi which she tied herself, signifying her symbolic marriage to Jamadagni, husband of the goddess. It is a popular misconception that jogatis are married to the goddess. 'We are Rēṇuka Devi's children,' Manjamma clarifies.

Coming back home as a jogati, her parents had a hard time accepting her. 'I am like a plant that grows on the seabed, nobody wants comfort in my shade. I decided to end my life.' Twenty days after her dīkshe, she bought a bottle of poison and consumed it. Hours later, smelling the poison on her, her mother rushed her to the hospital in Davangere. She spent a fortnight comatose—her parents were by her side, as she was later told. The next two weeks she was awake and convalescing but alone. Her family had abandoned her.

She returned home to be shunned by her entire family. 'We made you a jogati like you wanted. Yet you tried to commit suicide. You cannot stay here anymore, I want you to leave the house,' her father said in front of a gathering at home. 'If she were a girl, we would have married her off. If she were a boy, we would have got his marriage arranged and bought a house for him. If he was disabled, we would have taken care of him. But he has done wrong by us, and we don't want him at home.'

'They're asking you to leave home, will you go?' the people gathered around Manjamma asked.

'I will do as they want,' she replied.

After completing another jogati ceremony, where five jogatis are invited home for a meal and are gifted cloth, fruit and grain, her family severed ties with Manjamma. 'Taking only one set of sari and blouse in my basket, I left my natal home. Neither of my parents asked me where I would go or what I would do. My mother had me in her womb for nine months, but she no longer had space for me in her life.' She boarded a bus headed to Davangere, where soon, the encounter with Basappa and Paraśurāma would kindle her longstanding love for the Jogati Nritya.

'Ï Candragiri paṭṭinadoḷge huṭṭāḷo Yellamma, beḷedāḷo Yellamma
Huṭṭidi marudinakke koṭṭāre Yellammana, māḍāre lagnavanna.
Maduve āda marudina kanase kanḍāno, horavāsa hogyāno ...'

[In this town of Chandragiri she was born, Yellamma, she grew up, Yellamma,
The day after her birth, they gave Yellamma away, they fixed her marriage.
The day after they got married, he had a vision, and he deserted her ...]

With these verses, Manjamma and troupe begin the story of Yellamma. This story of rejection, of abandonment, of being cast out, is a trope that is central to her chronicle—resonating with the lives of most jogatis.

As Manjamma sings different stanzas, she dances here and there: a graceful swaying of the arms that becomes more vigorous, shifting on her feet, she lets the pallu of her sari flow behind her. Her every movement is practised, carrying with it innumerable performances from the past. A particular twist of the wrist or a tilt of the head lights her face up with a broad smile, seeming to remind her of another time, another night when she had danced and smiled. For those attending her performance for the first time, she allows a glimpse into her past, the movement of her body taking us back with her to her younger days. In these moments she embodies the timelessness of the folk artform, effortlessly making time stand still for a brief while.

Sung stanzas are punctuated by narration. All roles—Paramēśvara, Pārvati, Paraśurāma, Rēṇuka, Jamadagni, Kārtiviryarjuna and his companions, even bystanders whispering 'What will they say?' to one another—are brought to life by Manjamma, each with a distinct voice further communicated through different body language. As Yellamma, she does not make her voice more feminine but fills it with infinite compassion steeped in suffering. As Paraśurāma, her voice is loud, cruel and uncompromising, her bangles and ankle bells fall silent. As Kārtiviryarjuna she is cunning and deceitful yet animates the pell-mell of the six kṣatriyas in his entourage.

That day, we got to listen to only a tuṇuku of this lengthy story, the duration of the performance being only an hour and a half. Manjamma and troupe were performing at the Bangalore International Centre (BIC), as part of the 2019 edition of the Bangalore Queer Film Festival. Six years later, I try to find videos of her performances online and find instead clips of Manjamma receiving the Padma Shri, or snippets of interviews after she was appointed president of the Karnataka Jaanapada Academy in 2019. One has to dig deeper to locate videos of her performing. Eventually, I came across videos from the Pravaasi Mahila Janapada Mahotsava in 2017, the Bengaluru Poetry Festival in 2024, the Kinnar Mahotsava in 2022 and the Karnataka Arya Vysya Sanskrutika Sambhrama in 2020.

'Each of our performances are slightly different. Back in the day when we used to sing and dance the whole night, we would choose to tell different stories to different audiences. And like I inherited one version of the Yellammanāṭa from my guru Kāḷavva, different communities of jogatis, jogammas and jogappas have kept alive different versions of this story,' Manjamma had told us at BIC.

Across all these versions, what remains the same is the suffering and anguish Rēṇuka-Yellamma faces in her life: Princess Rēṇuka stuck in a loveless, sexless marriage to Jamadagni, who kicks her out of their house and curses her because she is no longer chaste. Society that rejects her, calling her barren and childless. God Śiva bestows upon her a child who will end up killing her. This notorious child, Paraśurāma, starts making demands of his mother right from the womb, and later makes her go through ordeals like jumping into vats of boiling oil before beheading her on the order of his father. And then her resurrection by her son's hand, when she comes back as Goddess Yellamma.

These stories constitute a powerful living archive of affect and resilience, which have been retold over centuries by different cis women, trans women, gender non-conforming persons and cis men, each adding a little bit of their own suffering into the story. These folk stories stand testament to the transmission of social and cultural memory across generations. But this artform is critically endangered and risks being forgotten. Many jogatis are no longer interested in learning the Nritya or the Yellammanāṭa: 'Unlike us elder jogatis who had very few ways to support ourselves back then, the younger ones have today found other methods of making more money in a day than they would from a week of performing,' Manjamma said, explaining why the community was abandoning the art form.

My first reaction when confronted with the tragedy of a dying artform, especially a queer one, is: how do we archive this? Having worked for three years at the queer archive in Bangalore, the QAMRA Archival Project, National Law School of India University, my understanding of the archive has changed fundamentally. Physical, community archives play a significant role as sites of memory. When I talk of the traditional conception of an archive, I posit that to relegate the Yellammanāṭa to such a physical form—recording its entirety in video or penning all verses on paper—will sound the death knell for the artform. I think of Cameroonian historian Achille Mbembe, who equates the archive to 'a cemetery in the sense that fragments of lives and pieces of time are interred there, their shadows and footprints inscribed on paper and preserved like so many relics.' The Yellamanāṭa is not just a performance, or a static collection of stories that have been passed down, it is a part of different social communities from Karnataka, Maharashtra and Andhra Pradesh. To remove it from its context of production, to remove it from the bodies and the tongues of people who carry it within them would be an act of dis-membering, not one of re-membering.

As it exists, and has existed, it has been in constant use by its different proponents as an archive already—an archive that doesn't exist only as a repository of the past, but as a contemporary living one that is continuously added to and reinterpreted. 'Archive' here, is not a noun or a place to visit, but a verb, a practise that confers cultural identity and continuity. This might negate the Derridean insistence that the archive requires a physical site,[9] yet confirms the jogatis, jogammas and jogappas as archons in their own right.

Kāḷavva's and Manjamma's modifications to the form of the Yellammanāṭa can be seen as an essential archival exercise—adapting its format to make it more accessible. When I asked Manjamma about the impressive athletic feats she and her troupe perform as part of the performance, she elaborated how she has shaped the Jogati Nritya: 'I wanted people to be fascinated by me, by jogatis. I wished to make the same people who abandoned me, who rejected me, want to sit by me and learn more about me instead. So, I started demonstrating my physical prowess through dance: all while balancing the bindige on my head, I balanced on one foot, I would bend backward and forward. I would lie down on my stomach/back and get up again without the bindige slipping. I would run around.' In an astonishing feat that I have seen in only one video, Manjamma stands with the decorated bindige on her head and with small, regular tilts of her head and neck manages to turn the bindige in one complete rotation atop her head. She not only mastered the repertoire of her teachers, but added to it with her own flair and has grown the archive of the Nritya.

The Yellammanāṭa performs a fundamental archival function for the jogatis, it refers to what Derrida describes as 'the originary, the first, the principal, the primitive, in short, to the commencement.' The Aravanis of Tamil Nadu find their origin in the story of Aravāṇ in the Mahābhāratha, the Hijras in a story in the Rāmāyaṇa and the legend of Bahucarā Mātā. The jogatis of North Karnataka trace their lineage to the following story which was sung by Manjamma and the Jogati Nritya was danced for by her troupe, marking the climax of the performance at BIC:

> The last of the ordeals the teenage Paraśurāma demands of his mother to prove her purity is for her to jump into a vat of boiling oil, find his

> ring inside and return unscathed. Deeply disheartened yet striving for her son's love, Rēṇuka jumps straight in. And from within the vat, ascends to heaven, unwilling to come back. When she doesn't come back out, Paraśurāma starts searching for her high and low, screaming for her. She hears his voice in heaven and, unable to stay silent, reveals where she is. When he asks her to come back, she says that a curse prevents her from doing so and to break the curse Paraśurāma must 'wear the saree and bodice that I wore, adorn your feet with my anklets and your arms with my bangles, tie my pearls around your throat and pierce your nose with my ring, carry my basket on your head, with your forehead coloured with kuŋkuma and bhanḍāra, become a napuṃsaka,[10] sing and dance in front of me, and come feed from my breast.' When he comes thus dancing, Rēṇuka descends to earth but instead of accepting her, Paraśurāma denounces her, calling her a bitch and a slut.

When I ask her if this is the only story which denotes their mythological origin, she narrates another from later in Rēṇuka's life:

> When Jamadagni, furious with Rēṇuka wants her beheaded, he first orders his children Eknatha and Joginatha to do so. When they refuse to kill their own mother, Jamadagni curses them to be reduced to ashes. Next, he orders Paraśurāma to behead Rēṇuka, who unflinchingly does so. Pleased with his son, Jamadagni offers him three boons. With the first one he asks for his mother to be restored to him, and she comes back as the Goddess Yellamma. With the second one he asks for his brothers Eknatha and Joginatha to be restored. Jamadagni tells him that he would restore them, but because they had not fulfilled the wishes of their father, they would come back as napuṃsakas. Would Paraśurāma accept them? Yes, he says, they are my siblings no matter what. And thus, Eknatha and Joginatha come back to life as napuṃsakas, singing and dancing and wearing saris.

The former is a story which demands that someone become queer to be accepted, and the latter where despite queerness being considered a punishment, there is acceptance from the family. Only a version of the latter appears in canonical texts. These stories become vehicles for powerful social messages, the former especially potent through its reversal of roles—it is usually the queer individual who is asked to abandon their queerness in order to be accepted.

Curious about the demands Paraśurāma had made to his mother while in the womb, I asked Manjamma to tell me a few stories and discovered that the subversion of social power dynamics extends to challenging caste as well:

Seven months old in Rēṇuka's womb, he supplies her with a long list of vegetables and dishes, threatening her that for the next two months if she does not eat what he wants, he will come out into the world by breaking her back. Disguised as a jogamma, she goes in search of these to a Gowda's farm. On the way, as night falls, she approaches a matangi's [woman from a caste that cured leather and was thus considered socially inferior] hut and asks her for shelter. 'Holy jogamma, why have you come seeking shelter in the meat-eating, alcohol-drinking house of a low-caste woman? It will be better if you stayed the night in a temple or a tent outside. Do not come here.' 'No, I want to stay in your house.' 'There is not much space. I have some intestines drying there, I will hang them for you like a chappara[11] and you can stay here.' In the middle of the night, Rēṇuka wakes up the matangi. 'I want to go to the Gowda's farm and steal his vegetables. I hear that he does not give alms to jogammas but he shames them by tying their anklets around their necks, filling their baskets with cow dung and cutting off their noses.' The matangi refuses to accompany her, saying, 'I might have to lie to survive sometimes, but I will never steal.' So, Rēṇuka goes to the farm alone, where she enchants all the guards to fall asleep. Then, she eats all that she needs, and taking fourteen bushels of produce with her, she erects a magical sky-high hedge of thorns around the farm as she leaves. Some vegetables fall on the way, leaving a trail. When she comes back to the matangi's, she heaps the vegetables outside her door and crawls into the tanning den, using the hides as a blanket and falls asleep. The next morning, the Gowda, enraged that not only had he been robbed, but also cursed to not have access to his farm, follows the trail of vegetables to the matangi's hut. Assuming it was she who had robbed him, he cuts off her nose and her breasts and ties her up. Her father, realising that they had been visited by the goddess Rēṇuka herself last night, and not any ordinary jogamma, appeals to her. Honoured by their devotion, Rēṇuka restores the matangi and blesses her, saying, 'Until the end of Kaliyuga, I will keep you in front of my shrine. Your puje will be done before mine.'

The Yellammanāṭa thus becomes an archive of belonging, of relationships which transcend social hierarchies Containing verses composed by devotees like the nineteenth-century social reformer poet–saint Shishunala Sharif,[12] and embodied by jogatis who come from all castes and faiths, it imparts through its various stories a vision of society where our differences do not cause division, and encourages compassion when faced with oppression.

⁂

'One day in 2021, I was teaching a class of school and college women in Karuva, a small village in Honnavar. In the afternoon, I got a call from somebody: "Manjamma, congratulations *aap ko Padma Shri mil gaya hai.*' I thought somebody was pranking me. "Wrong number," I said and cut the phone. I didn't tell anybody about this. That evening, I got a call from another man asking me to send my biodata. It was only then that I told my colleagues at the Jaanapada Academy. By that night, my name was being announced on the TV, and it was only when the registrar of the academy called to tell me how delighted she was by the news that I finally believed that I had gotten the Padma Shri. I was alone in a lodge in Honnavar that night. I had nobody to share the news with. My limbs started trembling. I was shocked that I had been given this award, my first thought was—why have I got it? What have I achieved? Isn't it only given to the big names, the uber famous? I had lived my life without ever aspiring to such lofty heights, I had never thought I would even qualify for something like this. Until 1.00 a.m., I was taking phone calls, I hadn't eaten any dinner. I stayed up till 5.00 a.m., replying to messages. In the morning, I was swarmed by journalists,' Manjamma recounted in a 2021 interview with Niranjan Narayanaswamy of Republic TV.

That November, she travelled to Delhi to receive the award with Vikram, her adopted son, and Prakash, a representative from the Karnataka Jaanapada Academy. At the Bengaluru airport, she had a plate of idlis: 'I am somebody who sold four idlis for a rupee and now am eating a plate of idlis for ₹218,' she joked to Vikram.

The State had offered them suites at The Ashok. 'When I went to the bathroom, I had no idea how to use the shower! I had only ever used a bucket and mug. And they had given such small bottles of shampoo and other things—I couldn't even read what each was, the text was so small. So, I just used whatever I had taken with me, I didn't want to put the wrong thing in my hair, I had to meet the President!' she laughed uproariously on the phone with me, even though she must have told this story innumerable times to others.

She wanted to have flowers in her hair when she went to receive the Padma Shri, so they searched around, but couldn't find anything nearby. 'At a faraway temple, Vikram spent ₹400 to buy the most fragranceless jasmine!' The programme was three days long, and she was given a rehearsal.

'What benefits have you received after getting the Padma Shri?' Rajesh Gowda, host of the podcast *Rajesh Reveals* asked

Manjamma in an interview in January 2025. 'My travel was reimbursed, but I have received nothing else,' she told the stunned host, who had assumed that the award came with a cash grant.

'The "crown jewel of our zilla", "pride of Karnataka", "lifetime achiever"—these are hollow congratulatory words people use while introducing me but they only feed me words as sweet as jaggery without actually giving me anything,' Manjamma continued. I recalled what she had told me three years ago, as a humble admission—'The Padma Shri was awarded to my art form, not to me'—but it held an alternate meaning now.

After she got the award, Manjamma met many politicians and requested them to give her two-and-a-half acres of land to start an institution to be governed by the Manjamma Jogathi Charitable Trust. She even scouted out land—identifying two acres beside the Hampi University campus. 'Then, with the elections, the government changed in Karnataka. They kept stalling, asking me to come back yet again. It is now the third year running after the registration of the trust, but no work has been done. On this land, I wish to build housing, an auditorium and classrooms, and teach performing arts to the transgender community. My hope was that by learning here, each and every one of them could become famous artists. But this has not been possible. I also wanted to conduct a transgender survey under the trust. Older working-class trans people who are rejected and abandoned by their biological and queer families for no longer being able to contribute financially, die in places like bus stands and railway stations, on the road, in some unknown temple! I wanted to build a home for people like this.'

Tears stream down her face, overcome with emotion. Regaining composure, voice still quivering, she continues, 'The government has not given me land for this. They gave me the award, that's it. I am famous, I get respect, I am recognised everywhere. But I did not benefit from this materially. It is ridiculous the number of shawls, turbans and garlands I have. I have numerous fans, but I have still not been able to achieve my dreams.' Her voice sounds deflated on the phone.

Manjamma continues to face new struggles—last year, Kannadigas in Sharjah had invited her to a programme they were organising in her honour. She applied for the visa, but it was rejected because she is a trans person and doesn't have the appropriate documentation. 'I was asked to change my gender on my passport to female, visit the country and then change it back to transgender upon returning. I appealed to the Indian government for help, but my requests fell on deaf ears, again.'

When I asked Manjamma what her plan for the future is, she replied: 'I have not been given the land to build an institution. My main concern is who will sustain my work after I am gone?'

Her work, her legacy, has been to liberate the jogatis, jogammas and jogappas from being the sole custodians of the Yellammanāṭa and the Jogati Nritya, sharing them with anybody who wishes to learn. Over the years, Manjamma and her troupe have been teaching the artforms to a large number of students. 'When I visit schools and colleges, in which my biography is taught as part of the syllabus, they perform for me. Sometimes, they perform a play about the story of my life with the form of the Yellammanāṭa. I also see both boys and girls dancing with the bindige on their head. This brings me great pleasure—that which was born amongst the jogatis now lives everywhere!'

Notes

1. The chowḍki and the śruti are twin instruments which are essential to the folk artforms of Yellammanaāṭa and Jogathi Nritya. The chowḍki is a percussion instrument with a stringed drum played with a plectrum or with the fingers. The śruti is a single-stringed instrument which produces a drone sound.

2. The Goddess Yellamma is also known as Renuka, and the two names will be used interchangeably here.
3. A pale yellow powder (like turmeric) made from a type of maize.
4. A traditional water pot made of metal.
5. All three refer to different groups of Yellamma worshippers. Jogamma refers to cis women who live their lives in worship of Yellamma, often practising the Yellammanāṭa; jogati refers to transgender women (assigned male at birth) who are dedicated to Goddess Yellamma, and live their life in her worship. Traditionally, they did not undergo castration/sexual confirmation surgery; jogappa are cis men, who are dedicated to and live in worship of Yellamma. They do not wear the sari nor are effeminate.
6. Lingayats are a sect of Śiva worshippers who belong to a distinct social and religious reform movement led by Basavaṇṇa, a tenth-century poet philosopher from Karnataka.
7. Literally meaning 'words of the chowḍki', these are a set of diverse songs accompanied by the instrument.
8. A black string that male children/men wear around their waist.
9. Jacques Derrida, 'Archive Fever: A Freudian Impression', 1995.
10. Sanskrit term for 'hermaphrodite' or 'neither man nor women, but in between'. Here, it is being used to refer to individuals who are born male and undergo a sex/gender change to female.
11. A temporary structure of leaves and poles erected in front of the house on auspicious occasions.
12. Santha Sharif composed the song 'Elli Kaane Yellamma', which Manjamma's troupe sings while dancing the Jogati Nritya to depict Parashurama as a *napuṃsaka* searching for Yellamma.

WALK YOUR OWN RAMP

Kenny Awomi

As early as I can remember, I lived and breathed fashion. Growing up in a town called Zunheboto in Nagaland, I was in my pre-teens when I started mixing up different items of clothing to create my own looks. I would spend time posing and practising my walk in front of the mirror, completely absorbed in the world of style.

I moved to Delhi in my late teens to be with my cousins, as I knew no one in the Capital to help me navigate a big city. I started making connections in the fashion industry, which led to a job as a stylist for an e-commerce platform. It was a hectic job, styling up to thirty looks a day. I often helped the models with posing and learnt a lot from them. It was during this time that I came to believe that I could make a living as a model myself.

As a transgender woman, it was difficult to get jobs in the beginning unless a brand was specifically looking for a trans model. I remember my first show—it was for Indian wear. Walking in a heavy lehenga is a challenge because you have to move slowly, making it look like the fabric is floating. I nailed the walk and received a lot of appreciation. My job as a stylist gave me many contacts with scouts, and I took every opportunity that came my way from designers who were inclusive. Eventually, my work began to speak for itself, and the shift from inclusivity campaigns to regular modelling jobs started to happen.

On a day of a shoot or a ramp walk, the most important thing is to be in the best state of mind. It starts with a good night's sleep. I skip my regular gym workout and instead stretch, do some light yoga and practise a few minutes of mindfulness. I don't eat heavy meals; I hydrate with a healthy smoothie and snack on fruits and nuts throughout the day. I always make sure to arrive on time and socialise with the team while I'm getting my hair and makeup done. That backstage rush and hustle fills me with an excitement to step onto the ramp or in front of the camera and do my best work.

For a model, it's crucial to stay healthy, both physically and mentally. It's also important to build a strong portfolio, know your angles and poses, and understand the business side of the profession. To prepare, aspiring models should focus on perfecting their walk, practising poses and grooming. Building confidence through self-care and mental well-being is also key to handling the demands of the job.

My top fashion tip is to wear clothing that fits you perfectly and to find your own personal style. When you take the time to learn about different materials, colours and patterns, you'll slowly develop a unique style that works wonders for you.

For young people entering fashion, I want to tell them to be a thorough professional. Always be punctual. Practise self-care and grooming. Be resilient. When you know you have the skills, don't let rejection waver your determination. Do your homework. Be interested in the designers and campaigns you work with, and understand their aesthetics. Build a strong portfolio with a reputable photographer who understands the industry. Don't be unprofessional or unprepared. Don't fall for scams. Always research and network to find established agencies and photographers. Don't take rejection personally. You won't book every job, and that's fine. Sometimes, you are simply not what they are looking for.

In this journey, challenging at times and uplifting in others, my mom has been my rock—a single parent who always encouraged me to explore my truth and supported me in the face of adversities. Since I appeared on *Naga's Got Talent* at fifteen, dancing with abandon on stage in women's clothes, I have always been blessed by support—whether it was from my cheering teachers and classmates who voted for me during the talent show, or my mother who has always stood by me.

I have had to do everything on my own, including auditioning, castings and even battling transphobic discrimination. People's knowledge about trans persons is still poor, even within the industry, and sometimes, I have had to fight my way into an audition. As more of us fulfil our dreams, headline shows and walk the ramp, I hope this veil of stigma will be lifted.

A HOUSE WHERE EVERY CHILD CAN BE

Dit Thoudam

I came to know that I am intersex after completing Class 12. At that time, I was trying to fit into whatever possible category I could. I thought maybe I am a trans man, but when I joined an organisation of trans men and spent time with the community, I felt different from them. A trans woman activist helped me understand where I belonged, what my condition is and even introduced me to Intersex Human Rights India (IHRI). But I haven't stopped meeting or working for trans men because I continue to identify as a trans man. After my graduation, I started working for a youth-based organisation where we put together a football team of trans men, focusing on playing the sport and representing the community.

Over time, I realised our community holds a variety of experiences as there are forty-plus intersex variations. Growing up, doctors treating me weren't aware of intersex people. When I went to a gynaecologist, concerned that I hadn't had my period after turning fifteen, they conducted an MRI and ultrasound. That's how they realised I didn't have a uterus or ovary. But instead of discussing what we should do, what I want or what the best scientific recourse is, they directly told my parents that if I wanted to live as a girl, I should get a castration and remove the mini penis. So this was the kind of lack of awareness about the intersex community.

In my school, I often got bullied. At the time, I was enrolled as a girl. My voice changed and became deep and masculine. Classmates taunted me. 'What happened to your voice? You sound more like a man.' The teachers were surprised. Even my friends openly said that they were suspicious of my body. But they didn't understand the experience I was going through. Where did I fit in? I had a gender identity crisis, a problem that I long struggled with. Till now, the one problem that I continue to face is in accessing medical care such as some necessary surgeries that I need, but can't get due to my financial condition. And the medical system is such that there are high chances of an unsuccessful surgery. Even that is a scary thing.

Thankfully, things are slowly changing. I'm very happy about the progress in how transgender and intersex rights are being talked about, but the two should not be unnecessarily mixed. If intersex people want to identify as transgender, they can do so, but if an intersex person doesn't want to identify as transgender, they should not be forced to be included. They should not have to depend on the transgender tag to have a stable and secure life.

Since 2022, I have been associated with the Aura home for trans boys in Imphal. This is a home run by a non-governmental organisation, Mirage Foundation, but funded by the Ministry of Women and Child Development. At that time, I was told that this was a pilot project because it was the first children's home specifically for the transgender community. I joined Aura as a counsellor at first; since 2024, I have worked as the superintendent of the home.

This job is very hectic. There can't be any mistake because the superintendent is going to be blamed if a surprise inspection is conducted. The superintendent needs to wake up early and check on the children—whether they are brushing their teeth or using the washroom. Even small things need to be monitored, such as breakfast, timely cooking in the mess or paperwork. In the evening, when the children come back from school, we look after the physical training, playing with the kids or teaching them football, table tennis and badminton. We check whether the home tutor is performing well, if the children are doing their homework or if they need help in studies. And then we ensure that they're in bed by 10.00 p.m.

Since the home is funded and regulated by the ministry, the home comes under the District Child Protection Unit. We have held sensitisation sessions for them, talking about policies, terminologies and what can and cannot be said.

Yes, some colleagues have faced hostile attitudes—some officials ask how a child can be trans, or how they can know if they are trans—but they're not very widespread. So, sensitisation needs to be an incessant process; just conducting a one- or two-day workshop can't change the mindset of society. We need to continuously sensitise, if not the whole public then at least the people who work with our communities, because a little mistake can ruin a life.

Children placed in a home are those in need of care and protection—maybe a single parent can't afford to look after the child, or both parents are incapacitated, or the child is an orphan. But in our home, there are many cases where parents are present but don't know how to look after a child expressing their gender differently. And they realise that not knowing how to deal with the child affects their child as well as them. Plus, the society, neighbours and school authorities don't make it easy because they complain about the child's clothing, or their behaviour. If they send their child to school, the teacher or their friends bully them, instruct them or scold them just because they behave differently.

The child returns home and says that they don't want to go to school anymore. Some parents feel helpless, and after knowing that such a kind of home is there for gender non-conforming children, they come to us and say that we know you can look after the child.

Among our eleven children living here, aged between seven and eighteen, is an internally displaced person and a victim of the conflict going on in Manipur, a child who had been living in a relief camp for a very long time.

Sometimes the challenge is to send these children to schools that will not stifle their choices and expression or bully them into following dress codes. Moreover, we don't want to push any child, who could choose to identify as any gender. They need to explore and, afterwards, decide for themselves. We need to give that space, making them feel safe and secure. Sometimes, principals have refused admission to our students, saying it will hurt the reputation of the school. Sometimes, a child has not been allowed to sit for an examination.

My hope for the future is that we don't need to mention our gender when we introduce ourselves. I hope we live in a place where we are not seen just for who we are—not as a man, woman, intersex or transgender person—but where people look at us as human beings, and focus on our potential. A place where homes such as ours are only the last option for children who are different.

SILENCE, FAITH AND (IN)VISIBILITY

Dr Aijaz Ahmad Bund

To be queer in Kashmir is to inhabit multiple margins of sexuality, religion and geopolitics. It means existing within a deeply conservative, conflict-ridden, patriarchal society where identity itself becomes a site of negotiation. Queer existence in Kashmir is not merely a question of sexual orientation or gender identity; it is an on-going struggle for survival and recognition in a context defined by silence, social control and political instability. The Kashmiri queer experience is simultaneously local and global, shaped by religious moralities, postcolonial anxieties and the geopolitical realities of occupation and militarisation.

To me, queerness in Kashmir is a form of resistance, a quiet yet radical assertion of selfhood against structures that deny identity and intimacy. In a region where conformity is enforced and difference is feared, the act of being queer becomes a deeply political, even spiritual, act of defiance.

The first and most pervasive feature of queer life in Kashmir is silence. There is no public vocabulary for non-heteronormative identities and few safe spaces for expression. This silence, however, is not neutral; it is a social mechanism of control. It is enforced through religious morality, cultural codes and political repression. The absence of public discourse on sexuality indicates not acceptance, but erasure. As Michel Foucault notes, power does not simply repress sexuality; it produces certain kinds of discourse while silencing others. In Kashmir, this silence functions as both protection and punishment. Queer individuals conceal their identities to survive within a society that stigmatises difference, yet this concealment perpetuates their marginalisation. Silence becomes a means of survival that ensures safety but denies voice. The militarised context of Kashmir deepens this erasure. Under continuous surveillance, curfews and conflict, the politics of sexuality are often dismissed as trivial compared to 'national or religious' struggles. In such a climate, the discourse of queerness is viewed as a distraction from the collective political cause. The queer body thus becomes doubly invisible, silenced by both societal morality and nationalist ideology.

Religious discourse plays a central role in shaping the perception of queerness. Islam, as practiced and interpreted, is deeply intertwined with cultural and moral life. While the Qur'an emphasises compassion and human dignity, heteronormative interpretations have often framed non-heterosexual desires as sinful or deviant. This moral framework places queer Muslims in a position of spiritual conflict, torn between their faith and their lived identity. Scott Siraj al-Haqq Kugle the author of *Homosexuality in Islam* (2009), argues that this conflict arises not from Islam itself but from patriarchal readings of scripture. The Qur'anic story of Prophet Lot (Lut), for instance, has historically been misused to condemn homosexuality, when the actual sin described is sexual violence and coercion. However, such progressive interpretations rarely penetrate conservative religious spaces in Kashmir. Here, religion functions not only as personal belief but as a mechanism of social regulation, reinforcing gender binaries and controlling bodies. For many queer Muslims in

Kashmir, faith remains a site of negotiation rather than rejection. They often construct a personal relationship with the Divine that transcends rigid orthodoxy, a form of what Kugle calls 'inclusive spirituality'. This individualised religiosity allows queer believers to reconcile their identity with their faith, resisting both external condemnation and internal guilt. In this sense, queerness becomes not a denial of Islam but a reassertion of its ethical essence: compassion, justice and divine love.

The family occupies a central position as the moral and social nucleus. It is within this institution that gender roles are defined, sexuality is policed and honour (izzat) is preserved. The notion of honour is deeply intertwined with the regulation of women and, by extension, all non-normative sexualities. Queer individuals, therefore, are seen as threats not only to religious morality but to the integrity of the family and the community itself. The result is often coercion disguised as care, forced marriages, emotional manipulation or conversion practices intended to 'cure' same-sex attraction. Coming out is rarely an option, as disclosure can lead to ostracisation, violence or psychological harm. The family, which serves as a refuge for most, becomes for many queer Kashmiris a site of surveillance and control.

To be queer in Kashmir is inherently political. Visibility itself challenges the normative foundations of society, where gender and sexuality are tightly linked to religious and cultural identity. In a region marked by occupation and conflict, where the dominant narrative revolves around nationalism, purity and sacrifice, queerness disrupts the moral order that underpins both state and societal control. In her 2007 book, *Terrorist Assemblages*, Jasbir Puar's concept of homonationalism, the selective acceptance of certain 'respectable' queer identities to reinforce nationalistic ideals, provides a useful contrast. In Kashmir, queerness is also co-opted and entirely excluded from the nationalist discourse. The queer subject is rendered incompatible with the collective imaginary of either side, precisely because queerness introduces differences where purity is demanded. This exclusion, however, gives queerness its radical potential. The very act of asserting one's identity within such an environment becomes a form of resistance against both religious orthodoxy and state power. The queer Kashmiri body, surveilled and stigmatised, becomes a living critique of all forms of domination: patriarchal, political and epistemic. As noted queer theorist Judith Butler argues, vulnerability can itself become a site of resistance: '... to be injured, to be exposed, is not to be powerless.' Queer existence in Kashmir exemplifies this politics of vulnerability, where mere survival is an act of defiance.

Militarisation, curfews and socio-political instability have deeply affected the private and public lives of all Kashmiris. For queer individuals, these conditions create additional layers of insecurity. The militarised male gaze, the dominance of patriarchal authority and the moral policing of communities combine to create a suffocating atmosphere where deviation from normativity is equated with betrayal. Queer Kashmiris experience discrimination not only because of sexuality but also due to religion, class, gender and political subjugation. Their marginalisation exists at the crossroads of faith-based morality, social conservatism and state violence. The compounded effect of these forces limits access to mental health support, community networks and safe spaces, perpetuating cycles of isolation and despair.

Being queer in Kashmir means living at the convergence of silence, stigma and struggle. It means negotiating one's identity within structures that deny its legitimacy. Yet it also means embodying a profound form of resistance: to exist as queer in Kashmir is to claim visibility in a world that insists on invisibility. Queerness here is not simply about sexuality; it is about reclaiming agency in the face of erasure. It challenges the binaries that define Kashmiri life, sacred/profane, moral/immoral, loyal/traitorous, and reveals the fluidity that lies beneath them. At the core of queer existence lies the yearning for belonging within one's family, faith and homeland. Yet, each of these spaces poses challenges. The family demands conformity; religion demands repentance; the nation demands silence. Queer Kashmiris navigate these conflicting demands with strategies of concealment, coded communication and selective visibility. In the midst of political occupation and social conservatism, queer Kashmiris assert their humanity through love, faith and survival. Their existence demands a rethinking of what it means to belong, to believe and to be free. It reminds us that liberation cannot be complete without acknowledging those whose voices remain—silenced not because they are apolitical, but because their very being is political. The queer Kashmiri, in this sense, is not merely a marginalised subject but a symbol of unspoken truths: that love, in all its forms, persists even in the most repressive conditions, and that visibility, no matter how fragile, is itself a revolution.

IS THAT ANY WAY TO TREAT SOMEONE?

A CONVERSATION ON HEALING

DR AQSA SHAIKH AND ARYAN SOMAIYA

What does healthcare for trans and queer people entail? What is the relationship between mental and physical healthcare? Exactly how affirming should therapists be? Does queer healthcare look different? What are the pitfalls in the current paradigms? Dr Aqsa Shaikh, professor of community medicine, Jamia Hamdard, and Aryan Somaiya, psychotherapist and co-founder of Guftagu Therapy, sat down for a conversation. The following text is an edited excerpt.

AQSA (Aq): Congratulations on *In Transit,*[1] it was really very touching to see the first episode.

ARYAN (Ar): Thank you! We have known each other for some time now. Of course, through community, and you are a doctor and well, who doesn't know you? But I remember first meeting you through Sangath.[2]

Aq: Yes, it was at one of the events where we were studying the barriers that trans and queer people face in access to healthcare. I was tasked with taking back findings about trans men because trans men are extremely underrepresented, unfortunately.

Ar: I am so glad that trans women have always led the fight, been on the ground and done the work of making transness visible. Now it's our chance to take on this fight too.

Aq: At Hamdard Institute of Medical Sciences and Research (HIMSR), where I work, trans men approach us for gender affirming procedures in the gynaecologist's Out Patient (OP) department, which predominantly caters to cis women. We conduct hysterectomies for trans men, but we haven't started performing surgeries on trans women yet, which is surprising. That makes me wonder, and maybe you can talk more about it, whether it is technically easier for trans men to transition as compared to trans women, but the social acceptance for them is less?

Ar: It could be because when it comes to trans women undergoing surgical transition, you need certain specialist doctors like plastic surgeons, whereas for the most common procedure for trans men— the removal of the uterus—we have in-house gynaecologists.

Aq: So, what I understand from this is that I would not want to take credit for this being available for trans people. I think it is available for assigned females at birth.

Ar: Yes exactly. Hysterectomies were never made for trans men in the first place. It was always about the female person. In vitro fertilisation (IVF) treatment, abortion, childbirth—the whole field of gynaecology is for assigned females at birth. We have the privilege of using those benefits. Of course, to also call them benefits is, in itself, very controversial, because IVF for women is an altogether different political issue. If it is even beneficial for women, or not, we cannot say.

Aq: That is very interesting. You know, the Surrogacy Act does not allow trans people legally to use the option of surrogacy to have children. The Assisted Reproductive Technology (ART) Act, which provides the system for implementation of the laws on surrogacy, does not allow trans people to undergo ART procedures on their own unless they are legally married. So, we have options available. We have the technology. We could even have gametes that we have frozen, but we are helpless in the face of such laws. I am one of the petitioners in the Supreme Court challenging the Surrogacy Act because it says that single women—women who have never been divorced or widowed—cannot undertake surrogacy. Trans people cannot undertake surrogacy.

Ar: A thought that often comes to my mind is that thanks to testosterone, passing—though I don't like that word very much—but passing as a man becomes easier in society compared to a lot of trans women, especially those transitioning later in life.

Aq: Do you think that passing helps trans men in accessing healthcare better?

Ar: I have been on testosterone since 2019. I still don't pass because I am five feet tall. I now have a beard but it doesn't matter because I am five feet tall. The window is too narrow to be legible as a man. Even if you don't appear to be a man for a tiny reason, you will be called 'namard' [non-masculine]. This is a pseudo-privilege that people assume trans people have, which we don't. Because we are constantly reiterating our gender, and telling people that we are men, please count us as men. But one thing I would definitely agree on is that masculine women are a little more acceptable than feminine men.

Aq: Yes, I agree.

Ar: Isn't it? Because, I think that if any man leaves his masculinity, that is a bigger social problem than if a woman behaves in a masculine way.

Aq: I totally agree. In our society, being masculine is socially supported in both genders. It's considered to be a strength.

Ar: That also makes me wonder—for trans men who are transitioning, does this feeling that men have to be strong, prevent them from seeking mental health advice, because seeking help is considered a weakness?

Aq: That's a brilliant question. Mental health in itself is so stigmatised in our country and being in a more masculine position makes it worse, you know? And not just being masculine, but being in any position that upholds the norm, because going to therapy would also mean that you are questioning your existing norm.

Ar: I think the more powerful you are, the more privileged you are, the more it is seen as a weakness. So, in the gender hierarchy, if you are on top in terms of sexuality, class, caste or any other social marker, the more your privilege, the greater the stigma to take mental health assistance.

Aq: It's interesting to me that a lot of your clients are trans men. Now, do you feel that a trans-masculine mental healthcare provider helps attract more trans men as clients? Are they more comfortable talking to another trans man?

Ar: Whether it is because I am a trans person who also happens to be a therapist, or because I am a therapist who also happens to be a trans person, all kinds of trans people are interested in coming to me. I think it's symptomatic of the fact that we don't have trans therapists, i.e., therapists who are trans or non-binary.

Aq: When it comes to medical doctors providing physical health, we don't think it matters if they are male, female, able-bodied, disabled, or what their religion or class is, because at the end, they are doctors. But when it comes to therapy, particularly, your identity suddenly matters. What do you think about that?

Ar: This takes me to the first question you asked—if we have the upper hand when it comes to surgery. What I wanted to add was that if trans men had an upper hand in gender surgery, then there would be some capacity for bottom surgery in our country. We don't have that. On the other hand, bottom surgery is more easily available for trans women. Even in traditional systems, there is a provision for bottom surgery. But when it comes to trans men, there is no research, no funding and it's not easily available. I have not gone for a bottom surgery because there is no understanding of cost or success rate.

But going back to the question about therapists, if a therapist is good and ethical, then no matter what issue is taken up, they will not discount it. We need to ask why are trans clients not keen to go to existing therapists. The answer is that therapists pathologise, medicalise and stigmatise them. They out them to their parents or send them to the asylum. So, people prefer to seek a trans therapist because they feel that at least they will not face any judgement. A trans therapist will not tell the trans client that they are not trans.

Around 80 to 90 per cent of my clients are trans. I would say 95 per cent are trapped. Everywhere, I have to begin differently because every person is coming from a different level of understanding of their trans identity. You know, somebody is starting from the fact that they have met nobody similar to them before or never felt like they could talk to anybody because of social stigma. So, with them, I have to start from the basics. But with some who are empowered, they are aware and have fought to live their life. For them, everyday navigation is a problem.

Transness is just one way of living your life. Gender is the biggest site of ambivalence. As a culture, regardless of what gender or sexuality we are coming from, I feel that we are all traumatised around our gender. In the trans experience, it just unfurls further ... like, you may have problems with your family, but when you are experiencing your transness and there is no hiding it, and no place where the family can hide from it, then it seems larger as a problem. For trans people, rejection is something they have faced since childhood—of their love, attention, needs and basic childhood requirements. It's not just restricted to when they are asked to leave the family home. They are not strangers to rejection from their family.

We are not taught to hold the ambivalence of transness and sexuality, because at the core of it, we have to confront pleasure and desire and we all have a terrible equation with these two things to begin with. We start with shame and stigma. Very simplistically, I am saying we are living in ambivalence. We are everything— we have a good side, a shadow side, a pretty side, an ugly side. Transness, I think, is a symbol of ambivalence.

I know I am approaching this in a very psychoanalytical way, but it is true that people find ambivalence threatening. They wonder how do trans people have the audacity to live with such ambivalence? How do they have the audacity to accept their authenticity? Because everybody has had to compromise so much to conform. They have squashed so many desires in their own hearts, and when they see people not do the same, then it's a threatening thing for them, for the family, for the entire system. So there's a lot at stake.

And, as a therapist, sometimes I get frustrated knowing that there is so much pain and we are so invested in our differences, and in scarcity mode, that I am victimised because I am queer or trans. But we are not able to see that as a society, we are all in pain. We have all died inside and sacrificed so much to get some acceptance, some love from our systems. It frustrates me sometimes—why can't we come together in pain?

Aq: Relatively, I would say that the acceptance for physical health treatment is more. But still, when it comes to trans people, I believe that they prefer to take treatment from unlicensed practitioners, ask friends or go to a chemist for self-treatment, rather than a government hospital where free services are available. They go to a hospital only when they are in dire need. On the other hand, in the mental health space, people don't go even when it's a dire situation because of stigma.

Ar: Yeah, a lot of people say this to trans people—now that you have transitioned, which is what you wanted, you should be happy. Why are you having anxiety or depression now? Why do you need therapy? So is there a burden of being happy, post transition? Absolutely.

Aq: Do you face challenges right now in navigating a hospital, let's say, for a physical examination?

Ar: Well, as you said, I want to avoid it at any cost because people, nurses—everybody starts looking at you weirdly. Like, I recently moved to Goa. I didn't know any gynaecologist here. So, I went to this group by chance and thankfully found a person who pointed me in the right direction. But when I was at the reception, and she was writing down the names, I said, 'I am the patient, Aryan.' So she was like, 'Aryan, you know that you are asking for a gynaecologist?'

I am all right because I have learnt to navigate such spaces but I know so many trans people who just cannot. Before my top surgery, I had some issues in my breast. I had gone to a doctor and the doctor spoke to my mother and said I had issues because of the way I looked. I was stunned. Did her scientific knowledge fly out of the window on seeing me? It shows just how much social bias exists in science. Even if you are trained, your personal values or beliefs remain important.

Sensitisation programmes are so necessary, not just through training programmes, but also in school syllabi and medical curricula.

Aq: When you were talking about what you faced at the hands of the reception staff at the doctor's, I want to add that it is a blind spot we carry. The doctor may be the face of an organisation but there are so many stakeholders involved in healthcare. And until they are all sensitised and affirming, the experience of getting a consultation may not be great. I'm probably more privileged and blessed that I work in a hospital and have been in a medical college since I was seventeen. Being in that space gives you an upper hand because you have a personal connection with the providers, they know that you are a medical student, doctor or a professor. And I would say that makes them more respectful as compared to a patient who does not have that privilege.

I remember when I was twenty, when I went to my psychiatrist, in fact, I was referred to her because I was diagnosed with high blood pressure. That was the first time I found a very humane, compassionate, and understanding doctor with whom I could talk about my gender, sexuality or anything I knew about myself. And I wish that more people were like her. In that sense, I feel the default is a discriminatory doctor, an ignorant doctor, with biases and stigma. But then there are some doctors, occasionally, you know, who shower you with a lot of compassion and understanding. Is there a magical formula to make more such doctors, therapists, healthcare providers?

Ar: I have also come across doctors who are not stigmatising. Or at least they are able to regulate. They have probably never come across a trans person but they at least don't want to do any harm. But there are people who intentionally harm, and they are different from people who know that they are not aware. Neutral practitioners are way better than harmful practitioners who tell you that you are abnormal.

The government should also take this seriously. Those who actually are stakeholders, like education institutions, those who make the syllabus, teach it, those in positions of power—this is actually the work that they need to do. This is how systems work. At the moment, this heavy burden is being taken up by the community but I am also seeing more and more organisations speak to us. I think it is changing, it's not as hopeless anymore. I think it is very hopeful. We also hold sessions with doctors, corporates, NGOs. We talk to them about what they can do, what is affirmative and what kinds of problems trans persons could approach them with.

The way I see it, because many are on Hormone Replacement Therapy (HRT), there are other issues that they face too. One of my friends has developed something in the pancreas. I have a fatty liver and a build-up of uric acid, and because there is very little research in the field of trans healthcare, we don't know the connections. It is frustrating, because, at one point, doctors didn't even believe there were serious side effects of hormone therapy. I feel that doctors need to take our feedback and believe us rather than dismiss our experience of taking testosterone. Are soft skills even taught in our courses? How to talk to patients, how to be affirmative, how to build relationships with clients? How to hear them? This is not a one-person job.

This should start from school, and go all the way to the media channels. Parents should be taught how to talk to their children, particularly trans or non-binary children. And, on a larger theme, we need to start talking within families in a language that acknowledges vulnerability. We have to normalise telling each other our feelings—today I'm sad or upset. I had a bad day. I am hurt. This is about mental health.

Parents should also start talking about sexuality and gender. It's not like we are islands. We have friends who can come to our house for lunch. We can go to their house for lunch and that's how they can start communication with their children. You know, like an uncle–aunty couple, an uncle–uncle couple is possible as well as an aunty–aunty couple. Home is the first place. Then, the educational institute. Then, the medical institute. Then corporate. Then, organisation. Then, society. This is everyone's job.

Aq: I remember when I first went in for a physical health check-up, it was for high blood pressure. They ran a battery of tests—hormonal, endocrinal, looking at kidney health, etc. Not even one person talked about my sexuality or gender. They thought probably the two are not related. There was an endocrinologist who asked how I was feeling in terms of all those aspects. And I remember how uncomfortable he was, he was literally shaking. And when I spoke about it, he attributed a lot of it to low gonads and low hormones. He took me to his senior and she said, 'Oh, you are normal.' That was the first time someone in my life told me that I'm normal. And then I was referred to the psychiatry department, which was very helpful. This was almost twenty years ago.

When I was diagnosed with Covid-19, I was in hospital in isolation for ten days. I was being treated by doctors, who were, in fact, taught by me. My students are now doctors and I have transitioned in front of them. But I remember that as a patient, they didn't even take my transness into consideration. They treated me as a cisgender woman, which was medically incorrect. They did not take into consideration that I was on HRT and had also undergone certain surgeries, and these would have had an effect in their choice of treatment. Because of that I was misdiagnosed as having pneumonia when what the X-Ray was showing was actually the shadow of the breast implants. It was only a wise radiologist, who was a friend, who realised that the shadow was not due to pneumonia. This was an example of how only knowledge is not going to translate into better healthcare. You need much more than that.

Just three months ago, I had a severe headache. I have had migraines before. I have been taking those drugs for five years but this time the migraine was not settling down. I had to undergo an MRI scan of my brain and they found a blood clot. I was given blood thinner medicines, and my HRT was stopped, because it was thought that estrogen may be leading to that blood clot. So, when the clot was diagnosed, we were not sure whether it was due to Covid or the vaccine or hormones. But the doctors blamed hormones. I remember a friend, who is a paediatric surgeon, said, 'Oh you have had enough of your femininity. You have proven what you wanted to prove, now stop all this HRT, look at the harmful effects.' I felt that I will be used as an exhibit of the side effects of HRT to potentially scare trans women.

Both approaches are very harmful—completely discounting the side effects of HRT or thinking of it as carcinogenic or life threatening. When you talk about the burden on the community to educate our healthcare providers, I have done that job a lot as a patient and a fellow doctor. But one danger I have noticed recently in doctors who have undergone some kind of sensitisation or who think they are sensitised is that the humility of ignorance is replaced by arrogance of knowledge. They say, 'Oh, I know trans people, I know HRT, I know transition and I am very friendly to trans people and so I am not discriminatory.' They inadvertently end up sometimes pushing people towards certain gender-affirming procedures that they don't want or pulling them out of the closet by saying, 'Oh, it's normal to be queer, why are you afraid, you should come out to everyone.'

Ar: You're so right. People do courses and think, if I have XYZ course or certificate, then I will get new clients. But we have to be wary because a course doesn't automatically mean that they offer a viable alternative. You cannot do analysis without doing self-analysis. No healing can happen unless you have worked on your own healing, right? You will unfortunately still hold the power and stay in the dynamic of being the doctor who knows everything.

Aq: I am wary of government-run trans care, because I feel that it's a slippery slope and I say this because of the experiences from other countries and the US. When you give the authority or responsibility of taking care of trans people to governments, they are going to make very good use of that opportunity to medicalise your bodies and rule them through laws and legislation. And to even create a hierarchy within, such as who is truly trans and not trans. In 2019, things started changing a lot because the Transgender Persons Act[5] came in, replaced the NALSA guidelines and made life more difficult for many trans people. Along with it came the Surrogacy Act and the ART Act.

At the same time, I wish more doctors knew about the kind of stress that we go through because of intersectionality. A lot of my mental stress nowadays is not due to my transness but due to my other identities as being a Muslim living in India, the turbulence of the endless war in Gaza[6] and a lot of other things in which religion or identity plays a role that's hard to talk about. Within the community, there are divisions on ways of being trans. I wish more people, more doctors, more caregivers were informed by these experiences.

Ar: Yes. Like I said, for mental health practitioners or any healing professionals, the first thing is that you get into self-analysis. You have to do that work. You have to heal yourself first. If you can see your scars, you will be able to see my scars. So, first we have to work on this grief. This is the emotional work that needs to be done. As much as I agree with you, we are living in a world where there will be some government structure.

Representation is very important, especially in places that make the laws for us. And finally, continuous and regular sensitisation needs to keep taking place. As humans, we carry so much in our minds that we can forget things. So, time and again, we should be taught how to love. After all, we are taught how to hate time after time. If the state is able to sponsor more love, more inclusion, more positivity, more support, resource building and if we can head in that direction, that would be better for everyone, especially for those on the margins.

In a statement put forward by mental health professionals, which I helped draft, regarding the Transgender Persons (Protection of Rights) Act, we wrote, 'It is essential to name what this amended Transgender Persons Act is dismantling. For most transgender persons in India — particularly those rejected by families of origin, expelled from homes, pushed out of schools and workplaces — the safe circle is already vanishingly small. It is a therapist who uses the right name. A friend who accompanies them to a hospital. A chosen family member who answers the phone at 2 a.m. This is not a robust support system. It is the minimum. Under this Act, that minimum becomes criminal. And when the circle is gone, what remains is isolation—the single most consistent predictor of suicide in the clinical literature. The state is not protecting these people. It is removing the last thing between them and the worst possible outcome.'

Gender is a psycho-social experience and medicine's approach must be to support gender affirmative care, not to validate or legitimise gender. The new Act makes biology essential [to the definition of gender], whereas the medical syllabus has never discussed gender outside the realm of sex assigned at birth. Science has always been used to control the bodies of persons assigned female at birth, and this law (by leaving out trans men among other gender identities) is an additional example of that control, violation and shaming.

Aq: It is correct to say that in the core medical curriculum, gender is not taught to medical students. We are taught about sex or sex differences. This reduction of gender to tangible, evidence-based attributes is a trend we are seeing around the world. Physical evidence is considered the truth, and our mind, psyche, socio-cultural lived experience is not given any value or considered untrue. This is an extremely regressive view even scientifically speaking. This narrative also percolates into other aspects of our lives, and I fear it will affect mental health services in general. We've seen these reversals happen in other South Asian countries, like Pakistan, and they are used by right-wing governments to punish those who are breaking social and cultural norms.

Notes

1. *In Transit* is the title of a four-part docuseries that was released on the OTT platform Amazon Prime in June 2025. It showed the lives of nine trans and non-binary individuals in India, including Aryan. It was produced by Zoya Akhtar and Reema Kagti under their Tiger Baby production banner and was directed by Ayesha Sood.
2. Sangath was established in 1996 and offers community-centred, evidence-based intervention on mental health initiatives. During the pandemic, it started iHEAR, an initiative on health equity, advocacy and research for queer and disabled people.
3. India's Surrogacy (Regulation) Act, 2021, regulates the practice of surrogacy and establishes an assisted reproductive technology framework. It restricts the options of surrogacy to couples, defining them as 'the legally married Indian man and woman above the age of 21 years and 18 years respectively', and that too proven infertility. It permits altruistic surrogacy but prohibits commercial surrogacy, thus leaving out same-sex couples, trans persons in relationships, single persons and live-in partners (irrespective of gender).
4. Nirvanam refers to the traditional ritualistic castration or removal of male genital organs (penis and testicles) conducted within the Hijra and other traditional trans women communities.

5. The Transgender Persons (Protection of Rights) Act, 2019, was widely critiqued by members of the trans community for violating the spirit of the *NALSA vs. Union of India* judgement of 2014, which guaranteed the right of self-determination in gender identity. The Act created a procedure to acquire legal documentation for transgender identity which, in turn, was tied to reception of entitlements. Furthermore, it divested the trans person of the right to self-identify, and established a medico-legal mechanism for establishing identity. It also necessitated surgery in the event that the trans person sought to identify as either woman or man.
6. Israel launched an offensive against Palestine on 27 October 2023, with the stated aim of destroying Hamas, the military wing of the Islamic Resistance Movement, a Palestinian political organisation. This came after an attack launched by Hamas and other Palestinian groups on 7 October, in which at least 1,000 Israelis were killed, and over 100 held hostage. Israel's military response, which lasted for two years, led to the deaths of hundreds of thousands of women and children through direct military offensive as well as by cutting off food and medical supplies, preventing aid from reaching Palestinian settlements and destroying hospitals. A ceasefire was declared on 10 October 2025.

THE MEDICAL LANDSCAPE OF TRANSITION

A PERSONAL HISTORY

DR SAMEERA JAHAGIRDAR

As a child, I felt most comfortable around girls. I never perceived any difference between us—behaviours, thoughts or even playtime activities like collecting parijat flowers to make tiny garlands to adorn our hair with. I believed I was a girl until one day, when I was around seven or eight, I accidentally walked into the bathroom while my cousin was bathing and noticed that my body was different from hers. This realisation marked the beginning of a decades-long internal conflict regarding my gender identity.

As puberty hit, everyone, from my parents to the school bullies on the playground, insisted that I was a boy and needed to behave accordingly. This social expectation clashed with my internal sense of self as a girl and only served to intensify my struggles with gender identity.

I come from a middle-class Muslim family, born in a small village nestled in the heart of Maharashtra's Solapur district. Seeking better work prospects, my parents migrated from this close-knit village to the bustling metropolis of Pune and that is where I spent my innocent childhood, filled with joys and discoveries, my adolescence, which was marked by the complexities of self-discovery and growth, as well as my early adult period, which was a time of significant personal and academic development.

Being born into a conservative family, a heritage deeply ingrained with traditions and values, I was raised within a framework of rigid norms, traditions and values, particularly around gender roles and expectations. As a child assigned male gender at birth, I was immediately subject to a multitude of societal impositions, unspoken rules. From a very young age, these expectations began to shape my understanding of the world and my place within it.

The commencement of my medical education marked the beginning of a significant new chapter in my life's narrative. The rigorous journey of pursuing my Bachelor of Medicine and Surgery (MBBS) degree, followed by the demanding postgraduate studies in the specialised fields of anaesthesia and critical care, occupied a considerable portion of my energy and attention. However, concurrently, another journey of self-discovery and increasing clarity regarding my sexual orientation was unfolding, too.

It is somewhat astonishing to reflect that even at the age of twenty-six or twenty-seven, the concepts of gender identity and sexual orientation remained blurred in my understanding. I now recognise that gender identity is deeply personal and internal, representing the gender that one feels oneself to be. It is about the intrinsic sense of being a man, a woman, both, neither or somewhere else along the gender spectrum. Sexual orientation, on the other hand, pertains to whom one is attracted to, with whom one experiences emotional and physical love and desire, regardless of that person's gender. Understanding these two seemingly basic yet profoundly important concepts eluded my grasp for a considerable period.

Living as a transgender person in India, particularly twenty odd years ago, was enormously challenging. The transgender community faced and, to a significant extent, still faces, profound prejudice. However, the level of stigma prevalent at that time was truly immense. Furthermore, as a doctor who had completed postgraduate education and was working in a medical school, I understood that coming out as a transgender person could likely have a substantial impact on my career, job prospects and overall standing within the medical community and the academic environment of the medical school itself.

Nevertheless, over the course of a decade, I reached a point where I knew I needed to transition. The institution where I was working at the time boasted a truly excellent library. I began by immersing myself in psychiatry textbooks, seeking to understand the historical and contemporary perspectives on sexual orientation and gender identity. Initially, my exploration revealed the significant progress that had been made in depathologising sexual orientation, with the medical community having largely removed it from the context of being considered a mental health pathology or disease. However, I also observed that the medical literature, while progressive in its understanding of sexual orientation, was still grappling with gender identities. In particular, gender dysphoria in adulthood was still frequently pathologised, recognised and registered as a distinct disease within the diagnostic criteria of many prominent psychiatric associations.

Now, significant advancements in medical understanding have led to the depathologisation of gender dysphoria in adults as well, reflecting a more nuanced and accepting view of diverse gender identities. However, the knowledge available during my initial period of exploration profoundly shaped my personal transition journey. I meticulously considered the potential impact of my transition on various facets of my life, including my professional career and my social interactions. This careful consideration was the primary reason behind my proactive approach to developing allyship within my workplace. I thoughtfully identified individuals who I believed would be supportive and understanding during my transition.

In the early stages of my transition, I entertained the notion that I could simply self-medicate as I was a doctor. This proved to be a terrible misstep and the self-administered hormones had a rather erratic and unintended impact on my body. Despite my efforts, I was not achieving the physical changes I desired. It took me nearly a year before I came to the stark realisation that I was actually causing more harm to myself than good.

Once again, I began to research. I was determined to find qualified specialists who possessed the necessary expertise to support my transition, including mental health professionals who could provide psychological support, endocrinologists who could appropriately prescribe and manage hormone therapy and surgeons who specialised in gender reassignment surgery—these were the key areas where I recognised I needed professional guidance and support.

A psychiatrist, who is a very dear friend of mine, connected me to a plastic surgeon who initially refused to operate on me. Six years later, they got back in touch and said they felt ready to assist me. This surgeon said that they had personally gained significant experience and expertise in performing gender affirming surgeries during the intervening time. This selfless offer was deeply touching and exemplified an exceptionally high level of moral and ethical conduct, both as a medical professional and as a compassionate human being.

Ironically, and for reasons that remain unclear and felt discriminatory, the hospital where this surgeon worked declined to grant me permission to undergo the operation there. This refusal was a powerful trigger.

I brought the situation to the attention of my mentor and the administration at my institution. Simultaneously, my supportive surgeon friend also reiterated their offer, stating that they would be willing to perform my gender-affirming surgery at my own institution where I worked—the Mahatma Gandhi Medical College and Research Institution, or MGMCRI, in Puducherry. This was a truly pivotal moment, and it felt as though many pieces of the puzzle were finally falling into place.

Furthermore, during this period, as my colleagues at the workplace gradually became aware that Sameer was transitioning and wished to be known as Sameera, an interesting development occurred.

We housed an HIV clinic, where transgender individuals—*thirunangais* from Tamil Nadu, *kinnars* from Chhattisgarh and Bihar and *hijras* from Maharashtra—often sought care. The surgeon who was associated with this clinic had been performing some gender-affirming surgeries, but these procedures were often rudimentary and primarily involved emasculation, unfortunately leading to complications in two patients and resulting in medical and legal issues. Consequently, the hospital administration decided to place restrictions on the types of surgeries this in-house surgeon was performing. It was at this juncture that the administration approached me, believing that I could offer valuable assistance, particularly considering my own ongoing medical transition within the workplace.

Thus, my personal journey of pursuing medical transition became intricately intertwined with the hospital's need to establish a more comprehensive and ethically sound gender-affirming surgical care programme.

The setting up of a gender care team received the boost it needed because of a supportive hospital administration. The multidisciplinary team, comprising a dermatologist, a psychiatrist, two general surgeons, a gynaecologist, an anaesthesiologist, a legal expert, an administrative officer and a community representative, comprehensively addressed the gender-affirming procedural needs of transgender individuals seeking care at MGMCRI.

The foundation upon which the Sexual Reassignment Surgery, or SRS, protocol was meticulously drafted at MGMCRI was laid through a period of extensive and dedicated research (the term used now is Gender Affirming Surgery, but the term SRS was prevalent at the time we wrote the protocol in 2016). I diligently reviewed a wide array of resources and established guidelines, with the primary source of guidance being the recommendations put forth by the World Professional Association for Transgender Health, more commonly known as WPATH. Specifically, I relied on the earlier versions of their guidelines, as this was the prevailing standard at the time. While these guidelines have since undergone significant reforms and updates, it was this foundational knowledge from the earlier WPATH recommendations that served as the bedrock for organising the protocol.[1]

In addition to this academic research, another crucial element that significantly shaped the development of the protocol was my growing involvement with community-based support networks.

The protocol offered a five-step process which involved self-identification as a transgender person, initial contact with the Transgender Clinic with a request for gender affirmative procedure, mental health professional screening or counselling, certification, ensuring surgery readiness (surgical counselling, dermatology check-up, anaesthesia clearance, necessary blood investigations) and consent preparation.

The day before I was wheeled in for my surgery, I finally wore a churidar kurta to work. On 4 November 2016, I sat on the other side of the desk, not as a doctor, but as a client. Not in a shirt and pants, but in a bright blue kurta, a white dupatta draped over my shoulder. It was wonderful. I was so happy telling my colleagues that I will be undergoing surgery tomorrow. I was the first person to be operated under the protocol.

The experience of becoming a patient within the very system I had helped create revealed dimensions of gender-affirming surgery that no amount of clinical expertise could have prepared me for. The vulnerability of being a patient, even within my own institution, exposed how power dynamics, institutional hierarchies and personal relationships intersect with medical care in ways that can either support or undermine patient dignity and autonomy.

The recovery process taught me about the importance of comprehensive aftercare that addresses not only physical healing but also the emotional, social and professional adjustments that accompany surgical transition. My experience as a patient revealed gaps in our protocol that were invisible from a purely clinical perspective, particularly regarding the long-term support needs of patients navigating workplace transitions and family relationships during recovery.

I must emphasise that the MGMCRI protocol in 2016 was not where my advocacy journey began. It was actually the institutional culmination of foundational community-centred work that started years earlier through SAATHII's Vistaara project.[2] This distinction is crucial because Vistaara helped me build the transgender healthcare advocacy roots that made institutional changes like MGMCRI possible.

My work as a resource person for SAATHII's 'Vistaara: Medical & Health Domain' project—'Ending Discrimination and Expanding Access to Inclusive and Stigma-free Services for

LGBTI Communities in India: a Four-State Initiative'—provided the community engagement framework that would later inform everything I did at MGMCRI. My role involved providing advice and insights on how medical curricula, medical education programmes and broader health-related initiatives addressed the topic of transgender health.

This mentorship spurred me to delve even deeper into researching and understanding the various guidelines and resources available, and to consider how these could be effectively tailored and adapted to the specific needs of the local population we served at MGMCRI.

The ripple effects of this work began to manifest within just three years. In May 2019, the National Health Mission designated our MGMCRI protocol as 'a role model worth emulating in transgender healthcare nation-wide'. This recognition was profoundly validating, but more importantly, it catalysed systematic expansion across multiple states that I could never have imagined when we were developing those initial protocols in relative isolation.

Tamil Nadu's leadership in implementation has been particularly inspiring, building on its foundation as the first state to establish a Transgender Welfare Board in 2008. Their provision of free gender-affirming surgeries in government hospitals, comprehensive social support systems and educational scholarships demonstrates what systematic commitment to transgender healthcare can achieve when political will aligns with adequate resource allocation.

The immediate impact was systematic expansion that built upon the foundational principles we had developed through Vistaara's four-state initiative. The documented replication began directly with Tamil Nadu, where the National Health Mission team that visited MGMCRI in May 2019 also established transgender clinics at Rajiv Gandhi Government General Hospital in Chennai and Rajaji Medical College Hospital in Madurai, explicitly using our protocol as the template.

The over 500 patients from sixteen states who have registered through MGMCRI and the over 300 surgeries we've conducted demonstrate demand that extends far beyond our institutional capacity. This success has created challenges, as we've become a referral centre for patients who cannot access quality care in their home states, highlighting how institutional recognition without comprehensive educational reform and community advocacy infrastructure can create unsustainable bottlenecks.

Things are changing fast, though. The evolution of medical education regarding transgender health represents one of the most significant shifts I've witnessed in my three decades in medicine, but this transformation was catalysed by the foundational advocacy work I undertook through SAATHII's Vistaara project, which helped me understand how discriminatory medical curricula perpetuate healthcare barriers for transgender communities.

A direct result of Vistaara's project was the development of transgender health curriculum for nursing and allied health professionals at SBV University. This achievement represents something even more transformative than clinical protocols because nursing education touches every aspect of healthcare delivery. When you transform nursing education to be transgender-affirmative, you influence thousands of future healthcare interactions in ways that extend far beyond any single clinical protocol.

When I completed my medical training in the 1990s, transgender health was literally invisible in our curriculum—not mentioned, not acknowledged, not even pathologised in ways that would have at least provided a framework for understanding. My work with Vistaara involved analysing medical textbooks commonly prescribed by Indian medical institutions from the perspective of absences, misrepresentations and inaccurate information pertaining to sexual orientation, gender identity, expression and sex characteristics. This systematic analysis revealed how medical education actively constructed transgender identities as pathological while providing no clinical guidance for respectful, effective care.

The textbook analysis work I conducted through Vistaara became foundational to the broader national movement for medical curriculum reform. When we discovered that gynaecology textbooks characterised homosexuality, transvestism and transsexuality as abnormal sexual behaviours, and that psychiatry textbooks still listed homosexuality among sexual disorders, while stating that transsexuals may have high degrees of concomitant psychiatric disorders, we documented systematic educational discrimination that was shaping healthcare provider attitudes and clinical practices.

This documentation work contributed directly to the National Medical Commission's eventual mandate to remove discriminatory LGBTI portrayals from textbooks following the Human Rights Watch's recognition in 2021. The same government that directed that reform has, five years later, passed legislation reinstating state control over transgender identity through a medical board constituted under the NMC's own regulatory framework. The tools of reform have been turned into instruments of erasure. The recent curriculum reforms, introducing AETCOM module competencies in 2019–2021,[3] represent progress that emerged from years of advocacy documenting educational gaps and developing alternative approaches through projects like Vistaara.

The Transgender Persons (Protection of Rights) Act, 2019, established unprecedented healthcare rights that transformed this experimental approach into a legal mandate. The integration of transgender healthcare into schemes like Ayushman Bharat TG Plus, providing 5 lakhs of annual coverage for hormone therapy, gender-affirming surgeries and post-operative care, represented a policy shift that fundamentally altered the landscape of accessible transgender healthcare in India.

However, the gap between progressive policy and discriminatory practice remains a persistent challenge that continues to frustrate me professionally and personally. The certificate requirements that contradict the 2014 *National Legal Services Authority vs. Union of India* judgement's emphasis on self-identification have, as of March 2026, been formally enshrined in statute. The Transgender Persons (Protection of Rights) Amendment Act, 2026, has not only retained those contradictions but has deleted the right to self-identification entirely. What I described here as bureaucratic tension is now completed legislative reversal. I continue to witness discrimination in healthcare settings despite legal frameworks, and the complexity of accessing benefits through bureaucratic processes often defeats the most vulnerable patients who need these services most desperately.

Reviewing current implementations reveals that much of the mandated transgender health education focuses on awareness rather than clinical competency. Students learn that transgender people exist and deserve respectful treatment, which is foundational, but they often graduate without practical skills for hormone monitoring, surgical aftercare or the complex psychosocial aspects of transgender healthcare that define clinical practice.

There are no formal Indian Council of Medical Research (ICMR) guidelines yet, though a few government documents and white papers do exist. Indian Standards of Care, version 1 (or ISOC v1) for Persons with Gender Incongruence, developed by medical practitioners, was released in November 2020. These guidelines have not been adopted on the national scale, as they require ICMR to mandate it.

Since 2020, I have been a part of the United Kingdom's National Health Service (NHS).

My journey through the multiple roles of protocol developer, patient and ongoing advocate has fundamentally transformed my understanding of gender-affirming surgeries from technical procedures to deeply personal experiences that intersect medical expertise, community advocacy and individual autonomy. Here are three learnings of mine. First, transgender health education must move beyond awareness to clinical competency, with hands-on training that enables general practitioners to provide comprehensive care rather than reflexive referrals to overwhelmed specialist centres.

Second, the integration of transgender health education throughout the curriculum rather than as isolated modules would normalise transgender patients as part of routine medical practice. The educational transformation requires systematic change rather than add-on training that reinforces marginalisation.

Third, involving transgender community members and transgender healthcare professionals in curriculum development and delivery ensures that medical education reflects lived experiences rather than theoretical frameworks that may not align with patient needs and priorities.

My perspective as an NHS clinician, who has navigated both sides of the gender affirmative care equation, reveals paradoxes that continue to challenge my understanding of how healthcare systems can simultaneously advance and restrict transgender healthcare within different national contexts. The theoretical frameworks appear contradictory—India's developing healthcare system has embraced community-centred, accessible approaches while the UK's advanced system has evolved towards increasingly restrictive policies that contradict international best practices.

My advocacy now emphasises the importance of community-centred approaches that prioritise patient autonomy and self-determination over medical gatekeeping, while simultaneously ensuring that patients have access to comprehensive information and support systems that enable informed decision-making. The balance between removing barriers to access while maintaining appropriate clinical safeguards requires constant recalibration based on evolving evidence and community feedback. Globally, the next decade requires community-engaged, longitudinal studies examining health outcomes and intervention effectiveness that can inform evidence-based policy development and clinical practice improvement. The systematic integration of transgender health competencies in medical curricula must become standard practice rather than optional training that varies by institution and location.

Post Script: I wrote earlier in this piece that the gap between progressive policy and discriminatory practice remains a persistent challenge. With the new Transgender Persons (Protection of Rights) Amendment Act 2026, that framing no longer holds. The gap has been closed—not by bringing practice up to policy, but by dismantling the policy itself. The 2019 Act, the NALSA principles, the self-identification framework: these are now formally reversed in statute. What I described as a tension has become a complete rollback.

The law does not protect. It erases. It removes the right to self-identification—the very right that the Supreme Court upheld in *NALSA vs. Union of India* in 2014, the constitutional foundation upon which everything I have described in this piece is built. It replaces self-identification with a state-appointed medical board, headed by a chief medical officer, whose recommendation is required before a transgender person can be legally recognised.

The law specifies that the board must examine a person's biological characteristics—primary sexual characteristics, external genitalia, chromosomal patterns, gonadal development—but does not prescribe what that examination involves. The procedure is left entirely to the discretion of the board.

Under this law, to be legally recognised as the person I have always been, I would need to undress in front of medical colleagues who hold state authority over my identity. I have spent my career fighting for patient dignity and autonomy. I am now the patient this system would strip of both.

The law also criminalises 'alluring' a person to adopt a transgender identity—language broad enough to encompass a doctor advising that gender-affirming care is clinically appropriate. I write this from the United Kingdom, where I practise under GMC jurisdiction and the protection of a different legal framework. That distance is not incidental. The criminal provisions of this law—carrying up to life imprisonment—have effectively silenced the professional voice of every Indian doctor who might otherwise speak. I am writing from the only position from which this can currently be said without criminal exposure. My distance is not a choice of safety. It is the structural condition of this argument being made at all.

I have dedicated three decades to the proposition that medicine can be an instrument of dignity rather than control. That proposition is now a site of active political contest in the country where my work began. The next decade will not only be defined by curriculum reforms or insurance schemes. It will be defined by whether the medical profession—in India and internationally—has the courage to refuse when the state asks it to become the agent of erasure. The Declaration of Geneva says doctors must not use their medical knowledge to violate human rights and civil liberties, even under threat. That clause was written because history showed what happens when medicine forgets whose side it is on. We are at that moment again.

Notes

1. Read a ground report in *Hindustan Times* about the creation of this protocol: 'The making of a standard protocol in gender care', Dhamini Ratnam, 'https://www.hindustantimes.com/india-news/the-making of-a-standard-protocol-in-gender-care/story-bbncDzdQX3CIZD 76doHS0L.html.
2. SAATHII (Solidarity and Action Against the HIV infection in India) is a Chennai-based NGO that works in the field of stigma-free healthcare across the country.
3. The Attitude, Ethics and Communication (AETCOM) module, introduced by the National Medical Commission in 2019 focuses on shaping professional qualities and communication skills in the undergraduate medical training programmes.

SUBSPACE

Written by Ammel Sharon
Illustrated by Sharanya Ravi

Subspace

Written by Ammel Sharon
Illustrated by Sharanya Ravi

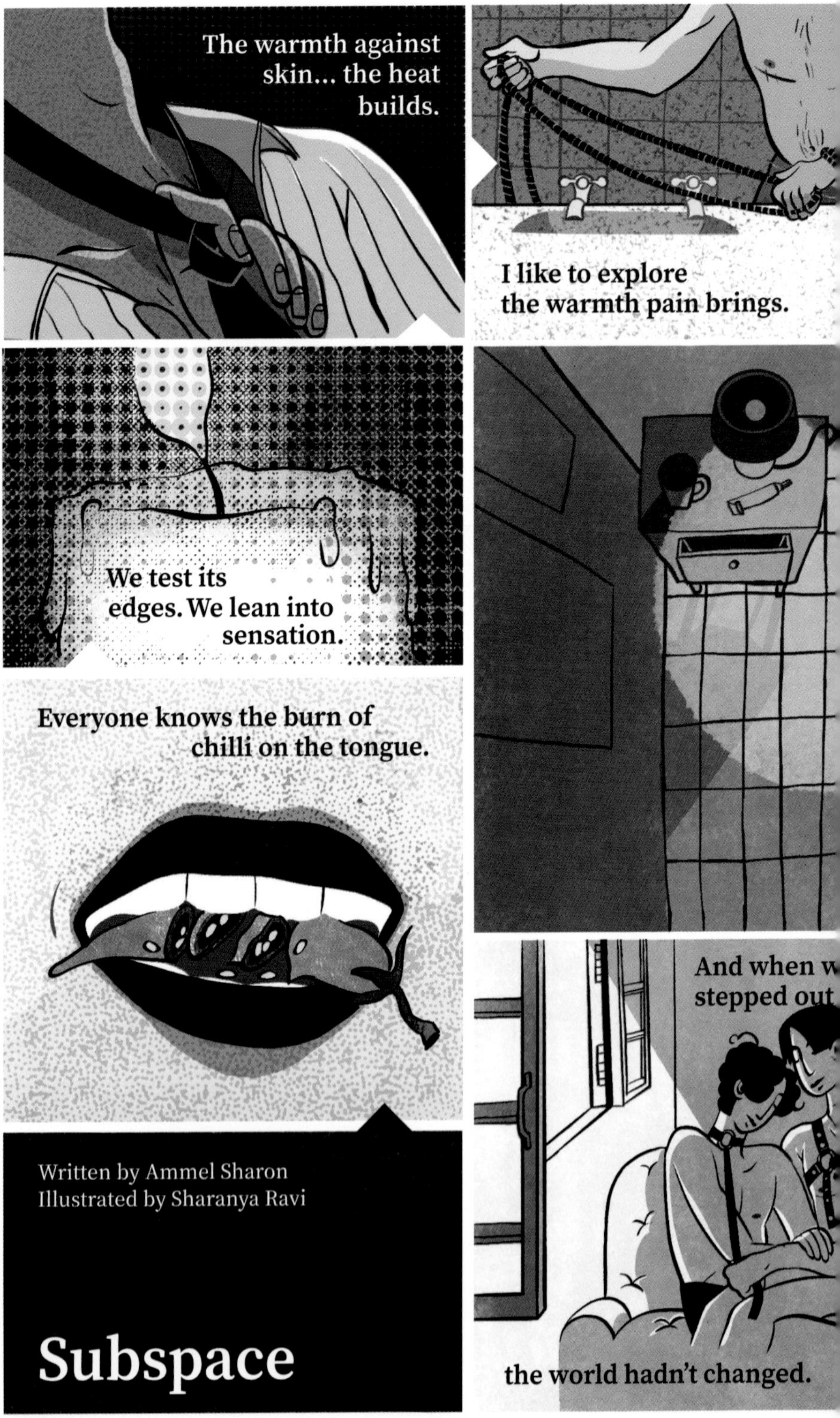

Tanu:
same safe word?
es, *blue*.
We discuss our limits before play.
I've been told porn seeks release, but pleasure in kink lies in restraint.
Rafi gave me what
I asked for.
He also tended to my wounds.
'Make it burn,' I asked. They answered with rope and rhythm.
Subspace: *where sensation replaces thought.*
I had.
Not every knot leaves a mark.
Some just hold you long enough to soften.

THE 11TH DIRECTION AKA DISHA PINKY SHAIKH

Written and illustrated by
Priya Dali

The 11th DIRECTION AKA DISHA PINKY SHAIKH

Written and illustrated by Priya Dali

School had taught young Disha that there are only ten directions, so imagine her confusion and amusement when she saw a sign that said '11th Direction'.

As someone who couldn't see herself reflected in any direction she looked, she felt like she could relate to the unusual sign. Lost in the noise, unheard of, unacknowledged and dismissed.

Disha was born in Yeola, Maharashtra, in a nomadic family, and knew from a young age that she looked at the world differently.

When you have to find your own way in a world that doesn't let you take a step towards yourself, pushing past the boundaries, questioning the norms, taking risks and diving in become the tools to create your own map.

Adopting the name 'Disha' became an early step in her journey of envisioning the 11th direction. And the questions led her path.

“Why are sarees, jewellery and make-up all for women?”

Much to her father's dislike, Disha had always enjoyed dressing up and playing dandiya instead of sports like the boys.

Eldest among the siblings and burdened by how her choices could hamper her siblings' future, she ran away from home at the age of twenty. She found shelter in the company of her trans sisters.

“If I had been born without any imposition, not conditioned by gender norms and had gotten the chance to exist as my current self since the beginning, maybe I would have been wearing a saree and a beard, and I'd still be a woman and acknowledged as one.”

Disha considers them as her first family and hence took up their name 'Shaikh'. She believes that those who accept you just as you are and back you up are your real family.

From having to go out onto the streets to attending family events to give out blessings, she moved through the world with the support of her trans sisters.

“If I had the power to bless people and grant them their wishes, why wouldn't I bestow that hand on myself?”

“Why worship me as a devi when you can't respect me as a human?”

Constantly being boxed as the third gender irked her.

“If I ask for more, beyond entertainment and blessings, if I ask for equal rights, it's too much.

Too much more than what's convenient for society. Why?”

“How can I be upset with the lovers gone by when it’s the society that keeps tearing us apart?”

Disha developed a deeper understanding of the various challenges of being a trans woman in India during the painful process of her breakup with her long-term partner.

“Why is my relationship not recognised in public?”

A separation that was caused due to her lover’s unaccepting mother, felt even more isolating when she couldn’t find films, books or stories that looked like hers.

“Heartbreak connected me to poetry, but once again, why do the words sound familiar but still make me feel unseen?”

While poetry healed her heart, she made her way into politics to speak about trans issues such as employment, livelihood, lack of choice and the need for rights.

She didn't want to sit on the sidelines. She wanted to be the change.

> "What does it mean to be a community?"

Disha built a community home in Srirampur, the Tritiyapanti Samaj Seva Ashram, to support her trans sisters and ensure a safe and comfortable life for them.

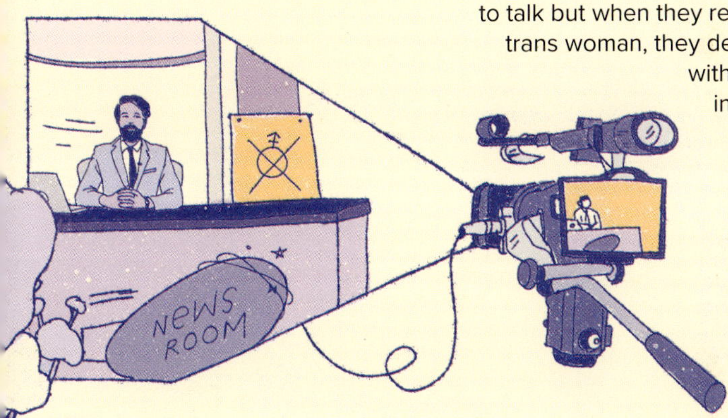

Once she was invited to a news channel to talk but when they realised that she's a trans woman, they decided to move on with the show without including her voice. A strong protest by her party, the Vanchit Bahujan Aghadi, made the channel change its stance. Today, she is the party's spokesperson and state vice-president.

> "The minute they know about my party affiliation, they offer me a chair and my words are suddenly audible. Funny, isn't it?"

The party association ensured that one couldn't simply ignore or push her aside anymore, and she made sure to address rallies and public talks, thereby ensuring that her voice travels far and wide.

Today, students and supporters want to take selfies with her, hug her and wish her well.

A sign of progress, she calls it.

The opposite of what life was like on the streets where people would change their direction upon seeing her.

Disha now spends most of her time and focus on improving the position of transgender people in politics and how to ensure more trans people get basic rights.

> "We don't want to be the dhaniya in the salad—mere decoration. We want to reach a spot where no one can ignore us."

Disha Pinky Shaikh is the 11th direction.

THE FOREST

Written and illustrated by
Payal Rathva

After Rupa's birth, her parents named her Raju. They always felt something that no one knew—not parents, not friends, nor sister. They only wanted to live by their own rules. When no one was on the road, they would walk with a *thumak*, talk with a lilt. They liked it very much.

When no one was at home, they would wear the sister's or mother's clothes. But that happiness was only inside closed walls. And that happiness was nurtured by tears of pain too. Because he knew he couldn't take that happiness out of the four walls into freedom. Because in front of him, danger hovered—the parents, the friends, the sister; society itself.

One day, when no one was home, a neighbour peeked through the window. They told everything to the parents. The parents thrashed Rupa. Now, life became a lot more difficult because the parents would not leave the house. But whenever there was a wedding, or some festival, Rupa would put henna on the fingers and apply nail paint. The parents didn't like this at all. Sometimes, they even beat them in front of people.

One day, one of the priests in the tribal village, the Badwa (who guards the shrine), told them that their child had an evil shadow. They took Rupa to the temple. There, the Badwa unleashed a torrent of thrashings. But Rupa was steadfast and her mouth shut, not saying anything. As time went on, the parents became sure that their child had improved. But only Raju knew that she was still Rupa. And she no longer wanted to be confined inside the four walls of the house. She wanted freedom.

The family lived by raising goats, cattle and such animals. In the tribal areas, often in the summer, the green bushes dry up. Then there is no fodder for cows and buffaloes. So, the parents asked them to take the cattle to the forest to graze. After doing this for fifteen days, they thought: *I am alone in the forest, there is no one here. Here, I can bring out Rupa.* The next day, they packed the sister's clothes, mirror, bangles and makeup into a bundle along with the tiffin for the forest. They wore the clothes, applied the lipstick and, looking into the mirror, felt happy: *How beautiful my lips are.* After putting on a bindi, they exclaimed again: *How beautiful my face looks.*

Someone saw them in the forest. The family came to know. When they came home, the parents threw them out of the house. But Rupa had begun searching for people like them. They started living among them. And now, Raju is no longer Raju. She is only Rupa.

Rupa.

SURVIVING HOMELESSNESS AND A LIFE OF CRIME

L Ramakrishnan, Randhoni Lairikyengbam, Swetha Shri, Khush Pahuja, Amit Bisoi, Rahmathulla, Sharmista Das and Biswa Bhusan Pattanayak

In February 2024, a member of SAATHII's team got a call from a social worker associated with the Juvenile Justice Board in a southern state. The call was about a seventeen-year-old 'girl who behaves like a boy' who was in conflict with the law and apprehended by the police.

The minor, Noor (name changed), was arrested along with members of a local gang of young men who allegedly drove around on motorcycles and snatched mobile phones from pedestrians. Upon discovering that the individual was below 18, the authorities incarcerated Noor in an observation home for female juvenile delinquents. In the home, the social worker noticed that Noor, while assigned female, was gender-nonconforming, preferred to wear clothes meant for men, and had a masculine demeanour. Further, the child did not seem to have any supportive family members or address of residence.

We visited the Juvenile Justice Board, and met the judicial magistrate in charge of the case. We explained diversity in gender expressions and the challenges faced by gender-nonconforming children at home and in educational and childcare institutions. We also touched on the lacunae in the current legal system, with the Transgender Rights Act being mostly focused on rights of adult trans persons and the Juvenile Justice Act not considering the issues of gender-nonconforming children. We took care to point out that not all gender-nonconforming children go on to identify as transgender, and we would not know the child's self-affirmed gender without asking them.

The judicial magistrate arranged for us to have a private meeting with Noor, as she felt the child would be more likely to open up in our presence than with her and the social worker. Sure enough: Noor appeared greatly relieved to meet us, and opened up instantly. He shared that he had always known he was a boy and recognised himself as a thirunambi (local term for trans man). He came from a dysfunctional family: His stepfather was physically abusive to both Noor and Noor's siblings (both assigned female at birth). Noor had dropped out of school at fourteen because of bullying, and left his natal home, spending the last three years on the streets, living in a slum and sleeping in auto-rickshaws parked there. The only people who affirmed his gender and accepted him as one of their own were some of the cis male teenagers and young men in the slum. Unfortunately, this group consisted mostly of youth who had dropped out of school, and earned money by selling stolen mobile phones and drugs. Noor said he was interested in the fine arts, wanted to become a tattoo artist and showed us paintings he had done on the walls of the observation home.

Listening to this account, the judicial magistrate was deeply moved. She called Noor to her chambers, apologised to him on behalf of the juvenile justice and education systems which—according to her—had failed him because these systems were not designed to account for the challenges faced by gender-nonconforming children. She hoped that he wouldn't put himself in a situation where he would need to cross paths with any law enforcement agency again. She also requested that SAATHII and its community partner, Nirangal, support Noor till he reached the age of eighteen, and asked us to help him get into school and subsequently get employed.

Over the past year, we met Noor frequently for peer support, introducing him to other young trans masculine persons, and helping him apply for jobs on turning eighteen. While he remains interested in completing his school education, and pursuing the fine arts, he prioritises earning enough money to be able to get off the streets, and save up for future studies.

He has now been able to find a job in the pantry of an Information Technology (IT) firm, where he has disclosed his trans identity to the human resources team and immediate colleagues. He is now staying in an apartment with a group of young trans men, all of whom share the rent and other costs.

In the past year, we have engaged with over 1,000 government officials from juvenile justice, child welfare and legal service authorities on the issue of safety and protection of gender-nonconforming children. The judicial magistrate, who helped with Noor's case, went on to deal with another situation of a transgender girl, where she summoned the mother to the juvenile justice court, explained gender diversity to her, exhorted her to respect her child's gender expression and identity, and ensure that the bullying from the siblings stopped. On our part, we have learnt that while laws, policies and court directives are vital to the work we do with trans persons, it is equally important to sensitise government officials who engage with trans persons because they are the human face of the system.

YOUR NAME, THEIR RULES

Kavish Kaushik

A trans man living on rent suddenly faces the police that have arrived to investigate a domestic dispute in the landlord's home. The police find out that the renter is transgender. Immediately, they're rude and threaten him to leave. A small remonstration and the trans man is slapped.

A trans woman, originally from Haryana, lives in another state because of family problems and her job. She applies for a transgender card, but the application is stuck for over a year. Every time she inquires, she is asked to re-upload the same documents. Eventually, officials stop taking her calls.

A trans man ekes out a living as a mehendi artist. He decides to apply for a transgender card because he lives in Haryana, which pays a monthly pension of ₹1,000. It's enough to get by, he thinks. But every time he goes to the government office, he is told that no guidelines have been issued and just the transgender card will not do—his Aadhaar card and medical examination are also needed.

Another trans man is a central government employee who just needs to change his identity in his department. He has already made the change in his education documents. But the department rejects his Aadhaar card every time, despite attaching all supporting documents. No amount of re-applying appears to work.

These are the battles that transgender people have to experience on a daily basis. The Supreme Court's *NALSA vs. Union of India* verdict, which affirmed the rights of the transgender community, came eleven years ago. The Transgender Act, which expanded our rights and provided a framework for their realisation, was passed six years ago.[1] But how much have they worked on the ground? Our work across rural Haryana doesn't paint a pretty picture of their implementation.

Take the transgender card. The online application process was created so that a person didn't have to disclose their identity while applying. But despite submitting the application online, officials ask for numerous documents to be submitted offline because the staff have no clue about transgender identity. Not just that, officials will regularly ask for documents not mentioned in the Act because they feel like it. No priority is accorded to work related to transgender people. The Act mandates a period of one month at the maximum for such applications, but in reality, it takes years. And this was even before the new amendments to the law.

The real rub is that without a transgender card, no trans person can change any other document. They are left hanging without a recourse.

Or take the Aadhaar card. The Act says that based on the transgender card, other documents can be updated without a gazette notification for name change. But from every government office, the demand is for gazette notification, ensuring unending harassment for the trans person who has to repeatedly visit the local office as well as the head office in Chandigarh.

The same situation exists with education documents too. For example, the Central Bureau of Secondary Education demands cards as well as a gazette notification and a recommendation letter from the school. But how does one get any document out of a school when the staff of the institute is not even aware of gender and sexuality?

Unfortunately, these are not academic questions for us. Without these documents, we cannot go anywhere to clarify our identity. Think of a trans man who is taking hormone therapy and has facial hair now, but whose identity documents still list him as female. How does he survive everyday situations? How can he get ahead in life?

Note

1. In March 2026, the Transgender Persons (Protection of Rights) Amendment Act came into force.

ON THE FORCE

Ronit Jha

Run a kilometre in six minutes or under, jump three feet or higher and nine feet or longer and then throw a shot put ball at least ten feet away. I had already qualified the prelims and then two papers—general knowledge and Hindi—in the mains before I stepped up on the starting block for my physical exam. Since I was ten years old, I had dreamt of being a police inspector. I was confident of doing well, I had practised for years for this recruitment examination.

But I didn't know that the real hurdle would come off the sports field. When I first reached the examination venue, the people behaved as if an alien had shown up. They kept me and the other trans candidates sitting on the side. An hour went by, then another. After I cleared the physical examination, they hit me with a barrage of insulting questions in the document verification process. Mentally, it was torture. No officer there had heard about the 2019 Transgender Rights Act. They challenged me repeatedly on my name change. 'Here on this document, the name is something else, and here it is something else. Why did you change your name? What was the need?' They asked and asked. They did not even read the transgender card, on which was clearly written my birth name and my chosen, current name.

This went on for more than three hours. Two other transgender candidates—both had cleared the examinations, mind you—broke down in tears. But I didn't. I had dabbled in student politics in college. I stood my ground.

They kept asking in Hindi, 'Why did you get it done? What is this thing?' Their mindset was that a transgender person only sings and dances. Even on my Aadhaar card, the same questions cropped up—why this name, why was it changed. Other candidates were checked quickly and left. But we were kept waiting.

This was not limited to the junior officers. After I cleared the verification, one top officer gave me a warm welcome. But another cross-questioned: 'You are born in a Brahmin family, how can you get OBC reservation?' They troubled me, but others had my back and I got the joining letter.

I was ecstatic. But people turned this happiness into sorrow by trolling me. It was frustrating for me and my parents. People had no idea about trans people, and the local media splashed my photo with misleading news. On social media, people accused me of trying to 'steal the benefit of being both a boy and a girl'. In my home town, my parents were tense and rumours were flying. People were calling them and asking all sorts of questions. I could not even celebrate. I stopped going out. This went on for months. The months between the selection in June and my joining date in August were among the toughest of my life.

I was born in Sitamarhi. It's not a big place but my schooling was good. From my childhood, there were always the little things. When I was in Class 6, a little frustration set in because my body started to develop. After Class 10, I went to Patna. I opted for science because I had topped in it. In Patna, I started breaking out of the cocoon my life had been in back in Sitamarhi. I shared things with my friends. But I was also felt different from all of them. When I started menstruating, I cried a lot. I felt very uncomfortable. When someone treated me like a girl, I felt very frustrated. But still I could not do anything, because this is Bihar. And in Bihar, especially in the villages, no one understood.

I was still doing well in studies so my parents bought me a mobile phone. So, I started to search about things. I read about Aryan Pasha bhaiyya.[1] But when I tried to share it with others, they shut me down. 'No, you are a girl, it doesn't matter what you are feeling.' This was new for them, this world did not exist for them. So they reacted poorly.

Just as I had cleared Class 12, the shadow of the pandemic descended on us. I was forced to take admission in a girl's college. Only a few friends knew about me. They never revealed anything, because it could nuke my education. So, I too kept everything to myself.

After my masters, I saw the posts for the Bihar police sub-inspector exam. I decided that while I wanted to come out, I wanted to do so from a big position. It would give me some societal legitimacy—especially in Bihar, where police officers are respected and reputable—and people might react less strongly.

I told my mom I am filling out the form, that I'm applying for the transgender card. If it hadn't been for her, maybe I could not even come out, maybe I could not even live my life due to frustration and depression. She is why I am here today. My papa also said, 'No problem, if you're our son, then for us, it's a plus point.'

Still, I was depressed. One day, I asked my mom, 'When you gave birth to me, did you see a boy or a girl? You saw a child. Now tell me, if my happiness is at stake, would you want me to live happily, or suffocate like this all my life?'

I never gave up; I kept showing my family videos of other trans success stories, marriages, books and whatever other relevant material I could find. The biggest plus point for me: I started preparing for a job. Every parent's dream is for their children to be settled. I want to tell everyone struggling with this to please first get a job and focus on your career. Your parents will accept you eventually, even if it takes them time. But never stop trying.

I'm now posted in Supaul, where people don't have much idea about these topics. Still, I have never faced problems. The department is supportive. People who get to know my story say we want you to move forward. Hours are erratic. We go on flag marches for eight to ten hours. The call for inspection can come anytime. Once my probation is over, I will become a sub-inspector.

My work is challenging but full of adventure. I always wanted to become an IPS officer. But I became serious when I saw my community struggling. I saw some policemen misbehaving and humiliating many. Since I've joined, there is more awareness. Now people don't have the courage to misbehave, because they know if they do, Ronit will not spare them. Our image has changed.

Note

1. Aryan Pasha is a Delhi-based trans man activist, athlete and bodybuilder.

QUEERING THE LAW

AN ADVOCATE'S TALE

AMRITANANDA CHAKRAVORTY

It is 10.15 a.m. on a hot summer day at the Delhi High Court. X's hand is tightly held by a woman police constable, who is stressed about the long line outside the High Court for entry passes. There are fifteen minutes to go before the judges walk in. Suddenly, a middle-aged woman comes in front of X and starts crying. '*Tune humari naak katwa di … ghar ki izzat nilam karwa di*,' [You embarrassed us and dishonoured our household] she wails. The woman constable is empathetic towards the middle-aged woman, as she knows that she is the mother of X. But she sternly tells her, '*Aunty, yahan nahi … court me batana*.' [Not here, speak in the court.]

Outside the airless courtroom, X's lawyer is pacing furiously. She has filed a petition for *habeas corpus* (produce the body) before the court for X, a young queer woman of twenty-one, at the behest of her partner, ZY. The police have been directed to bring X before the court. Neither ZY nor the lawyer knows what X will say before the court, given that X is being unlawfully detained by her family. ZY is on high alert when X is brought by the police. At 10.30 a.m., as X walks by ZY, she blinks.

Relief courses like a waterfall through ZY, who is certain X will speak up for both of them before the judge. The lawyer is puzzled. 'Are you sure? She did not say anything to you.'

ZY nods confidently. 'Trust me. She will.'

When the matter comes up, the judges walk out of the open courtroom into their chamber. Since it is a *habeas corpus* case, it is in-camera, or away from the prying eyes of the public and the media. For about forty minutes, the courtroom is filled with loud whispers about the nature of the case.

Things move fast. In an hour, X is released and the court says she is free to go anywhere, including with ZY. It turns out that she told the judges that she wanted to be with ZY and knew what she was doing, despite her parents' attempts to convince the court otherwise.

But the battle is not yet over. After ensuring that the order would be uploaded shortly, the lawyer whisks the couple away from the court premises, where X's parents are still hovering around, to figure out options for a safe shelter. It will be an uphill struggle.

The lawyer in question is me, and the wild swings of this sultry morning comprise the sobering reality for queer people who choose to exercise their rights to live as per their own wishes, and not under parental diktats. Our experiences of navigating the law and courtrooms has been a bizarre mix of emotions—oftentimes jumping with joy or crying in absolute agony or holding one's head in sheer frustration. The Indian queer community's tryst with law is more like a toxic love affair, where each decade comes with its own share of heartbreak and loss, and the unbelievable contortions we are required to perform to access a modicum of legal protection, whether through courts, police or other state authorities.

The landscape of LGBTQ+ jurisprudence in India was transformed on 6 September 2018, when the Supreme Court struck down Section 377 of the erstwhile Indian Penal Code, which criminalised penile-nonvaginal sexual acts between consenting adults. The seeds of *Navtej Johar vs. Union of India* were first planted in the landmark decision of the Delhi High Court in *Naz Foundation vs. Union of India* in 2009, and the groundbreaking 2014 Supreme Court decision in *NALSA vs. Union of India and others*, which granted legal recognition to transgender people in India. From Naz to NALSA to Navtej, it seemed to be all about loving the 'N', but when it came to marriage, the community and its lawyers realised the jurisprudence did not extend to 'M', when in 2023, the apex court refused to uphold the right of same-sex couples to marry under secular or religious law.

LGBTQ+ jurisprudence over the last thirty years can be divided into two phases—the legal campaign against Section 377, and the demand for legal recognition for transgender persons and queer relationships since.

The seeds of the first phase were sowed by the 1994 constitutional challenge to Section 377 in *AIDS Bhedbhav Virodhi Andolan (ABVA) vs. Union of India* in the Delhi High Court, which was later dismissed for non-prosecution. Naz Foundation India challenged the colonial law in November 2001, which culminated in the High Court reading down the provision on 2 July, 2009. I witnessed first-hand the effect of the Naz verdict—thousands of queer persons came out to their families, friends, peers and colleagues, support groups for queer people rose exponentially, police harassment plummeted and, for the first time, queer persons felt they were an equal part of a democratic country, with its constitutional promises of equality and dignity within their reach.

However, this promise shattered before the Supreme Court, which overruled the Delhi High Court in December 2013 in

Suresh Kumar Koushal vs. Naz Foundation, and reinstated Section 377 in its full horror. The memory of that day still haunts me. The recriminalisation triggered the sweeping 'No Going Back' campaign, as queer individuals who had finally tasted freedom refused to go back to the closets of life and law. Their grit garnered the support of a wide swathe of mainstream society. Yet, the impact of recriminalisation cannot be understated—a spike in extortion/blackmail cases faced by gay men and transgender persons on dating applications like Grindr, often in collusion with the police, and a rise in forced marriages and violence against queer women. After almost five years later, Navtej brought the curtain down on one of the longest litigations in the history of independent India.

Before Navtej, when queer persons approached us—whether to report violence or about wanting to leave their abusive natal families or to live with their partner—we largely refrained from divulging the sexuality of the clients or their relationship, framing the issue as that of family violence or portraying the couple as close friends. The biggest challenge was in cases where gay men faced extortion but could not make a police complaint, owing to the fear of prosecution under Section 377. In one case, a gay man met another man on Grindr, and called him home after a few days, but there was no sexual contact between them. Still, the second man asked for money, but was unhappy with the sum given by the gay man, who lived in perpetual fear that he would be outed to his mother. In another case, A met B on Grindr, invited him home and they had sex. After B left in the morning, the police came to A's house and said there was a complaint of sexual assault against him. Scared, A went to the local police station, where B was sitting. The police told A that B had complained against him, and if they sorted it out among themselves, the police would not interfere. In front of the police, B asked for 10 lakhs to withdraw the complaint; eventually, A paid 8 lakhs. A did not want to file a complaint, as he felt the policemen were involved in the ordeal. Often, even after gathering the courage to make a complaint, many clients backed out at the last minute, as they were not out to their families or in their workplaces.

Navtej was a watershed moment. Queer persons came out to their families, workspaces, educational institutions, and started claiming public spaces, though battling family backlash, violence and police harassment. High Courts affirmed the rights of queer couples, particularly queer women, by protecting their right to sexual identity, and the choice of their partner. We no longer shied away from disclosing our clients' sexuality or gender in court. The emphatic articulation of queer rights in Navtej made it imperative for lower courts to respect the exercise of choice and autonomy by queer individuals.

The personal attitudes of judges and law enforcement, however, have been slow to change. In one case, I was told by a judge, 'Counsel, you might have the law on your side, but we don't approve.' In another, the police told my colleague, '*Supreme Court ne to judgement de di, par hum nahi mante. Yeh rishte samaj ke khilaf hai.*' [The Supreme Court may have delivered a judgement but we don't approve. These relations are against society.]

Queer lives are still fragile, survival concerns often overpower constitutional rights and court attitudes are uneven and unpredictable. Still, if the dominant sentiment among queer people before Naz, and then Navtej, was fear and survival, today it's hope and survival.

In one case, we persuaded a very reluctant Delhi High Court to free the female partner of a trans man from her parental home. The woman was in an abusive marriage and found companionship with a colleague at a salon. When their love blossomed, the family found out and separated them. Initially, we were reluctant to go to court, as she was already married, but changed our mind when the partner told us the details of her abusive marriage. In the chamber hearing, the judges could not hide their disapproval of either the extramarital relationship or the fact that a married woman was in a relationship with a trans man. But the couple stood their ground and the woman assured the judges that she would file for divorce soon.

In another case, a lesbian couple from Punjab and Delhi sought shelter in a women's safe house in the capital, fleeing severe family violence. The High Court granted protection to the couple easily, but failed to understand the intensity and degree of the family violence. It told the queer women to adjust with their families and not 'disappoint' their parents. The hearing was marked by high drama—the mother appeared to faint in the courtroom and one relative broke down, saying, 'We don't know why she's doing this, we have never stopped her from anything.' Unable to bear their dishonesty, the daughter cried out, '*Yeh sab court me drama kar rahe hai, ghar jate hi mujhe marenge*!' [They're doing drama in court, they'll beat me the moment I get home.] The judge's sympathy clearly lay with the parents, but the judge was bound by law and had to grant protection to the couple.

In a third case, the Delhi High Court released a young transgender woman detained by her family, facilitated her access to medical care at a government hospital and even ordered some maintenance by her family. In contrast, another High Court, while dealing with a similar *habeas* case of a gay man detained by his family for five months, did not have a chamber hearing, allowed the father to level vile allegations against the son in open court and told the gay man to 'respect his parents' and that there was 'no immunity if detenu has done anything wrong'. Finally, the gay man was released but the police were directed to enquire into any complaints from either parties, if they found it fit to do so.

Thus, there is no way to know how a *habeas* or police protection case involving a queer person will go, as many judges and police instinctively disapprove of queer relationships and back familial objections. It is only when the lawyers or queer persons themselves articulate their decisions in the language of rights and equality that there is sometimes a halt on the imposition of patriarchal heteronormative values.

Often when young queer persons contact us, mostly from working class backgrounds, they either want to leave their homophobic/ abusive natal families or live with their partner. We ask them extensive questions about their background in order to assess the risk of familial backlash, including filing of a missing persons complaint or a false police complaint.

Then, they are informed about their rights and legal options. Accordingly, a legal strategy is devised, with security as the primary concern. In many cases, when one partner is detained by their family, the other partner has had either no (or very) limited contact with them and we don't know what pressure the detenu has been under or what they will say in court. Further, when the police bring the detenu to court, they are often emotionally blackmailed into not speaking against the family. If the detenu (surrounded by police and family) makes eye contact or smiles at the partner, then we know that mostly they will speak their mind. In some cases, the detenu are in no position to withstand familial pressure and tell the court that they are voluntarily staying with the family.

In order to avoid such outcomes, we request the court to let the detenu stay at a queer-friendly shelter home, to calm themselves down, get access to counselling and generally be away from pressure. After a few days, they are again produced in court to speak their mind, free from coercion or threats.

But staying in a shelter home is also not easy. Most are designed to protect cis heterosexual women fleeing either their abusive husbands or in-laws, and have strict rules about phone usage and mobility, which are not conducive for queer persons looking to talk to their partners or close friends. Queer shelter homes are few, have limited space and are always in high demand. In one case, the detenu was kept in a government-protective home, which was essentially a mini-jail with no phones or ways to contact anyone. She wanted to be with her partner, but the judge kept on adjourning the matter, while telling the detenu that if she did not go back to her family, he would not release her from the home. After spending almost two months in that home, the detenu told the judge that she wanted to go back to her family and was immediately released. We were extremely upset, but her partner, a trans man, assured us that the detenu would contact him again soon. This is what happened. The detenu contacted the partner, who managed to reach her hometown and they came to Delhi. We then were able to secure police protection for them from Delhi courts.

The wildly varying standards between different High Courts prompted the Supreme Court in 2024 to mandate certain guidelines in *Devu G. Nair vs. State of Kerala*—priority in listing and avoidance of adjournments; no roving inquiry into the nature of relationship; chamber hearing; creation of an environment for persons to express themselves; acting with empathy and compassion, not morality; and avoiding sending persons for 'corrective' therapy, amongst others.

These are significant directions that can go a long way in streamlining court procedures and making it less traumatising for queer persons.

One significant hurdle remains. In many cases, we make the parents parties to the case, as they are either the abusers or enablers of abuse. No matter how horrific their actions are, the parents/family members are perceived as victims in court, as their 'beloved child' has turned out to be queer and dragged their parents to court. In one case, the judge empathised with an abusive father and said, 'I understand your emotions, I am also a father.' In another, the judge sarcastically remarked, 'Why are you forcing your child? Let the child make her mistake, eventually she will realise, and will come back to you.' Even in chamber hearings, the partner or the queer relationship is scrutinised, and not the natal family violence.

Lawyers representing the queer persons are seen with suspicion and accused of 'brainwashing' their clients. In one case, the parents complained to the judge that the 'lawyers were too aggressive' and should be asked to 'back off'. Often, in court proceedings, we have to physically surround our clients so that the family members cannot get access to them, literally acting like bouncers. No one teaches this in law schools.

Even in police stations, many officers dislike that queer people have access to lawyers who insist on following the law. In my seventeen years of practice, I have been repeatedly asked why I was helping 'break up the family' or how I could do this for money. A station house officer once asked me, 'You are saying parents have been violent. How is it possible? I have never heard of parents beating their children. Parents only love their children.' This was when the trans person was sitting in front of the Station House Officer with an order of police protection from the High Court. When I was leaving his room, he said, 'Ma'am, you will earn your fee, but think about the parents whose child has left them suddenly.'

Many queer persons suffer from mental health issues, and parents often weaponise this by alleging that they are taking drugs, or that one partner is forcing the other to take hormones or undergo gender affirmation surgery. In court, this information is misused to state that the person is not in a stable mental state, and incapable of taking independent decisions. Often, the court's concern for the well-being of the queer person is valid, especially if they are still in college, and not yet financially self-sufficient. But that concern cannot override the decision of the individual. In moments like this, one feels the absence of an enabling environment or state infrastructure to facilitate the exercise of queer rights, whether shelter homes, queer affirmative mental health services, legal/crisis intervention services and educational/employment opportunities. More legal time is spent looking for safe shelters than honing arguments.

Against this backdrop, many queer couples came together before the top court in 2023 seeking marriage equality, with the understanding that for many from marginalised backgrounds, legal recognition of their relationships would act as a shield against natal families and police harassment, and make life slightly easier with access to state benefits and legitimacy. The Supreme Court rejected the demand, but recognised the right to relationship, noting that if the queer persons' right to relationship is under threat of violence, the State is bound to extend necessary protection.

Still, approaching the court is not easy. One needs queer-friendly lawyers, the ability to claim their rights in palatable ways, appear as perfect petitioners and brave intense scrutiny of their relationships and lifestyles. This is aggravated for transgender persons as their identity itself becomes a matter of trial, especially for those whose documents are incongruent with their gender identity. They are asked to notarise an affidavit in their self-identified gender, get a pass made to enter the courts (not district courts), get misgendered by the police/court staff and even by judges and battle constant backlash from the family. In one case, the sister of a trans man deliberately filed a property case against him in his deadname, despite knowing fully well his legal and chosen identity, and made allegations of impersonation against him on the grounds that she never had any brother.

Homosexual and bisexual men face harassment by law enforcement and private non-state actors, including extortion, entrapment, illegal detention, abuse and threats of outing. There appears to be an organised pattern of extortion of gay and bisexual men in cities, by contacting them on social networking sites, luring them into sex and then subjecting them to blackmail and threats. In most cases still, such violations aren't reported to the police.

Even in cases of sexual violence against queer women, navigating the criminal justice system is a herculean task, particularly if the survivor is from a marginalised community; the police is routinely hostile, and the judges are indifferent, if not biased. Neither the police nor the judges have kept up with changes in law (definition of consent in the Indian Penal Code and now the Bharatiya Nyaya Sanhita) or understand the sexual practices of young persons. Any mention of dating applications or an active sexual past further complicates the situation. In fact, sexual history often becomes a matter of court gossip when a survivor has met the accused on a dating application and exchanged messages (with sexual connotations). In one case, the defence lawyers made a big deal about the identity of a sexual assault survivor, as she had written non-binary queer on her Tinder profile, and argued that she was not a woman, so Section 376 of the IPC, which punishes rape, was not applicable. In another case of sexual assault of a gay man, the judge asked the complainant's lawyers if 'gay sex was legal' and then asked them to submit a copy of the 2018 Supreme Court verdict.

Despite the challenges, the massive strides are indisputable. It is easier to talk about gender and sexuality in schools and colleges. Many queer collectives have stamped their presence, creating visibility and safe spaces for LGBTQ+ individuals. Specific provisions in the Transgender Persons (Protection of Rights) Act, 2019 and the Transgender Persons (Protection of Rights) Rules, 2020 have been put in place to prohibit discrimination against transgender students in educational institutions. The High Courts of Karnataka, Calcutta, Madras, Uttarakhand and Allahabad have passed directions to change the educational certificates of individuals, in compliance with the Act. Both public and private sector establishments are mandated to comply with the Act. Significant cases of discrimination against LGBTQ+ persons continue, but not many want to go to courts, as they don't have the time or resources for long-winded litigation. Some transgender persons have approached the courts seeking reservation in public employment, and some High Courts have ruled in their favour, though not many cases of employment discrimination have been litigated yet.

Be that as it may, queer persons and their lawyers continue to exist, live, work and claim their rights. More judges are now exposed to queer issues; it's not always a positive interaction, but an interaction nevertheless. Sometimes, I wonder if I am being typecast as a queer lawyer, either as an identity or an area of law, but honestly, it's who I am. The clients relax when I tell them that I am from the LGBTQ+ community and understand their issues well. They start trusting us more with sensitive information. At the same time, we are mindful that we do other cases too, both to run our practice and to not get typecast. In fact, when young queer lawyers join us, we make sure that they get exposed to different areas of law. One day I might be deep in a regular civil suit poring over the provisions of the Code of Civil Procedure, 1908, and then suddenly receive a call at 7.00 p.m. that a person has been forcibly taken to the police station. With no time to spare, I immediately switch to crisis mode, contact an organisation and either go myself or send a colleague to the police station. Every morning, when I walk into the office, I have no idea how the day will turn out.

At the same time, this work would not have been possible without the support of organisations who are on the ground providing safe shelter, counselling and just emotionally supporting the individuals in their most trying times. Each crisis is as much about the queer person as about the collaboration between the queer organisations and the lawyers. Moreover, queer emancipation is deeply connected with the empowerment of other marginalised groups, including Dalits and Muslims, among others. In recent years, there has been a sharp rise in hate crimes against Muslims. Increasing Islamophobia in the public discourse has created a culture of fear and insecurity amongst many Muslims. Accordingly, this has had a huge impact on queer Muslims who have to navigate both homophobia and Islamophobia together, and sometimes find themselves constrained to remain silent, to safeguard themselves. Thus, queering the law is as much about protecting queer rights as about protecting the secular democratic ethos of the country. I don't know about the future of queer rights in India, but it's definitely connected to the future of minority rights, and as long as the two are fought for together, the dream of a rainbow nation is still alive.

WHAT A DRAG!

REFLECTIONS ON QUEER JOY, EUPHORIA, TRANSGRESSION AND PERFORMANCE

Vikram Phukan

The tagline read: 'Love burns. Revenge bleeds. Kings rise.'

It was the third edition of the drag revue, *Kingdom of Anarchy*, taking place in a Mumbai five star hotel's discotheque, and standing in the wings, twenty-six-year-old Arjoon Kabir Kakkar adjusted his pagdi, ready to make his debut as Papa Pancho, his drag king character. A trans man and a theatre artiste exploring trans-masculine embodiment, he first presented the work-in-progress *Jisman Ton Paar* (a Punjabi folk-tinged phrase which means 'beyond the body') at Delhi's Lok Kala Manch in 2023. In May 2025, he showcased a reworked version of the piece at OffCue,[1] an arts platform I run in Mumbai. But *Kingdom of Anarchy* offered a riskier, more unpredictable stage, and Papa Pancho was a whole new deal, as Arjoon had never performed drag before.

His character was a cocky Sardar who laid claim to land, women and weapons. While it was a parody of toxic maleness, it was also a fond echo of the Sikh masculinity he'd grown up around but never inhabited. It's a proximity shared by many non-Sikh performers who take on Sardar drag, often with affection, though not entirely outside the shadow of appropriation. Performing Papa Pancho presented a different kind of anxiety: not stage fright, but the unease of entering a space still unfamiliar, where identity is both expressed and scrutinised. Arjoon, who comes from a conservative Punjabi upper-caste Hindu background in North Delhi's Kalyan Vihar, was gender non-conforming as a child, growing into something more deliberate. For many trans men, this negotiation of masculinity involves embracing and questioning inherited ideas of maleness.

Papa Pancho exulted on stage to a mashup of Diljit Dosanjh tracks and Varun Grover's *Hunter*—that testosterone-soaked anthem from *Gangs of Wasseypur*. Arjoon channelled flamboyance, desire and menace. He drew on his acting training, but his joy came from feeling, even if fleetingly, what it meant to be unafraid of being looked at, he said. 'It is like theatre, but freer,' he told me after the performance. 'I wanted to know what it meant to become someone I don't usually show the world, or maybe someone I'm not.'

Queer spaces can be generous stages. Even an entry or a look can draw cheers and whoops, as if it's not about performing at all, but simply about being seen, however inchoate the act. The party raged well into the night, as queer ones tend to. But the sense of unguarded ease was not always something that queer nightlife in Mumbai was able to offer. For much of its history, the dance floor has carried the weight of risk along with the promise of release.

The LaLiT's plush nightclub Kitty Su[2] was, for that night alone, styled like a queer noir fantasy modelled on the hyper-masculine world of Frank Miller's *Sin City*. The night gave drag kings the full arc of spectacle and spotlight. The main acts that evening, choreographed and costumed for polished effect, were led by performers with spiffy stage names like Daddy Freddie, Inqalaab Singh and MX Stallion—personas respectively shaped by actor Toto Robin, Gay Gaze co-founder Winnie Chopra and multidisciplinary artist Siaan, each already accomplished well beyond drag—and all platformed by Gay Gaze Bombay, a four-year-old[3] Mumbai collective that was one among a handful holding gender-bending drag shows and parties for LGBTQIA+ folks. Many of their attendees were youngsters in their twenties.

Beyond any single event or space, the queer scene of 2025 is impossible to miss—especially during Pride season. June belongs to corporate HR departments kowtowing to global signposts and diversity diktats, while November and January host the parades, protests and parties. All year, the scene continues to thrum, alive with people pushing at the edges of gender, desire and selfhood, in a world where queer expression is reimagined through rituals and gatherings. Not always named as activism but political in its own right, a constellation of spaces make room for the city's queers to be together, to be seen on their own terms and to be joyful.[4]

A tantalising part of this is the shape-shifting drag culture, which bursts out of small bars, pricey discotheques, makeshift studios and Instagram Live feeds streamed from cramped bedrooms. Indian drag has arguably been defined by feminine aesthetics, led by the sequinned queens of yore, with their bouffant wigs and chakmak odhnis straight out of a *Zaveri Bazaar* bridal catalogue. But more visible than ever before are tapori masculinities, personas that slip between categories, flirt with gender ambivalence—the drag king with a contoured goatee and Bandra boy strut seen at club nights and shows like those hosted by Gay Gaze Bombay and other collectives.

⁂

It wasn't always like this. Beneath the celebration, the shadows of surveillance and repression have long reminded us how fragile these spaces can be. Around the turn of the millennium, when gay parties in Mumbai first began to appear in semi-public venues, they were still shrouded in discretion. Many enforced quietly draconian house rules that disallowed drag. Much of this stemmed from internalised transphobia—a policing of feminine expression in male spaces—but some of it was also strategic, as drag made parties more visible, and visibility risked exposure.

It's an ironic reversal today: where queer stages once dimmed the lights on femininity, they are now reckoning with how masculinity can be reclaimed. I remember the Queer Azaadi March of 2008, where women and trans folks led the procession, held placards with slogans and set the general tone of the Pride march in Mumbai. By sundown, the after-party at Girgaon's multi-roomed Liquid Lounge (now permanently closed) was steeped in hyper-masculine gayness. It's a pattern that lingers to this day. In many gatherings, to avoid triggering a raid, queerness was kept just quiet enough, and curated through a particular kind of masculinity. Frequent police crackdowns on private parties made queer organisers wary of moving into the open. The infamous White Party raid of 1999 saw gay men paraded out of a private beachfront bungalow in Patilwadi near Madh Island,[5] under the glare of television cameras. According to *India Today*, around 150 people in their twenties were in attendance, and the party featured fireworks, ecstasy, a drag queen show and male striptease. Among those arrested was a scion of a prominent diamond-trading family—proof that even elite privilege offered little protection when queerness was involved.

A decade later, in a raid on a villa in Jogeshwari, officers reportedly referred to the goings-on as 'chakkagiri', seemingly unaware that consensual same-sex intimacy was no longer criminal under Indian law—the 2009 Delhi High Court verdict reading down Section 377 had already taken effect. As I wrote in a *Mid-Day* article in 2011,[6] reporting on the raid, 'Some 133 people were detained and charged under a slew of laws—some about liquor permits, others about loud music—with organisers kept in custody for over three days.' In another raid in Mira Road, police subjected attendees to a school-style punishment: squatting while holding their ears in forced contrition. The indignities were many, and the message was clear: even the private pursuit of joy could come at a price.[7]

But joy cannot be trammelled, and some literally took to the water to party freely. Yachts set sail from the harbour near the Gateway of India, drifting out of reach to become makeshift party venues in the Arabian Sea. Fashion designer Inderjit Nagi, a gender non-conforming Sikh man still finding the full stretch of his flamboyance, remembered one such yacht party in 2002 as a rare, untethered moment of freedom. Then in his early twenties, he went dressed in his everyday clothes, turban and all, but underneath, it was a different story. 'We had entire sequinned ensembles waiting,' he said. 'The minute we were out at sea, we'd strip off the offending layers. It wasn't about hooking up. It was just about expression and being seen as ourselves.'

These boats, chartered from the Colaba jetties, became floating refuges where those made to feel unwelcome in city parties, especially gender non-conforming folk, could let loose. Occasionally, when the patrol boats of the coast guard made their approach, the most brightly adorned among them scrambled to the lower deck, crouching nervously in the shadows, until the patrol boat moved on. 'Because I had a turban, facial hair and my Helen-style outfit, I was designated as the first one who should be hidden,' Nagi recalled. 'But the moment they left, we came right back up—feathers, heels, the works.' There was no script or manifesto, just an insistence that joy could be cobbled together with chiffon and daring, even if only for a few hours offshore.

Some years later, Nagi cut his hair and shaved his beard. Removing the markers that made him visibly Sikh meant a complete rewiring of how he moved through gay Bombay. 'The way people saw me changed. How they approached me, how they desired me—it all shifted,' he said. Was it perhaps a quiet capitulation to the ethnophobia that still marks gay male circuits, I wondered? As someone from the Northeast, I've felt that same edge of being made hyper-visible and invisible at once in spaces where the mainstream of queerness rarely admits its own exclusions.

Nagi's recollection stayed with me. Not for its glamour, but for the raw permission those parties offered. We were unapologetically trying to live in full colour, especially because many of us were, for the rest of the time, in hiding. I later wove his yacht escapade into *Postcards from Colaba*, a promenade play I wrote that attempted to track Colaba's fugitive queer histories through memories of nightlife. The audience moved with actors through lanes and corners, glimpsing fragments of lives often overlooked. I haven't yet woven his Sikhness into the play. It feels like a missed chance to name what made his presence so powerful, so precarious.

That idealised memory met my actual, bodily limit when I finally got on a yacht myself, with all the elements in place: sea spray, sunset and a cluster of gay couples in coordinated linen—it was a private get-together for gay men. It should've been the setting I'd once imagined Nagi flourishing in. But I spent half the time in the cabin, nauseous from the motion, debating whether throwing up on the teak flooring would be more or less embarrassing than emerging to make conversation. I eventually resurfaced, clutching the railing like pearls in the wind, but the fantasy had already cracked. The yacht had exposed the limit of the image. It made me realise that glamour—like queerness—is sometimes a performance you can't always physically sustain.

Colaba yacht parties also stir a completely different memory: a ferry slicing across the water, carrying twenty-odd women towards something unnamed but urgent. In 1995, when much of India's emerging queer world still centred around gay men, a discreetly worded letter was passed from woman to woman—quietly, intuitively, often between those who recognised something sapphic in one another. It invited them on a ferry ride from Aksa Beach to Gorai. It looked like nothing more than a day out. But for many of the women who showed up, awkwardly hovering at the jetty, it was the first time they'd been in a space of shared recognition.

At Gorai, they gathered in a cottage for what felt like a cross between a picnic and a séance. They shared stories, opened their tiffins and began figuring out how to speak of things that had never been named aloud. 'Even sitting in a room with just five other similar women would've been like, oh wow. And yet, here were twenty. We simply wanted to meet each other,' writer Shals Mahajan, who was one of those attending, told me years later. That rented cottage, with its strewn food packets and outstretched hearts, was for many their first safe space, alive with the nervous, exhilarating thrill of recognition.

The same year, Mahajan and their friends founded the queer women's collective, Stree Sangam—a name generic enough to sit unbothered on postal mailers in a time when discretion meant survival, yet quietly echoing that first encounter. But by 2002, they were done with hiding. They renamed themselves LABIA (Lesbians and Bisexuals in Action), staking claim not just to space, but to language. The shift was emblematic: from quiet assembly to visible resistance, from coded solidarity to radical naming. Two decades after that first ferry ride, at Matunga's Mysore Association Hall, the collective hosted a raucous, overflowing anniversary event: four hours of programming, zines, manifestos, poetry and testimonies. The mood was electric, not so much nostalgic as still defiant, as queer women and trans folks gathered not just to remember, but to plot. Legacy was alive in that room, not only framed on a wall but also passed hand to hand. This was joy sharpened into subversive strategy: complex and intersectional. And, like most good queer gatherings, served with piping hot snacks.

But that was 2015. In April 2009, I came on board to edit my first issue of *Bombay Dost*, a magazine that made its debut in 1990, brought out by the Humsafar Trust. It had been defunct for seven years, and I, freshly returned from the United Kingdom, where I had worked a job in business consultancy, was looking for new impetus. I had barely interacted with the queer community in Mumbai, but in the UK, I'd been exposed to what felt like a queer renaissance of the performing arts—one that left me culturally primed, if still personally uninitiated. The chance to revive a queer magazine felt immediate and necessary. In my editor's note for the 2009 issue, I wrote about an 'unfettered, carefree optimism', not because the world had changed, but because something in the air had.

The court case against Section 377, the penal code that criminalised adult same-sex consensual intercourse, was dragging on, and the climate still crackled with fear, yet there was a buzz. You could feel it if you listened close enough: that maybe, finally, we were ready to 'awake to new possibilities'. Weeks later, on 2 July, the Delhi High Court verdict would come crashing over us like a wave. The ruling, which read down the section and offered up one of the best-written expositions affirming human rights, shocked us. In our circles, we'd always said we would never live to see the day. And suddenly, we had. For months, joy spilled out onto dance floors, through the city's bars and living rooms. Even as the police staged their usual raids, they turned a blind eye to many others. Parties proliferated like never before. The joy of no longer being considered 'unapprehended felons', as one of the justices who delivered the verdict put it, was of a wholly different timbre.[8]

A year on, we still wanted to celebrate. My friends Alok Gupta, a lawyer who had followed the case, and Simran Singh, co-founder (with Sabina) of Azaad Bazaar (or Az Baz as it was fondly nicknamed)—perhaps India's first openly queer boutique—and I, organised a gathering in a lounge space in Khar West. We sipped our drinks slowly, soaking in the quiet bonhomie. On the 377th day of the verdict—a mark too cheeky and too symbolic to resist—we returned. It was the same room, bore the same feeling, but the crowd was slightly larger. This time, we asked the venue if we could make it a regular thing. They said yes. And just like that, the Banana Bar Party was born, held on the first Tuesday of every month. 'We picked a day when bars usually had the least footfall,' Simran recalled. 'It was our way of taking over straight spaces, and showing them the power of the pink rupee. We'd just been talking about the new rupee symbol at the boutique and it felt like our moment had come too.'

From the start, it was clear this wasn't just another boys' night. The crowd remained mixed, with around 40 per cent women (a rarity elsewhere), alongside gay men, straight friends, artists and allies. And it worked. These weren't nights of utopia but they felt different. Elsewhere in the city, gay parties often tilted toward the transactional; cliquish and sleazy. The Banana Bar scene was looser, less coded. 'People came with their straight friends,' Simran said. 'It was their first step into queer space—with the safety of support structures already built in. You didn't have to come out before you came in.' It was a space where people lingered in smoking zones to chat long after the cigarette was done. Where a stranger could send you a drink and it didn't feel like a power move. For once, the room didn't ask you to explain yourself. Even the goodbyes had drama—someone might leave not with their crush, but with the crush of their crush, more theatre than romance. These were parties with aftershocks and the story didn't always end on the dance floor.

What began as a casual celebration quickly took on the shape of a proof of concept. 'Three months in, the owner told us he'd never seen that kind of business midweek; it even surpassed his weekend takings,' said Simran. Part of this shift was because, as word spread, the gay male presence began to dominate. The vibe got louder, more territorial. So we tweaked the model—charging a cover fee for men, keeping entry free for women. It wasn't perfect, but it helped steady the boat. Still, the lines were never clean. One night, a trans man stepped up to pay. The staff, reading him as female, waved him through. He quietly insisted on paying, and sent for me. I asked them to take his payment. It was a small moment, but it landed like an abrupt reminder that inclusion has to be lived, day in and day out. Words like 'sensitisation' were only just entering our lexicon. We were learning in real time.

The party didn't last long. Az Baz shut down, and Banana Bar turned into a paratha joint. That's the nature of queer space—liminal and impermanent. 'I feel like it was there when it needed to be there,' Simran said of both Az Baz and Banana Bar. For at least two years, Az Baz was a refuge for queer folk simply looking for somewhere to sit, to pause, to linger. Its absence hit hard. 'They asked us for a long time after that. And I think the void it left was of a safe, non-hookup queer space,' recalled Simran. That's how queer spaces often go: shimmering briefly into being, then vanishing, leaving behind the residue of memory, and maybe one or two inside jokes.

One belonged to a friend with a weakness for older men. He asked if he'd find any at the Banana Bar. I said yes, of course—a whole group. First seven. Then ten. Then fifteen. By the time we were pre-drinking, I'd confidently declared there would be twenty-three silver foxes in attendance. He lit up. Then paused. 'Wait, how would you even know that?' he asked. Just like that, the fantasy popped—when he realised I was testing the limits of his gay gullibility. But for a few brief hours, he believed. That was the Banana Bar Party: equal parts mischief and promise. Incidentally, this was the same friend who dragged me to that yacht party off the Colaba pier earlier this year and he turned up with not one but two husbands of a certain vintage in tow. He had, unmistakably, manifested his best life elsewhere.

During an interlude in *Postcards from Colaba*, audiences sit across from the Taj Mahal Hotel on Apollo Bunder Road and listen to a pre-recorded voiceover by actor Ratnabali Bhattacharjee, channeling a scribe on the queer beat. It doesn't describe the five-star façade in front of them, but points instead to a fisherfolk settlement a short taxi ride away. What they hear is the story of a very different kind of gathering I had once witnessed there—a transgender woman's wedding held in a narrow chawl courtyard, strung with lights and teeming with people, voices and something harder to name: a joy tempered by exclusion, but no less real for it.

In the heart of Macchimar Nagar one April evening in 2022, I had found myself drawn into what was essentially a consecration into a life that promised both recognition and exile. I was brought into this world by Bengaluru-based theatremaker Sharanya Ramprakash, who was organising a Mumbai run of her play *Nava*, a performance where an ensemble of nine urban trans women enact the full emotional range of the navarasa. Many of *Nava's* scenes were drawn from the performers' own testimonies, and here, it felt as if those stories had stepped off the stage and into the night air.

The wedding, however, was not theatre, but it carried the same defiance, humour and ache that had shaped the play, and many of Ramprakash's troupe were in attendance to witness the initiation of Aanchal (name changed), a nineteen-year-old trans woman marrying the goddess Yellamma in a Jogappa-linked ritual tradition. Her family was nowhere in sight, but in the meantime, her to-be-mentor ruled the night. Resplendent in a green sari and bold makeup, she presided with full command as emcee, matriarch, chef, priestess and stage manager. 'Aanchal ki Mummy ... Aanchal ki Mummy ...' [Aanchal's mother] she intoned into the mic over and over again, not pleading but summoning. Her voice was deep, assured and feminine in a way that refused apology. After more than two hours, the mother emerged from the shadows to place a hand on her child's head. And around that moment of belated acceptance bloomed celebration—mutton, fish and rice served on banana leaves, and a battalion of brusque trans hostesses who pressed seconds onto our plates. That night in Macchimar Nagar didn't make it into any archive. But it remains one of the clearest glimpses of queer futurity: not orderly, not official, but vivid, marginal and defiantly alive.

It was a gathering shaped by caste and class divides, where queer worlds live alongside one another in uneasy proximity but rarely intersect, revealing the fractured realities of queer existence beyond the urban elite.

In Bengaluru, Ramprakash was introduced by her *Nava* collaborators to Balaji Bar near the Krishnarajendra Market, which offered up a frenetic scene. 'Unlike the day with its prejudices, in the night the space becomes theirs, with all its companion associations and friendships,' Ramprakash said, showing how queer life in Bengaluru moves fluidly between sacred ritual and urban night-scape. She was in town when the Karaga festival was on—in it, Draupadi is worshipped as patron goddess, and trans women (including many of her collaborators) participate.

Such acts of reclamation, whether in smaller sacred sites or in the urban night, are part of a larger pattern in Indian culture where ritual provides a uniquely queer space for visibility and expression, even as broader society remains tight-lipped and averse to open discussions of modern sexuality. The gendered turf of the Karaga festival can just as easily segue into the sprawling, electric queer gatherings at Maddox Square in Kolkata during Durga Puja, where worship and desire coalesce.

Kolkata-based Amar Mukherjee, a sales professional in the medical devices sector, recalls how the square, already an urban oasis, became the go-to rendezvous point long before mobile phones existed. 'If I want to meet you, I told you, let's meet at Maddox,' he explains, emphasising how it served as a vital, unspoken code for gay men across the city—from South, North or Central Kolkata—who had no other way to connect. What started as a practical solution for discreet meetings has endured for decades, evolving into a vibrant tradition that is now a 'big thing' during Durga Puja, especially during Navami, the ninth and final day of the festival. 'During the festival, everyone spends time with their family, but we also want to spend time with our chosen family. That's why it became an important gathering spot,' said Mukherjee.

Maddox Square itself is marked by its own Durga pandal, organised by the Ballygunge Durga Puja Committee, where an unostentatious but tasteful idol, created in the old style presides—offering a familiar yet understated backdrop to these vibrant gatherings. Mukherjee recalls the atmosphere, 'Throughout the night, nobody will ask you to go. Till morning you can sit and chat.' The space is chaste in its way, where people revel in the corporeality of solidarity, the charged frisson of shared presence, while any other business is quietly taken elsewhere. Despite being an open secret, hiding in plain sight, Maddox Square's crowds remain a rare public space where the presence of queer men, kothis and transgender folk, is celebrated.

Yet, the radical queer possibility offered up by such spaces, is tinged with the threat of disrepute or violence.

Kolkata-based Shoumik Biswas has been part of the independent music scene for years, first as a drummer in bands and now through their solo persona Disco Puppet. It's a project that resists easy consumption, shifting between stripped-back electronic sets and more theatrical, costume-driven performances. After more than a decade in Bengaluru, they moved to Kolkata, working at a grassroots level and carrying an awareness and vocabulary that once came only as instinct.

A few months into 2025, they were exiting Girlfriend-Girlfriend—a queer party space in Bengaluru's Indiranagar for women, non-binary and trans people—dressed femme when they were harassed and assaulted by local drunk men on the street. 'Because I was the biggest person there, they beat me. It shook me because nothing like that had happened to me before. Since then, I've been more cautious about being visibly femme in certain spaces.'

'Earlier, I just thought all this was something I was doing. Now I know where it comes from, and I know the grammar and the language for it,' they say. The unreleased album they are working on is steeped in identity, friendships, chosen family and memory, a process they describe as both technical and emotional.

In their performances, joy is threaded with the knowledge that visibility can invite hostility, and that risk is the price of being fully seen. For Biswas, making music is not about arriving at freedom so much as, in my reading, staying in motion within it—testing how far joy can stretch before it frays, and noticing what survives when it does. Some nights it's just a loop or a half-formed lyric; other nights it's the sudden spark of recognition that passes between them and someone in the crowd.

Initiation can happen in many ways, shaped by circumstance, desire or just pure chance. For Aanchal, it came through a transgender wedding steeped in ritual; for Nagi, through the unguarded flamboyance of offshore yacht parties; for Mahajan, through the tentative solidarity of a first sapphic gathering; for Arjoon, through the community's charge of drag appreciation; and for Biswas, through an intensely personal practice of self-expression. All of them suggest how entry points into queer joy can be wildly different yet equally formative.

For me, two encounters are lodged in my mind, both in Edinburgh in the early 2000s, amid the swirl of August's overlapping festivals. The first was in a gallery, where Sunil Gupta's 1999 series *From Here to Eternity* was featured. I didn't know the work by name then, only by feeling. There were stark, deliberate images of an Indian man in domestic interiors, sometimes naked behind sheer curtains, sometimes lying fully shrouded on a bed, wrapped like a body prepared for cremation. I saw the stillness before erasure. Later I learnt that Gupta, a rare long-time survivor diagnosed with HIV in the 1980s, was staging the visual language of loss not to mourn but to reframe by showing a queer life narrated on its own terms, not only through obituary.

Years later, when I went looking for those exact images online, they had vanished, likely removed for the kind of 'indecency' institutions are quicker to see in queer bodies. That disappearance felt like a second erasure, a reminder of how easily queer images slip from view, even those warning us about disappearance. When I eventually encountered Gupta's Delhi-based work, it felt like the inverse of those Edinburgh interiors, bathed in tube-light glare, rooftops in morning haze, lives stitched together in bachelor pads and borrowed rooms. You can almost imagine Pegs and Pints, Delhi's long-running gay-friendly pub, as it appears in his frames, not as a centrepiece, but as part of the ecology that holds these lives together: glasses sweating on tabletops, bodies leaning close in dim light, the hush of being among one's own. Joy here is threaded through constraint, present in these low-lit refuges as much as in the open air of a rooftop morning. What I once read as an ending now feels like a rebuttal to the idea that queer lives only count once they've vanished.

The second touchstone came a few nights later in a small black box theatre at the Assembly Rooms: *Dorothy as Lad*, a cybernetic send-up of *The Wizard of Oz*. Behind me in the shadows, a drag queen in pink hair and green mascara waited for her cue; when it came, she emerged, flawed, resplendent, possessed by timing and glitter. If Gupta's photographs had held me in the stillness before erasure, this was its opposite, a burst of queer survival in motion, too loud and alive to vanish quietly. I was new to queerness then. The journal I kept from that time was full of performances I didn't know I was studying: drag queens erupting in fringe theatres, falsettos from the gay men's chorus, film festivals full of pierced bodies and defiant tenderness. I wasn't part of it, not yet, but I was watching closely, as if some future version of myself might need these blueprints. Two decades later, those blueprints have become practice. I wasn't in the wings but in rehearsal rooms, creating plays that lingered like that drag queen's entrance, now looking outward instead of in. Across works like *Postcards from Colaba*, *Those Left Behind Things* (a play on gay Iranian asylum seekers) or the fading cabaret world imagined by the Patchworks Ensemble in *The Gentleman's Club*, I've returned to such moments not as nostalgia but as cues for how queer lives were lived, shaped and shared. When the latter was invited to perform in London in October 2024, the irony was sharp: we were staging a fictional drag king show that had pre-empted Mumbai's drag scene in Soho Theatre, steeped in real queer cabaret history. Drag royalty lined the walls, yet our lovingly dishevelled play felt out of place beside the theatre's technically pristine drag, which was tight, high-decibel and unapologetically queer in its technical finesse. Ours was theatre, with wigs and sleight of hand, and the playful rhythm of gliding from one production number to the next with songs that were mostly oldies. Yet, our lineage was perhaps right down the road, in the vintage gay pubs where a queen in a sequinned gown still belts Celine Dion for the price of a drink.

I see these moments as part of a continuum. They are not milestones in a straight line but recurring cues, reminding me that queer life is made in the interplay between survival and celebration, solitude and collectivity, the private room and the public stage. What binds them is not medium but the insistence on telling our own stories before someone else erases them, and the knowledge that joy, however fleeting, can be both a refuge and a rallying cry. Queer joy remains a practice and it is in that persistence, not in any single party or parade, that our collective futures might be forged.

Notes

1. 'Mumbai Diary: Friday Dossier', *Mid-Day*, April 2025.
2. The LaLiT's Kitty Su is the name of a nightclub—in Delhi and Mumbai—with a bar and a dance floor. It has hosted several drag artists and shows, including internationally renowned ones. It is owned by Keshav Suri, who was one of the petitioners for the same-sex marriage petition before the Supreme Court in 2023. While it is definitely expensive, weeding a large number of queers out, it is renowned for being trans- and drag-friendly, something other nightclubs are squeamish about.
3. Inayat Sood, 'The Love Story of Winnie, Gurleen and their Gay Gaze', The Ideas Lab, June 2024.
4. In *Long Live Queer Nightlife: How the Closing of Gay Bars Sparked a Revolution* (2024, Princeton University Press), Amin Ghaziani writes about the nightlife in London and how it has changed. The present scene, contrary to popular perception, isn't 'dead', but, in fact, radically inclusive in the shape it takes now in the form of club nights, that are 'episodic parties, many of which are being organised by people who for too long have felt left out of gay bars'. (Interview to https://news.ubc.ca/2024/04/long-live-queer-nightlife/).

5. Sheela Raval, 'Mumbai Police raid Rave Party near Madh Island', *India Today*, June 1999.
6. Vikram Phukan, 'A Fine Line', *Mid-Day*, September 2011.
7. In 2022, a gunman shot and killed forty-nine people and wounded fifty-three more at a gay nightclub called Pulse in Orlando. He was eventually shot and killed by the police. This was followed by a spate of mass shootings at gay and lesbian events including other nightclubs, making it one of the more common targets of gunmen who have also targeted schools and shopping malls, and in one instance, a marathon.
8. Chief Justice AP Shah, one of the two judges to hear the Naz petition in the Delhi high court, used the phrase in his judgement to describe the impact that Section 377 of the Indian Penal Code, which criminalised non penile-vaginal sex, had on LGBTQ lives. The bench unanimously decided to read down the law such that it did not apply to consenting adults.

THE TRANS YOU SEE, AND THE TRANS I SEE (AND SHOW YOU)

Bonita Rajpurohit

Let me begin by saying that our stories matter and deserve to be told. But, having made films on shoestring budgets, I fully acknowledge that it is not a cakewalk. There is so much that goes into the process, behind the camera and before, during and after production that actors are unaware of—the politics of it, the hierarchy of it.

No doubt the place and intentions you're coming from matter when you're telling those stories. But when they say we want to 'humanise/normalise the trans lives' can that only be done by constant victimisation of those characters, as if that is the only aspect of their life? So basically a trans person has no depth and cannot evoke empathy if they don't go through pain and suffering? NGL, that sounds pretty sadistic to me.

I am kind of done with people approaching me for roles or stories that cater to the same old narrative built around trans people. Done with people telling me that I should realise why it is such a great thing that I am even getting a platform like theirs in the first place, done with being asked to appreciate their good intentions to 'include' such characters as if it's a favour, done with being told to take it as a 'passion project' for the sake of trans visibility because they really appreciate me and my acting chops, and because all they can offer me is a small sum.

I'm twenty-six now, nearly twenty-seven. I have made a film.[1] I have debuted in a Bollywood film as one of three lead actors.[2] I have participated in acting workshops, worked on sets and films in different capacities, and skilled myself in various aspects of acting, filmmaking, public speaking. When will I reach a level of undisputed worth in this industry? For how many more years will I be expected to start from scratch? What else does a trans person have to do in the industry to be seen as a professional and to be respected for their time and effort? Will I ever be seen as an actor instead of a trans actor? When will they write characters for trans people that take the story forward with layers of their personality besides gender?

There's a reason why there are such few trans actors in India, and why many who get into it are disinterested in continuing. Tangible support is necessary for survival, not just praise and sympathy. It takes vulnerability to embody transness and re-live the trans experience on the screen (for which you may be greatly appreciated as an actor, but for which you are an abomination in the real world).

I was born in a small village called Dornari in Pali, Rajasthan. My mother gave birth to me in our ancestral home, which had no electricity or running water. The first time I went online was when my older sister, Jyotsana, returned from her studies in Jodhpur with a cell phone. A new world opened up for me because of her. I found stories, people, news, medical reports and psychological studies that affirmed my gender, which gave me hope that I could live the way I wanted to. Close to where we stayed was a town where we were told, '*Sab hijra log rehte hain. Waha nahin jana.*' That's where hijras live. Don't go there. That was the extent of what passed as conversation about gender identities in my home, and it instilled in me an irrational fear of hijras while I was growing up.

Though the internet affirmed my sense of self, I also read stories of trans people being chucked out of their homes, rejected by their families. When I thought of coming out to my parents, I wanted to express myself as perfectly as possible, but I also began to prepare myself for the worst. I followed the old script and asked the very naive question, 'Do you still accept me?' after showing them an episode of *Satyamev Jayate*, where Aamir Khan, the host, interviewed Gazal Dhaliwal,[3] a screenwriter. They both looked at me blankly, as if I had spoken to them in Greek. They didn't know what to answer, because they had never imagined denouncing me.

My sisters, cousins included, are my lifeline. They turned my childhood from hell to heaven. When I moved out of home, I eventually went to live with them in Baroda. That's where I met Dhruv Solanki,[4] and we began to make films together. Dhruv, who is now engaged to Jyotsana, is my mentor. He introduced me to new forms of filmmaking, as well as to films that are not cinematically flawless or financially backed like Martin Scorsese's films, but still leave the audience feeling something, possessing the potential to shape generations of filmmakers through storytelling. We have made ad films together and we also began shooting a film series about us siblings and cousins living in Baroda, going through our lives, in touch with each other through chat, and, at the end of the day, in person. We fight and we're often irritated with one or the other, but we also help one another and offer each other advice and/or a shoulder to cry on. I acted in and edited the first film, *It's All In Your Head*.

In 2024, *LSD 2* was released in theatres across the country in April. The same month, my directorial debut, my baby, *If You Know You Know*, was screened at the Kashish Pride Film Festival in Mumbai. I spent 2025 working on another incredible feature film (not a Bollywood production) as one of the protagonists, which I am very excited about. More importantly, I reached the end goal of my transition journey after years of toil, sweat, tears, shedding blood and leather. This would not have been possible without the angelic donors who contributed to my fundraiser campaign,[5] helping me reach my goal amount in a mere four days, after I had lost all hope. That day changed the way I looked at life. It reaffirmed my faith in humanity. I felt like I really am loved, people do care, the world does have empathy. I will always be grateful for this for the rest of my life because I know I couldn't have done it alone.

I find playing trans characters like Kullu in *LSD 2* really tough. I am trans, because I identify as a woman and live my life as such. However, the roles I am offered require me to do the opposite of that. The roles are fixated on a trans character's transness; it is the only driving force of that character. The line blurs, and it becomes less about acting and more about their version of what trans is—neither masculine, nor androgynous, nor feminine enough.

LSD 2 brought me a lot of recognition and appreciation for my acting ability and I am proud of how I brought that character to life. Preparing for that role taught me a lot, but I still remember my father's reaction after he watched it. At first, he was eager to watch the film with the entire staff of his forest department team, a flex to show off his daughter who was in 'Jeetendra's daughter's film'. That never happened, though. When my sister showed him the film on her laptop, it disturbed him. He called me and told me not to do such kinds of movies, 'no matter how much the money'.

When you're in the Hindi film industry, life is fast-paced and full of competition, and you never get to celebrate the moments of real achievement that you might have dreamed of as a child. One thing that I will always remember is what my sister taught me: 'In life, you should do what makes *you* happy and not what makes you look happy.' I hold it in my heart. I am not here for fame but to make things that give me creative satisfaction, whatever it takes.

Since it is so difficult to create trans characters that don't have anything but their gender ambiguity to offer, it's a challenge I am willing to take up. If I don't get these roles, I guess I'll make my own films. I will find my own tribe, and work with people who share a similar vision of cinema. Rather than wait for a messiah to utilise my potential and skills as an actor and make use of everything I have to offer beyond my trans identity, I will create my own space.

I'll act, I'll dance, I'll write, I'll direct, I'll edit, I'll have fun with my friends. I'm exactly where I want to be.

Notes

1. *If You Know You Know* won the Best Emerging Indian Filmmaker at the Kashish Pride Film Festival in 2024, and was nominated in three major categories at the Critics' Choice Awards 2024. It has screened at Inside Out, BFI Flare, PÖFF Shorts and DIFF among other festivals.
2. *Love Sex Aur Dhoka 2*, directed by Dibakar Banerjee in 2024. Bonita starred as Kullu, a hijra woman who works as a metro railway station attendant.
3. Gazal Dhaliwal, a scriptwriter, appeared in an episode titled 'Accepting Alternative Sexualities' in the third season of *Satyamev Jayate* in 2014.

The episode was telecast on the Star Network as well as the national broadcaster, Doordarshan, thus taking the conversation about gender, dysphoria and self-acceptance to millions of households.

4. *It's All In Your Head* is director Dhruv Solanki's feature film debut. Its tagline is 'What if Kardashians were born in a rural Rajasthani family and lived in Baroda on a budget? 6 Siblings. 6 Problems. 1 day.' It made its debut at the Hurghada Youth Film Festival (Egypt) in September 2023. The second film, *Blah Blah Blah*, is in post-production at the time of writing this piece. Solanki and Bonita have co-directed the film. Bonita has also acted in it.
5. Bonita sought to raise ₹5 lakh through a fundraiser video, created on Milaap, in 2024. Within four days of sharing her video on Instagram and other digital platforms, she raised ₹5.40 lakh.

NEITHER MONK, NOR NUN

TASHI CHOEDUP

Thanks to my friend Katherine, two years ago, I had a beautiful opportunity to be part of a pilgrimage, tracing the first Buddhist nun's journey seeking ordination to be part of Buddha's ordained sangha. It was a surreal experience of revisiting the trails of my Buddhist ancestors, because of whom the ordained sangha is not just a cis male occupied space today. It was more special because my teacher and nuns from her nunnery were on this pilgrimage. Centuries ago, women fought and struggled to be part of the sangha; today, the struggle continues for access to full ordination, among many other Buddhist traditions. To walk in the footsteps of those historical Buddhist nuns in the company of my contemporary sangha felt inspiring and moving.

As a transgender person, my journey with faith is not an easy one, but it is a significant part of my life. Born and raised in a dominant caste Hindu family, I explored Hinduism as well as Christianity with the help of a teacher; but when I encountered the Buddhist faith and dwelled deeper, it was an obvious homecoming. Following that realisation, I made a commitment to study and practise Buddhist teachings as an ordained monastic.

Of course, that isn't the only way to do it, but that is how I wanted to engage with it.

Thanks to the kindness of my teachers, I received novice ordination in Tibetan Buddhist faith and because of my supportive sangha siblings, I continue to live a monastic life without shying away from my queer–trans identity. But that doesn't mean there are no challenges or setbacks.

A few months before the pilgrimage, I applied to be part of a Buddhist nuns' month-long retreat. In my application, I identified as a transgender monastic and said that in alignment with my gender identity, I see myself in more proximity with the nuns' sangha and that it would be a precious opportunity for me to study and reflect with a group of nuns. I sent the application with great reluctance and doubt, but pushed through because I hoped it would start a conversation about trans people in the ordained sangha, especially among some phenomenal Buddhist nuns who were part of the retreat and are my inspiration.

To my thrill, I received an email from the organisers saying that I could be part of the retreat, irrespective of my gender identity. My joy was boundless. I quickly blocked the entire month and made preparations. But then, a couple of months later, the organisers wrote back to me, saying that as a transgender person, I cannot take part in the gathering as it is only for people with 'female bodies' who were ordained as nuns.

Of course, I was hurt and upset. I hadn't expected this at the tail-end of what seemed like a done deal. After a few weeks, as the grief mellowed, I could begin to see that this is not a response to me as an individual, but a response to a subject matter that is unknown and unfamiliar to most in the Buddhist world. Except for passing mentions of 'gender' or 'sex change' in relations with the Vinaya—the monastic code—there has rarely ever been any meaningful mention or dialogue about transgender persons in Buddhist writings or discourse. The task for queer persons of Buddhist faith is to change this, one dialogue, one person at a time.

I am often asked why I chose to be part of a religious tradition as a trans person, knowing full well the harm that religion has wrought on queer folks across the globe. I recognise the strong historical and contemporary context from which this question comes, but I can't help but wonder where we queer folks are not harmed and oppressed. Even nascent feminist friendships are not an exception, right?

Just as it seems daunting to nurture our queerness in a cisgender-heterosexual world, a trans person navigating the Buddhist world of faith and religion can find it overwhelming at times, but I derive my strength and courage in the friendships that hold me as well as in the Buddhist teachings that are, in my opinion, queer in their own right.

A nun friend of mine, for whom I am the first queer friend who is open and out, has been a great source of support, care and guidance. She recently started talking about me using the pronouns 'she' and 'her' and introduces me to folks as her 'dharma sister'. The ease with which she does it, without bothering about how the people around receive it, all the while looking at me, brings me joy. It only reaffirms my faith in the potential of friendships and the transformative strength of Buddhist teachings.

My faith in Buddhism is because of my faith in queerness, and because I see the many reflections of queerness in Buddha dharma. For long, I navigated the world with faith in the queerness we embody. Today, I rely on the same faith to walk through the religious landscape and beyond, with courage and vulnerability.

NOW IT ALL MAKES SENSE

Oviya V.

In Class 12, while everyone talked about boys and girls, I opened my book and scribbled, 'Marriage is just a commitment certificate.'

Welcome to my head.

I grew up in Hyderabad, a city of lights and greenery, infused with the aroma of biryani. To me, Hyderabad is home. My family is the sort where obedience equals respect and no matter what, one must always respect authority.

When my classmates spoke about their crushes, I assumed they simply meant that they found them aesthetically pleasing. I never guessed that they felt differently; that they didn't just mean butterflies in the stomach, but also desired to be in a romantic or sexual relationship.

I mean, how do you even know you want to be in a relationship with someone after just a few dates? How can you even kiss them just because you've known them for a month? And sex? Let's not even go there.

One day, my friend asked, 'Who's your celebrity crush?'

'Tom Hiddleston?' I blurted out. 'He's so handsome. His acting as Loki! That smile, the outfits he wears! His beautifully chiselled face! His eyes, his presence!'

'Okay, I totally get it. Anyone else?' my friend persisted.

I thought for a minute and said, 'Tony Stark.'

Their face was questioning but not judgmental. 'Why Tony, when you have Captain America?'

I honestly don't get why people prefer Captain America. The only answers I ever got were: 'Just look at his arms, his muscles; oh my god, his abs! He's just so hot! Are you seeing it?'

I would just nod, thinking to myself that attraction wasn't just admiration in a way that is 'Wow, that's beautiful,' but rather, 'I find them sexy, and I want them sexually.'

That was really eye-opening for me.

'Why Tony?' I asked myself a year later. Everyone around me was feeling these romantic and sexual feelings so easily, and I just wasn't. Something stopped me. Or was I stopping myself?

Tony, the character whose alter ego is Ironman, is a Marvel Comics creation. As fictional characters go, Tony has brilliant intellect. He becomes an expert in thermonuclear astrophysics overnight. He builds a whole suit out of scraps, turning war tech into a life-saving device. He recreates a whole new element in his basement just from clues left by his equally genius father. That's a really interesting person, and I, for one, would want all his knowledge. I want to be that intelligent. He's a mechanical engineer, electrical engineer, physicist, computer scientist, inventor, a business strategist. So is it weird that I want his brain, and not anything else? All I want to ask him is: 'Tony, tell me how you know so much and teach me everything.'

So, staring at the ceiling, I thought, 'I like Tony Stark so much. But, why isn't this romantic attraction?'

A little digging of my own led me to read up about the Split Attraction Model (SAM). I don't know how many people know about intellectual attraction, but everything finally clicked into place, as though I had solved a 10,000-piece puzzle.

All this time, all the people I ever liked: did I want to be in a relationship with them or kiss them? No. I held deep respect for all of them, for their intellect. But kiss them? Absolutely not.

Intellectual attraction is when you see a person and say, 'Whoa, the way this person's mind works is fascinating. I could talk to them for hours about astrophysics.' (I say astrophysics, but really, I mean anything.)

That is why I loved Beth Harmon from *The Queen's Gambit*, V from *V for Vendetta* and Wednesday Addams from *Wednesday*. All these characters are beautiful with rich, complex thought processes. Beth dominates her chessboard quietly, V riots with a strong moral code and Wednesday decimates with wit and strategy. Each one dominates, but only through intellect, planning and perfect execution. That's the basis of what my intellectual attraction is all about.

It's easy enough with fictional characters. But what about Tom Hiddleston, whom I said I had a 'crush' on? I still don't want to date him or be physically intimate with him, so what am I even experiencing? That's when I found out about aesthetic attraction. It's when you find someone's appearance, vibe or movement beautiful or pleasing.

It's possible to find a person's posture or style appealing. You may not even want to talk to them or get to know them. This is just visual or sensory admiration.

Did I want Tom Hiddleston to know that I admired him? Absolutely not! I don't want him to know me, nor do I want to get to know him in any way.

I think the same way about Aishwarya Rai and Nayanthara, two actors for whom I have deep respect, for their work and skills and grace. I find them visually very appealing and hold immense admiration for them as people. This is an aesthetic attraction.

The two attractions we have discussed (aesthetic and intellectual) fall under tertiary attractions, which refers to types of attraction beyond romantic and/or sexual. Aromantics experience little to no romantic attraction, and asexuals experience little to no sexual attraction. That doesn't mean they can never find love or be happy. It doesn't mean they are cold, emotionless robots. It doesn't mean they'll die alone, living a lonely life.

There are other types of attraction—from sensual to emotional—that are not romantic and sexual. Sensual attraction means being drawn to someone for the feel of their body, their skin against your skin, their scent, their hair, the touch of their hands on your face. Alterous attraction is wanting a deep emotional bond with someone but not in a romantic or sexual way, rather, simply admiring them for their qualities and personality, enjoying closeness and trust. Emotional attraction is based on being drawn to someone's emotions, feelings and how they express themselves. It can be toward a romantic partner, a close friend or even a family member.

Over the past twenty years, and especially in the past few, a whole lexicon has grown around identities that step away from sexual attraction, romantic coupling, monogamy and heterosexual marriage. These words and terms have helped me and the aro–ace community more than I can put into words.

Knowing these terms helped me understand what I was experiencing. It helped me come to terms with my aromantic, asexual identity and feel comfortable without forcing myself to conform to society's expectations.

As I continued digging, I came across a concept by philosopher Elizabeth Brake, a professor of ethics, political philosophy and feminist philosophy at the University of Wisconsin-Madison. Brake coined the term 'amatonormativity', defining it as the assumption that a central, exclusive, amorous relationship is normal for humans, and that such a relationship is normative. The assumption that valuable relationships must be marital or amorous devalues friendships and other caring relationships.

Where heteronormativity assumes heterosexuality to be the norm, amatonormativity assumes romantic coupling to be the norm.[1]

Allonormativity, in the same way, perpetuates a social conditioning that people experience sexual attraction (an allosexual is someone who feels sexually attracted to another).[2]

Both assumptions indicate that I cannot exist, or if I do exist, then I must be broken or unhappy.

But I'm not. I have great friends who support me in my distress and root for my success. I have friends who try to understand me emotionally and listen to me talk about the various interesting things I learn. I have a sister whom I hold dear.

I'm in a beautiful relationship and yes, of course, aromantics and asexuals can get into relationships with informed consent.

Identifying as an aromantic asexual in this current society is hard. These identities always existed; they are not something new or modern. From the Golden Orchid Society in Qing-dynasty China—where women formed partnerships with one another, choosing companionship over the expectations of marriage—to the eighteenth- and nineteenth-century women of Europe who remained unmarried not because of misfortune, but because they chose to devote themselves to art, teaching, science, or community work: people like me have always been around.

I did not come out to a lot of people, but the few I did come out to didn't quite understand the identity. Some couldn't believe that a person can't experience romantic attraction because it's what everyone feels. One said, 'You come up with a new identity every month!' Another said, 'Coming out is bullshit. Humans are attracted to humans in any way, form, or whatever. That's normal.'

This entire sentence reflects the allonormative thinking often seen across aphobes. (Aphobic people express prejudice, discrimination or hostility towards asexual, aromantic or agender individuals.)

Not every coming out story was a bad experience. Some are very close to my heart. My sibling and I laughed for hours, and I was left thinking, 'Whoa, now it all makes sense.' And my partner never forced me to try things that I did not consent to; he wasn't unhappy when I came out, rather, he really tried to understand me and my identity in detail so we could better navigate our expectations. We remain each other's vision, and we are directing our relationship at our own pace.

Allonormativity still binds us in a world where diversity is constricted and freedom is allowed only if one follows the social script. For example, when I was harassed by my friend with her comment about human beings attracted to one another 'no matter what', it felt like a glimpse of the prison we have built for ourselves. That comment invalidated who I am as a person and reinforced a worldview that left no room for identities like mine.

She continues to disrespect my identity, insisting it isn't valid.

If you've ever received a response that invalidates your identity after coming out, just know it's not your fault. You are never wrong for coming out, because it's the culture that treats attraction as mandatory and everything else as non-existent.

Over time, I've learnt that I don't need anyone's validation to express my identity publicly. I also noticed how under-represented aromantic and asexual identities are as there aren't many books, research papers, YouTube videos or podcasts about them. That's why I decided to contribute my part to representation by writing a book about being aro–ace[3] which discusses how insights and representation around these identities can help shape a better, more understanding world.

Amatonormativity and allonormativity have always existed, so why can't aromantics and asexuals, who go against these beliefs exist, too? The world is more open to opposites than a singular path. When both sides believe their truth is the only one, no one wins. Inclusivity of diversity is the greatest empathy of all.

Notes

1. 'Amatonormativity, Aromanticism, and What Defines a Relationship', a paper by Rilee Granger of Bridgewater State University, Massachusetts. Granger quotes from Brake's 2012 book, *Minimizing Marriage: Marriage, Morality, and the Law*.
2. Amanda L. Mollet, '"I Have a Lot of Feelings, Just None in the Genitalia Region": A Grounded Theory of Asexual College Students' Identity Journeys', *Journal of College Student Development*, 2020.
3. Oviya V., *Being AroAce: Insights and Representation*, 2025.

BEDROOMS

Vasavi Kalluru

My mind is occupied with beds and bedrooms. As I prepare to go back to university after a sabbatical, I find myself circling back to a quiet grief. Grief for all the years I have lost to mental illnesses. All the time I spent (and spend) in bed, confined to the bedroom because my body and mind demand it.

Living with mental illnesses is a relentless battle, one that defies explanation or resolution. It doesn't follow the neat timelines that the world expects. It is not linear, not neatly boxed, nor easily cured. It is cyclical and often invisible. I am trying to learn that the time spent in bed is not wasted. Now, I remember my bedrooms, with fondness, grief, fear, embarrassment, but most importantly, curiosity.

There are bedrooms that remember me more clearly than I do. Trigger Warning: The one where I first tried to take my life still smells like Dettol and unspoken things. I remember the coldness of the floor more than my own hands. It held me without warmth, without questions. I remember the silence after being discovered in the bedroom in a pool of blood. Silence, not out of peace, but shame. That kind of silence wraps around you and pulls you down. It follows you to the hospital. Nobody says the word. Not aloud. Attempt. Suicide. Death. Instead, there are glances. Glances of disapproval, of discomfort, of fear. Glances that say *it would have been better if she died*. Glances that screamed I had crossed a line.

There is another bedroom where I had my first kiss. A and I were reading *The God of Small Things*. The book lay open between us, our fingers brushing occasionally as we turned pages. Estha asked Ammu, 'If you are happy in a dream, Ammu, does that count?' I turned to A and whispered the question, not entirely sure if I was quoting or confessing. They looked at me, eyes soft with something I didn't yet know how to name. And then we kissed. It wasn't dramatic. It didn't come with fireworks or music in the background. It was quiet. Gentle. Almost holy. The kind of kiss that makes you feel like maybe, just maybe, you are allowed to be held. For a moment, the world seemed to fold in on itself. No noise. No fear. Just breath, and lips and the warmth of another body next to mine. Happiness for a sentence or two.

Then there is another bedroom where I cut my hair short. I did not know what gender dysphoria meant yet. Just the constant aching feeling that the body I am in is not mine. The quiet alienation that throbbed just beneath my skin. A feeling not loud enough to scream, but sharp enough to pinch.

The haircut did not solve everything. It certainly did not make the dysphoria vanish. Gender didn't shift that night. It broke. It cracked open. Just enough for me to breathe.

And then there are bedrooms and hospital rooms in which I wasn't really there. Dissociation? Mania? Affective dysregulation? I don't know. The words came later, as symptoms. I remember floating above my own body. Seeing gods in ceilings. And the room knew before anyone else did. It had seen me pacing in the middle of the night. It had watched me stare at the ceiling for hours. It had heard the sobs swallowed by pillows, the prayers I muttered without believing, for having to perform sanity, success, gender, stability, all at once. When I ended up in a hospital bed, under lights too bright to lie under, they scribbled down symptoms on charts and clipboards. And I tucked them behind my ear like flowers. Not out of pride. Not out of shame. But out of survival.

And finally, the many transient bedrooms. Borrowed spaces. Shared mattresses. Floors scattered with pillboxes, poetry books and half-eaten snacks. Rooms where my friends held me while I was falling apart, who stayed while I was having a flashback. 'Eat first, then we can fall apart.' In these rooms, I was not a diagnosis or a burden. I was just me. In these rooms, we laughed out of exhaustion. We exchanged poems. We danced after taking our meds. Their love didn't fix me. Maybe love does not need to. It held me. And in that holding, I am.

Each of these rooms held versions of me I've barely survived, and some that I am still learning to love. Some rooms bore witness to grief that language refused to carry. Others held quiet, urgent joys, silly dance routines, shared playlists, the sound of a friend opening their pillbox next to me in the dark.

It has been years, and the faint traces of blood in bedroom never really left the tiles, even after they were scrubbed clean. Bedroom two is long gone, and A is someone I no longer speak to. The third bedroom holds a kind of sacredness I cannot explain. The doctors in the fourth bedroom called me 'treatment-resistant' because their pills couldn't erase the violence I carry in my body. Memory is like that, it seeps into corners and refuses to leave. The bedrooms still remember these memories, and on some nights, I do too.

I do not know what healing looks like yet. I don't even know if healing is the right word. But I know that some beds and bedrooms will hold me through it all. They held me when language couldn't. And there will be more bedrooms. Some warm, some terrifying, some playful, some sacred. Somewhere I will lie still for days. Some where I will dance, clumsy, joyful, flourishing, alive. Or maybe not. And that's okay, too.

SOME THINGS I LEARNT ON BAD DATES

Ankur Tangade

I came out as queer before I came out as Dalit.

I was on a third date with this guy, and we were not moving forward with the relationship, or anything else for that matter. And then he just casually dropped this gem: 'You should go to the doctor and get yourself checked up. Something is wrong with you.'

And I thought, *Damn, maybe he's right.*

Growing up, seeing all the straight couples around me made me think that's just how it is. For a very long time, I was an ally, the straightest ally you'd ever seen.

But the thought never crossed my mind that maybe *I* am queer. Being a woman myself, it's kind of hard to know because when you see a beautiful woman, you get confused. Do you want to look like her, or do you just like her? I started thinking about it and realised—oh wait, I *do* like women. So my journey as a queer person began. For a couple of months, I thought I was homosexual. Then I realised I also like men. I thought maybe I'm bisexual. And so I was bisexual for a couple of months. But that didn't feel right either. So I started reading more about queerness and came across pansexuality. Bingo! My parents, who are human rights activists, were *so* proud of me. All their life they've been working for gender equality, and now they discover their daughter is one step ahead: 'She doesn't even *see* gender when dating—gender isn't her criteria!' I'm basically the overachiever of the family, but make it gay.

I remember one of my father's friends had a trans daughter, and he tried to commit suicide because of that. My father told him, 'My daughter will be able to help.' But here's the thing: My father was talking about helping with the queer identity, connecting them to my queer network, whereas his friend thought I would be helping their daughter go back to being their son again.

Which was, at the time, a hilariously tragic misunderstanding. But I thought, whatever, at least I'll get a queer friend! In small towns, there aren't a lot of openly queer people. Three years have passed, and now my father's friend's family has accepted their daughter's identity and respects her choices.

It is difficult to be a queer Dalit woman from a small town. Often, Dalit spaces have no respect for your queer identity and queer spaces have no sensitivity towards caste minorities. In Dalit spaces, I was discriminated against because of my queer identity. In queer spaces, I was discriminated against because of my caste.

The reason I chose comedy as a platform to talk about my experiences as a Dalit queer person is because I realised that when you're on stage with a mic, cracking jokes about your life and these incidents, people laugh *and* acknowledge the problem. Normally, when you talk about discrimination, there's always an argument. With comedy, that's rarely the case. Laughter is basically consent to listen.

My mother keeps telling everybody that I am polyamorous, and I have to keep correcting her: 'It's not polyamorous, it's pansexual. I am pansexual, not polyamorous.' The aunties don't know either of the words. They just think it's some kind of advanced education course that I'm doing, which my mom keeps bragging about, like a master's in pansexual studies!

Dating women is also very, *very* confusing, something I'm still trying to learn how to do. I remember an incident when I went out on a date with a girl. I wanted to open the door for her, and at the same time, she had the exact same thought. We both ended up holding the door, expecting the other person to go in, just standing there like two very polite fools.

This kept happening all evening. We both kept pulling chairs out for each other like a choreographed dance of confusion. We both wanted to drop the other person home first because, you know, women's safety.

At my shows, I used to come across audience members who had coloured their hair, and I'd think, 'Oh, queer person!' But then I thought, I shouldn't prejudge someone. Maybe they're just straight people who love to colour their hair. But when I talk to them, it's *always* a queer person in the crowd with coloured hair. That's where one of my jokes comes from: 'If you haven't coloured your hair, you're not allowed in the community. Forget about your identity—the hair colour is the primary requirement.' It's like we all got the same memo; Step 1: Question your sexuality. Step 2: Buy hair dye.

IN OUR OWN IMAGE

SEX IN THE AGE OF APPS

Prathyush Parasuraman

His wife is at work, so he sneaks you into his home in the middle of the day, latches shut the 'servant's quarters' and shoves himself into your tunnelled throat, until air suddenly feels like a necessity, and your eyes leak, and you can feel the rising gas from your stomach, of the empty breakfast and black coffee, and you tap out, wiping the tears with the back of your hand, and soon dip back into it—why?—the throat throttled, then tapping out, dipping in and he finishes, leaking inside your throat, and leaving his house, you wonder—did I enjoy that?—and your friend responds that if you have to ask, the answer is, perhaps, no, but then you keep replaying the image of that pounding in your head, burping his aftertaste, when you look down and realise—you are hard.

Desire is not so simple, the memory sometimes overwrites the act. Desire can exist not only in the doing, but in the having-done. Desire's afterlife is part of, even pivotal, to its life.

You keep returning.

The opening line of Leo Bersani's seminal essay, *Is the Rectum a Grave*, poses an argument, 'There is a big secret about sex:

most people don't like it', simply because people are not able to distinguish between the questions, 'Do you like sex?' and 'Do you often feel the need to have sex?'

Complicating that position, and triangulating the doubt, the third question is—do you prefer the memory to the act? The ability to speak of it over its pleasurable, performative exertion?

Edmund White in *The Loves of My Life: A Sex Memoir* wonders if his friend might be right, that 'sucking cock is a purely cerebral pleasure', for unlike the lips, where a million nerve endings come to graze, making it one of the most sensitive parts of the body to touch, to heat, to ache, to bite, 'there are no such receptors in the throat'. Is the pleasure, then, merely the 'Pavlovian satisfaction' of kneeling in front of a man?

Bersani marshals feminist thinkers like Andrea Dworkin and Catharine MacKinnon who have made the case for the inherent violence of penetrative sex, that 'pornography eroticizes hierarchy', 'fusing the eroticization of dominance and submission with the social construction of male and female', and we perform this dominance—not as parody, but as piety.

Parody, as Bersani notes, is not sexy. We kneel because we love the act of submission, even if it runs counter to our ideals of socialised dignity. We laugh at men who perform 'roughness' and 'toughness'—Dom Top 9 inch asks you if you are his bitch, and you say yes, but you think, *oh god*—because they are not able to slip into the performance correctly or proportionately. Parody is sometimes that distance, when the reach exceeds the grasp.

When homosexual men take on the garb of heterosexual machismo, it is neither a perversion of that masculinity nor a subversion of it, because at the heart of 'gay-macho style [is] a yearning toward machismo'. You cannot inscribe your desires into your beliefs, sometimes, often, maybe always.

If we take seriously François de La Rochefoucauld's formulation that we would not have fallen in love had we not first read about it, then we must also take seriously the possibility of sexual pleasures being possible because of porn, and then to take it to the most absurd conclusion—sexual desire is mimetic; we want it because we saw it being wanted.

Sex is no longer had with bodies, but with images. And it is not just because he refuses to come unless he watches porn, while you are dangling with a slobbering tongue somewhere in his nether regions; nor just because he will insist on recording the sex, and replay the video while he is arcing into you, watching it again and again, till your body becomes a proxy for its image on his phone, sending the video to a diligent listserv of Snapchat users; not just because you realised over time that the best sex are the ones had in rooms with mirrors to look into; not just because sometimes during sex you imagine someone else and bite your tongue so their name doesn't come out in a moan by mistake.

It is also because everyone has turned themselves into strategies, the body's pleasures negotiated through its logistical plausibilities.

Top? Bottom?

Bareback?

Hairy?

High fun?

You are told off for being rigid, and not open to experimentation and possibility and play, and you know they are right, but you also know most men are terrible at sex, so it is better to know what you want of them, of yourself and perform that clarity at the outset. None of that vague versatile bullshit.

Grindr opened up a plethora of choices, and choice makes you keep wanting to make decisions, and every decision's weight is felt for what you did not choose in its stead, and possibilities—the ones met, the ones left dry—swarm into the moment, which has been leached off presence. When you cruise, the choices are immediate, the initiation, the repelling, the tugging, the eyes, it is impossible to do the algebra of the ideal guy at this moment when your eyes are fluttering about, hoping no one has sniffed out your desperation. At the local theatre in Trivandrum, you go to the toilet with men you would never have put a single thought to had they first emerged into your consciousness as an image.

Sex is no longer had as bodies, but as images.

'Sex is not intuitive,' Zachary Zane writes in *Boyslut: A Memoir and Manifesto* (Abrams Image, 2023). The act of conditioning our way into it—and this could be cleaning the folds of the foreskin regularly, shaving pubic hair, spending hours with a scissor snipping away at sproutings of hair on your ball sack, douching, fingering, figuring out what to do with pubic lice, procuring poppers, knowing that flavoured condoms is for losers—needs to be studied in order to understand what it is that we are actually performing.

Because for queers, sex is not necessary in an evolutionary sense, it is desired in an immediate sense. Our innate decoupling of sex from reproduction has meant that sex is no longer instrumental—to marriage, to family, to civilisation—and that sex can be pursued as an end in itself. It is the final institution that the body turns towards. When people look at queers as evolutionarily wasteful, the flipside is a kind of people who can pursue with the whole vitality and vulgarity of their being, a singular desire—pleasure. We exist only for pleasure.

Do we not want to probe this pleasure a bit more?

In Berlin, you will meet a guy who is visiting the city with friends, but has taken a day off from them, booked a hotel room and has lined up a litany of sexual partners, to decompress. When does the law of diminishing marginal utility kick in, if that law was even made keeping in mind the insatiable body's slurring limits? You come too quickly, and are kicked out to make room for the next man—men, really—before you even get to pose this question in between the grunts.

Simply put, are you enjoying yourself? Does the fifth man matter? The fifteenth? Fiftieth?

Berlin will knock any resolved notions you have on sex, where clubs have specified nights for 'piss and fuck', 'fist and fuck' and the much more benign 'fully naked, shoes only'. You will meet people who enter Berghain on Friday nights and emerge from its techno fuzz on Sunday evenings. That is why, you are told, Pfeffermint, of Peppermint Schnapps, is so common it is sold in the corner *spätis*, for it is both alcohol and mouth freshener. You wonder when you will shed this ethnographic desire to make sense of what you are seeing and become its subject. But when you do, stewing naked in a dark room for hours, the night collapses into images, and nothing will make sense. Time feels lubricated, and maybe it was not all pleasure, but there was a lot of that, too. Someone walks up to you, asking if you want some G, and you say no, because your friend told you to stay away from a particular drug, whose name was an alphabet, but you are not sure which one. Only lines for you—be safe.

Everyone does speed, and you have a vial of a glistening powder tucked into your socks, and you sit at the breakfast table, wondering if rigidity and routine has its own value. At what point, straying from the mainstream and the respectable, do you arrive at a place where life feels *more* difficult? Is freedom, as White writes elsewhere, 'a form of loneliness'? Also, what freedom is even possible after having exerted every inch of your body in the gym in order to look like a fantasy? Whose fantasy? And at what point, in this fantasy, do you renounce your race? At some point, rejection makes you rush towards the fantasy faster, and what was promised as freedom, is actually fiefdom. You keep moving up the ladder, hoping that one day, the abs will speak for themselves. Vanity will surf you through your insecurities. You know that it is false. You keep returning.

At the bar you meet a guy here with his boyfriend, who is in a dark corner somewhere, and this guy looks exhausted, waiting to go home, waiting for his boyfriend to emerge. *I want my sleep tonight*, he tells you, *I don't want my boyfriend to bring anyone over, so let him get done here, and we can leave.* They have arrived at an understanding, one that keeps getting negotiated every night. It is sweet that he waits. It is sweet that he won't bring someone over tonight. It could be easier. But where's the fun in that?

Queer is a verb. It can be the search for a horizon that is not yet manifest, as José Esteban Muñoz opens *Cruising Utopia*, 'Queerness is not yet here' (New York University Press, 2009). Because it is a desire, a longing, queerness is lacking, too. Because it is in the future, in the present it is expressed as impatience. Because there are no answers, does not mean the questions go unasked. Because you cannot live the future, only live towards it, the present is a site of torment.

How do you endure queer?

You look around at all your heterosexual friends, coupled off, birthing children like a socialised habit, and wonder, this can't be it, it is sweet and familiar but so reckless in its routine, reaching back to move forward, it turns life into a loop that must be repeated, not because it is desired, but because it is destined.

The same reason you kneel in front of men. Do you want it, or is it wanted from you? Every day you undo your queerness by practicing homosexuality.

This distinction between homosexuality as a sexual preference and queerness as a subversive politics was made at some point, in America. For queerness, homosexuality is a leaping off point towards, as Bersani writes, 'a political-sexual identity not "fixed" by, or in some way traceable to, a specific sexual orientation'. To be queer is to stand, as E.M. Forster wrote of Greek poet, Constantine Cavafy, at a slight angle to the universe.

Queerness came to be regarded as the renunciation of the three Ms—marriage; market; military. The failure of queerness was the politico-legal fight to fold LGBTQ+ people within the mandate of these very three Ms—gay marriage; working to include LGBTQ+ people within the non-discrimination tenets; repealing the military policy of don't ask don't tell.

Fenton Johnson writes in the essay *The Future of Queer: A Manifesto*, 'The assimilationists have won, with state-sanctioned marriage as the very mortar cementing the bricks of the wall of convention that separates us from ourselves, from one another, from all that is unfamiliar, strange, challenging, and thus from learning and growth.' When we speak of the history of queerness in India, what is often offered in response is a legal history. It is the easiest category to explain—rights. It is the easiest way to rationalise and secure your presence in the public imagination.

I want to add a fourth M, though, which is tangential to marriage—monogamy, or institutionalised boredom.

You will meet a guy who, in the past year, has been exclusively into threesomes and orgies, and you think, perhaps, he doesn't care much for the intimacy and the intensity of having sex with one person, preferring the performance of it, instead, but then you'll fall in love with him, and when you watch him have sex with others, watch his body take a nine inch dick you and him were initially nervous about, you can't stop looking, he looks so handsome, his lats flexed, his tightening biceps, and your stomach falls a little, in jealousy, as your dick rises to the occasion.

What future is here? You yearn to the tune of Julietta Singh, who writes in *The Breaks*, 'We are less preoccupied with capturing the theoretical form of our queer family than we are with existing in the felt rhythms of our lives unfolding.'

How do you exist without looking towards the future?

Panic-stricken, you text your friend as his eye wanders on the dance floor, 'How do I not imagine a future with him?'

You workshop possibilities, until you arrive at the only solution—tell yourself that there will be no future, and this is all there is, and chant it, every time your hopes stray.

The future is contested real estate. You don't want to raise its value by seeking its embrace.

You tell your closest friend about him, and he asks you the name, and then smiling, tells you that he had slept with this guy a few years ago. You laugh, because years ago, when a similar situation came up—your close friend having slept with a man you envisioned a future with—your stomach fell, but today, you shrug, not out of indifference, but inevitability. Not because you love less but because the pull of love clots the heart differently. The yearning is the same. You still re-read Neruda's *Twenty Love Poems and a Song of Despair*, still chanting

'You occupy everything
You occupy everything'

You will have to touch and feel your way into the future, seeing no future around you that you want to inhabit, or sometimes trying to blot out this future, and maybe, this future does not exist, or this future is irrelevant, and there will come a time when you put your boots to rest, but today is not that day, and who are you to speak for your tomorrow, anyway—that is another person.

After a night of being worn out by men, on the way to breakfast, you both stumble upon a temple and you pray—give me the clarity to find meaning in this, or the patience to reach a deferred meaning, or the courage to recede when I realise there was no meaning in the first place.

There are days you will hate sex and hate men and hate desire because nothing is sating what needs to be plugged, the appetite is elsewhere, ravenous, untended, and you think by feeding hunger with water you might be dimming something, but some days your body behaves unlike your training. It does not neatly fall into the silhouette of its image you chalked out—it spills around.

*

There is a ridiculous army of people trying to make condoms sexy, but anyone who has worn it knows its grip, and that the only reason it is worn is for safety. Men will keep trying to have sex with you without it—I'm just teasing the hole, they'll say—and you will empathise with their violence and their erectile dysfunction when rolling a condom over their rapidly softening dick.

You will be reminded of college, of those excitable evangelists who tell you that consent has to be enthusiastic, while here you are wondering if what you consented to was not the act but its memory. Sometimes sex is a thing you get done. Finally, you can have your dinner. Other days, you refuse to leave the moments you inhabited a few hours prior, making a monument in your memory to that man, whose name has been blurred out, but whose lower back gleamed with a clarity that no name could ever compensate with.

In trying to sell the idea of safety as a commodity, as a necessity, we keep peddling lies. He will ask you, if you don't wear masks in public all the time, why are you insisting on condoms, then? You will roll your eyes.

He is on PREP. Maybe you should get on it, too. But that only protects you from HIV—whose past violence has softened into melancholic anecdotes, whose name strikes a fear not of mortality but a life lived in its shadow—not gonorrhoea, chlamydia or syphilis, for which you take doxycycline, which is available over the counter in India. Your friend in Berlin, whom you were deeply in love with—but that's okay, those things pass from being humiliating to humourous—asks you to get him Doxy from India, and you supply him with enough. Your overly cautious friend in India takes Doxy even after blowing someone, the tablet always in his pocket. Your Berlin friend is shocked when you tell him this, and says, the body should not become immune to the tablet, so you mustn't take it so regularly, and like a diligent messenger, you pass on the advice to your cautious friend in India, who shrugs.

Nobody likes condoms, and if you think making it taste like chikki or strawberries will help—it won't. Sex without condoms is, perhaps, monogamy's singular comfort, but who in a monogamous relationship is even having sex?

Medication is not something you trust doctors with, because the proctologist you went to—which came highly recommended, from a gay man, that too—tells you that douching is bad for the anal lining and suggests taking an enema twenty-four hours before sex, and you look at him aghast, lacking the words or the confidence to tell him that nobody plans a day ahead for sex that is desired within the hour.

When your asshole tears, you instead go to the homeopathic family doctor you have been going to since childhood—not because you trust his medicines, but because you want to be told it will be fine. He asks how it happened, and you blame your poor diet. He suggests bananas and sitting on a plate of warm water every morning until it has healed in roughly six months. It heals in two, instead.

In the arms of a lover, you discuss your STIs—well, everybody has HPV, he tells you, and you wished he was in your life when you were in the oncologist's waiting room, because the stupid hospital misprinted your report, noting that the anal wart was cancerous. It can't be, it is something women should worry about, your lover tells you, and you know he might not be entirely right, but he feels right, and that is all you want from life sometimes. If he can make your toes curl till they feel like they will snap off, how wrong could he be?

Since you started smoking cigarettes, the erections have become intermittent, having a mind of their own, and so you decide, as a strategy, to become a bottom, because while it is high effort—all of that shit that needs to be scooped out of your body (impatiently, you just use your fingers instead of a douche), the diet that needs to be watched, the fibre pills to ingest—it is, ultimately, low pressure. You meet the sweetest man who, at the restaurant, takes a tissue, wipes the excess oil from the fries off your fingers and kisses you on your nose, and tells you—this cannot possibly work out, we both like getting fucked.

Do you like getting fucked or have you settled into it?

You stop smoking cigarettes, hoping the erections will become obedient. It doesn't particularly work. You start smoking again, and one afternoon, in the embrace of a man you have convinced yourself will be yours, you look down and think—well done. The cigarettes weren't the problem. It was love.

You might be wrong. But you aren't looking for a medical cure. There is always Viagra. Or the cock ring that you aren't entirely sure how to use. Google exists—to know is not the point. To want to know is.

❦

He will invite you to his house, where he lives in a crowded tenement, where you will have to snake through narrow gullies of wires hanging like snakes and a running drain, and when he sees you, he will panic, because your shirt is tucked in and you have a tote looped on your shoulders. He will take the tote, fold it and hold it in his hand like a parcel, and your shirt will now be untucked. You should not look so obviously gay, he tells you, but he doesn't use the word 'gay'. Instead, he says, 'community'. How can he explain my presence to his neighbours who live a nose hair's distance away from him? He won't want to see you again, but he will drop you home on his bike. His Grindr profile clearly stated, 'No champa chameli types'. You should have known. But sometimes even knowing isn't enough.

For the longest time you couldn't date people your age because they seemed silly, and you loved the idea of a relationship where you learn, where he slaps your head with a book from his shelf and you spend the night on his couch reading it. Knowledge is erotic, you tell everyone with an ear, but you don't tell yourself you like older men because they have set in their moulds, making you the pliable one. You walk into relationships where you have to bend to fit in. It is how you express love—by becoming unlike you, sublimating your desires.

Is the ease with which he allows you into his life part of a worldview where he doesn't need to allow himself into yours? His deep comfort in his set patterns being a version of his disinterest in yours—not disinterest in an active sense, but an ambivalence towards how he fits into your life, given you so easily fit into his?

Love is alchemy, though. Suddenly, one day, your dick is hard enough to fuck; suddenly, one day, you are no longer you.

No longer you? That is such a stupid idea—of a 'you' that doesn't negotiate itself, and remains a stable, predictable thing. Everyone uses the word 'authentic' these days—an ugly word whose logical motions run counter to life.

Love helps you become. What of that?

He says he is not attracted to hairy bodies, and you decide to shave your body hair, because some desires are better folded into than critiqued and challenged. To love is to negotiate which desires are worth folding over for. At some point, you become a pretzel of your earlier self, having folded over so much, you are something *else*—finally, an object of desire.

You will tell him to begin gently, before boring you like a deranged drill, and he will smirk, 'So you want romantic fuck, not hard fuck?' and you will turn to him in confusion and amusement, thinking of all the clarity that words can provide, slotting desires into neat nations of meaning, wondering if that is what the sexual economy turns us into—citizens.

BEGUMPURA

Shripad Sinnakaar

How many generations
does it take
for a dream to come true?
Long hair oiled, combed—
braid tucked tight to a ribbon
as if to secure into something.
Not some future
but a sense of moving
someplace
where sun is not overdue.
Hands don't reap
what hands didn't sow,
and water doesn't ask
what the caste of our thirst is.

2x2 Courtship

Hanging by the footboard of the train against the
direction of the speed in the fullest swannish bent,

gliding his back open to make a bypass
                                                            in the currents
of the contraction of the readying bodies—the profile of his
nape, cliffside, exploding against the high background
gliding fast past him
the points-of-view of zero bulb light, steel-glint
kitchenette eclipsed by the gyrating sidetracks—on
the edges
immaculate settlements an alignment of non sequiturs leaping
of one thing
                                                    over the other,
bearing sufficing trees in a distance, the serrated midribs of
palmyra fronds splayed green in stiff elevation embossed on
to the corrosive grid
of old, no-maintenance buildings—pilasters of staircase balcony
in columns—the dry down of balsam in the leathery
grease of the tracks in a bristling low sundown of
twilight that clasps like an incident
of assault in the morning newspaper manufacturing the dread
of its possibility—an action in repose at a fingertip—
clutched to the railing,
habit wants to thrive, recall over itself, glistening each minute
loosening into speculation—there are muttering of
suspicion that modulates into cadence of guttural
alighting pitch.
The train jolts in a graduation as in an afterthought—
next station—a dozen more flocking, buckled into a crook of
another
                                                    into the twisted signature
of shoulder blades and contours of burgeoning—a
                    strut, a prance, an itch, a little dance of
                    reshufflings and patience
—stubbornly burying of themselves into themselves in the 6–9
p.m.

after-hour rush—this is somewhere between democracy
and mob.
Only his ear particulate—sated in the ridge of its inner folds
sloping into a fleshy lobe as if an emergency cord to
stop the train—over the terminal bridges, they put
turpentine
in the ear pit as you crank your neck, they twist a
cotton stem, sending ebbs of shoots across the skin.
A lull riding the breadth of sleepfulness—next station—
the figures illume in white tube lights. Snaking hip-first
in the alley arrows of desire trail, we resemble less of
ourselves—
first the play of our glances replete with
drafts of scenes, then repetitive enough
to eliminate the surrounding—a white,
lowly moan in the underbreath of the
colony.
The elation is clear, the preference of you is always
plural, a physical state in its perennial
shift. The thousand valves
of turning around now looking ahead, the
luking frs erased, personal characteristics,
features, properties all gone—

THE HARDEST PART IS LETTING GO OF HOPE

SUSAN DIAS

My night terrors started when I was a child. Thoughts of the universe extending to infinity, of the limitlessness of consciousness and of the mystery of death and thereafter frightened the sleep right out of me. As a teenager, I discovered that this condition was known as an existential crisis and found solace in the books of philosophers like Emmanuel Kant, Friedrich Nietzsche and Jean-Paul Sartre, who had experienced similar thoughts. Good company to be in but there was no real cure. Was I doomed to a lifetime of sleepless nights contemplating the meaning of life?

No, as it turned out.

In my thirty-eighth year, my circadian rhythm is informed by my five-year-old's fantasies instead. His heavy head resting on my neck has replaced the weight of existential dread, and my dreamless sleep breaks only at his whim.

I love being a mother. Parenthood gives your life a grounded perspective. It leaves you with an appreciation for your own history and, in an oddly selfish way, it allows you to relive and redo parts of your own childhood that even therapy would not have fixed.

I suppose being a straight parent must be different from being a gay one—easier, in many ways—but, I have never found it to be particularly hard. Just like when I fell in love with a woman, loving wasn't the hard part. The issues came from someplace else. So it is with being a gay parent. Everyone looking in, sees a different family structure and of them, there are several who think that they have the right to impose their will on us.

The biggest concern in my home these days is what kind of birthday party our son wants. He is currently torn between a play area party and a pool party. If, like me, you grew up 'regular' or you do not have kids yet, let me explain. A play area is a designated space with padded flooring and various slides, trampolines and kids' zones that a child can frolic in for a steep hourly rental. Meanwhile, the parents sit in a viewing area sipping cappuccinos that are bound to trigger the anxiety in their bowels. A pool party, on the other hand, takes place in a swimming pool. Despite my misgivings, whatever he finally chooses, we will take action. But meet me at a play area for coffee on a Wednesday afternoon and I will chew your ear off about what birthday parties were like in my day. In this, I think, most parents will join me, whether gay or straight.

Over the thirteen years that my partner and I have been together, we have set up two homes, grown a puppy, brought our birth families together, faced financial troubles, built our separate careers and raised a child. Our love led to the creation of this world and, as we get older, we realise the importance of the choice we made to build a life together. What started off as a young friendship and an unlikely romance has given us years of love, learnings and gray hair. Do we have regrets? Perhaps. But all our choices—individual ones as well as those that we took as a couple—led us here. Is this what it means to be an adult and see the consequences of your actions play out? Maybe we have grown up over this last decade and are finally some sort of functional adults.

Now, as our son grows up, we see the complexities ahead of him. His world will be harder given that he has same-sex parents. We wonder every day if we are doing enough to equip him and also, somehow, make the world safer and better for him.

In 2023, Aditi and I were among the seventeen couples[1] who petitioned the Supreme Court of India to end the discrimination that we thought is written into the marriage laws of this country. Though we were nervous, we felt that it was time to take a stand and make an appeal for the right to marriage equality that we deserved. It was nerve-wracking and humbling. Meeting so many queer couples and individuals helped us see that we are part of something bigger than us.[2]

Straight citizens of this country take so much for granted. The simplicity of a joint bank account, or even of one's partner being able to weigh in on medical decisions around the other's health, and their child's health, brought home the reality of what this petition was about. For a while, when the court heard our petitions and the newspapers and television channels followed this seminal case, it really felt like queer couples were being seen and heard, the similarities and differences of their lives compared to the lives of straight married couples was out there for everyone to see. Now they knew why it was so hard for us. Now they knew how immensely privileged they were.

❦

One never imagines fighting a case in any court, let alone the country's apex court. Hearing lawyers argue about the rights you are entitled to by the Constitution of the country is disconcerting, because we all take so much for granted—our citizenship, free speech, freedom to practise our religion and, most importantly, our dignity. As adults, where do we engage in discussions on our eligibility to these rights? It was frightening at times when our lawyers argued for us before such an important forum. We were fighting for what we didn't have, but it also made me think, are we taking what we have too lightly?

Lofty sentiments, heightened emotions, august company, sombre environment. Put a five-year-old in the mix and life becomes a tragicomedy. I love narrating an incident from those days. Our visits to the Supreme Court involved a lot of paperwork and security checks. For entry into the main courtroom, a guard would instruct us to leave our phone outside—where, exactly, was unclear—and stay silent during the proceedings. During one of the hearings, I was kicked out by the guard for breaking the rules and using my phone briefly. This was a matter of great shame to my partner but what was amusing was that I was using my phone to order our son new shoes. His playschool teacher had texted to say his giant flat feet were pouring out of his sandals and he needed roomy shoes for his toes. Could my life as a partner, parent and gay woman get more domestic than that? Sadly, the irony was lost on the court. And, soon enough, so too was the case.

Everyone always knew we could lose the case but for most petitioners, including us, there was a buoyant feeling in the run up to the verdict that made it seem like victory—in some form or measure—was inevitable. The arguments, the conversations, the largely supportive media, all seemed to suggest that people were conceding to the radical idea that the LGBTQIA+ community deserves equal rights.

The opposition's argument regarding the social and cultural aspects of marriage seemed to many of us to be so droll—*we want to be part of this very fabric*, we wanted to shout sometimes—but even so, the mood was upbeat.

In October 2023, we lost the case. The court found that marriage is not a fundamental right, and it was not the appropriate forum to make laws for LGBTQIA+ people to marry their partners. The message was clear: you can be queer and live as you want to but it is up to you to work hard at convincing society to change age-old structures to accommodate your way of life.

What a daunting task for our short lives.

Our initial reaction was to return to default and go about our lives as quietly as possible. No more interviews, no more public speeches, no more ruffling feathers or wearing our queerness on our sleeves. This was how many of the petitioning couples responded in the immediate aftermath of our loss and how, as I realised, we are conditioned to live safely. Gradually, all conversations in living rooms and newsrooms ceased a few days after the verdict and the news cycle moved on to other pressing issues of our times.

What has changed since the court's verdict? As a queer family, we still have no legal status, but post-petition, it is hard to ignore the indignities that come from refusal to recognise us legally. The feeling that seeped in once we stopped pretending that everything was okay—we're doing great, we've built a life of benign innocuity—was not quite anger, no, nor frustration. It was a lump in the throat. An immediate recognition that someone was okay that we didn't have the same entitlements as them. It was a refusal to feel any more shame but also a grating at the core for having to participate as a citizen as though I have not just been shown what I don't get to have.

We now know that Indian society, polity and judiciary are not ready for same-sex marriages. Are my partner and I simply being tolerated by those around us because of our privilege? I wish I could ask those around me—extended family, friends, colleagues, all invitees to our son's birthday party—point-blank: Do you believe in equal marriage and will you stand up for it when it counts? Will you be okay if your child comes out to you as queer? Yet, I do not ask these questions because the answers may confirm what I know, or worse still, because they will kill the vibe of the party and my son may never forgive me.

All our choices, from falling in love to starting a family and fighting for equal dignity have rested on the hope that our tomorrow will be better than our today. As our little family moves on making weekly menus, trying to get in 10k steps and planning play dates, the hardest part is letting that hope go.

Notes

1. In October 2025, a five-judge bench of the Supreme Court ordered that marriage was not a fundamental right, and thus, the fifty-two petitioners seeking recognition under the Special Marriage Act of 1954, as well as other laws governing marriage, have not faced discrimination that could be constitutionally remedied by the apex court.
2. 'In petitioning the SC for marriage equality, we are asking this nation we love for our right to live our lives with dignity. And for our son to live in a country where his mind is without fear and his head is held high,' Susan Dias wrote in an editorial for the *Hindustan Times* barely days before the top court delivered its ruling.

QUEERING THE FAMILY, CHOOSING YOUR KIN

DHAMINI RATNAM

Recently, I helped my partner, L, empty a house. It did not belong to us, although it has been my home for some years now. It belonged to my partner's former partner, J. Once, many, many years ago, L and J bought it together. They lived in it. They made love in it. They threw dinner parties for large mixed groups of queers just as the language of identity was beginning to sprout. They fought in it. They raised dogs. They mourned the loss of their dogs. They held meetings about an offensive colonial law. They fought in those meetings (everyone did). They organised. They wrote manifestos. One wore skirts, large spectacles and oversized shirts, took copious notes and interjected with clarity and empathy. The other, short-haired and stocky, cooked elaborate meals and dropped truth bombs that sounded harsh but were vital. They sheltered runaway couples and friends in search of a quiet moment, away from the prying eyes of the birth family. They held taash parties in the Diwali season, cooked biryani for Eid and juicy roasts for Christmas. They preserved everything. A photograph of a friend who died in a car crash. A friend who died by suicide. Their dogs' bones. Their domestic help's old saris. Bed covers. Masalas. Rubber bands. Old black-and-white photographs. Decade-old love (lust) letters with curvaceous stick figure drawings that enumerated all the places one would plant kisses on the other.

We hollowed out this home of memories, packaged them and sent them to different locations: to a bustling colony in Thane, where I live, to a quiet lane in South Goa, where my partner and her former partner share a new home and to Vaga's apartment in Mumbai's western suburbs.

Who is Vaga?

Vaga is my partner's former partner's friend from the kinky community. Vaga is my queer family. Since I don't have a word to explain our relationship—he isn't a brother, a cousin or even a friend—I will only use his name. Vaga organises a multi-city kinky film festival and lives with his two partners—Vasundhara, a forty-year-old cis-het woman and Yaara, a twenty-seven-year-old Muslim trans man and a person with disability—and Vasundhara's partner, Aamir, a thirty-four-year-old Muslim cis-het femme-expressing man.

In an essay in the *Handbook of Feminist Family Studies*,[1] R.F. Oswald, K.A. Kuvalanka, L.B. Blume, and D. Berkowitz spoke of heteronormativity as the convergence of at least three binary opposites into a singular theoretical complex: 'real males and females versus gender deviants', 'natural versus unnatural sexuality' and 'genuine versus pseudo families'. However, they write, families of choice like queer families or polycules—the 'pseudo families'—complicate the underlying assumption that the binary is natural and universal.

The work of complicating underlying assumptions is never completed.

Back in Mumbai, Vaga's home will soon be filled with cartons from Delhi. If my cartons consisted of an old wooden cupboard, bedside tables and soup bowls, Vaga's cartons mostly contained art supplies and clothes. Yaara, an artist, constructs works where he can see his bodies like his own. Vasundhara reimagines fabric into newer, fabulous things. A sari may re-emerge as a bag, a diaphanous dupatta as a negligee or a collage on a frame. It seems to be a metaphor for family and queerness, although she doesn't identify as queer or like the word 'polycule'.

Vaga's flat overlooks a snaking metro line and a wide nullah where every other monsoon, a crocodile or two will give a nasty surprise to a passing pedestrian. It would have swum through similar drains—waterways created over 100 years ago for the rainwater to flow into—travelling the length of one of Mumbai's rivers, hoping to find its way to one of Mumbai's creeks. The adjacent one-bedroom flat, in which Vasundhara and Aamir sleep, and Yaara and Vaga work, is filled with boxes when I visit them a few weeks after our Delhi trip. The two flats share a kitchen, among other things.

'I have a discomfort with words like "polyamory", "polycule", "metamour", "queer", because it feels like we are trying to imitate how Americans or Europeans define their families. Here, family works very differently. So to extrapolate the concept without taking into account the context makes me uneasy. It seems facetious and performative,' Vasundhara says, adjusting her cushion on the diwan. We are sitting in a messy circle. Yaara's walker is beside his chair. Vaga is perched on a stool. Aamir, who has made a fresh round of tea, slips into a corner on the floor.

The first time she encountered the word 'polyamory', she 'hard identified' with it. 'I was married and lived with my in-laws and other family members of my husband at the time,' she says. Ten years on, she realises that she simply 'didn't fit in that box'. 'I spent years feeling guilty about not being monogamous, but I never thought of non-monogamy as a possible long-term situation either. So, when I heard about polyamory and relationship anarchy, it was liberating to find words that described what I inherently wanted. Now though, I just think of polyamory as an efficient term to describe my living situation,' Vasundhara explains.

Each of them has arrived at this flat through a series of fortuitous events. Yaara met Vaga in Chennai through a dating app, when Vaga was attending to his father, who was undergoing cancer treatment. Their first date was on the beach and Vaga travelled halfway across the city to meet Yaara, who has progressive pseudorheumatoid dysplasia (PPD) and walks with support. Earlier this year, Yaara moved to Mumbai. 'It's only after I visited Vaga in Mumbai that I realised that it was possible to manage my disability with much greater ease,' he says. Yaara's appreciation of the city's infrastructure may seem misplaced to those of us that have lived here longer, but it carries a far more damning indictment of Chennai's accessibility.

Aamir, who hails from Uttar Pradesh and works as a script writer in Bollywood, moved in to stay with Vasundhara, because he could not imagine being in a romantic relationship in which the partners live separately. 'I may sleep with whoever but I am monogamous when it comes to *ishq*,' says Aamir.

All four date other people who they meet on an app popular among polyamory practitioners. In fact, the app shows the four of them as a 'cluster', a feature that signifies a polycule. They negotiate timings of visits of new lovers, and joke that if any of them fall in love, they'd have to find another flat in the same building.

Imagine that. A seven-storey building in a crowded Mumbai suburb gradually filling up with a queer poly network of relationships.

The family has a 'revolutionary potential' and can act as a source of 'resistance, empowerment and change', Katherine Allen and company write in the introduction to the *Handbook of Feminist Family Studies*.[2] It is, at the same time, a structure in which 'oppression and privilege are systematically experienced and reproduced'. A queer family is revolutionary potential in action, because, at least in theory, we would like to imagine that it deviates from the normative and structural basis of the *savarna* worldview—access to networks and opportunities, intergenerational wealth and the material benefits of privilege—by calling into question the hierarchies implicit in a biological family.

But the praxis is an altogether different matter. Heteronormative families often weaponise money and inheritance against queer people. Several trans persons who leave their homes are disowned and written out of their family property, social circles and caste-based community ties, and often land up on the streets on account of their perceived gender or sexual variance.[3] The stigma is further compounded if trans persons and other queer persons turn to sex work to earn, which pushes them deeper into a tunnel of silence, exposing them to physical and mental health risks.

G, a polyamorous cis woman living in Bengaluru and a community organiser, draws a distinction between polyamory and queerness that I find particularly interesting. Not all who are poly are queer, G explains. Straight couples might find other straight partners, and form a polycule that is centred around shared resources or co-parenting, but they don't necessarily question the norms of caste-based patriarchal heterosexuality that gatekeep resources, or extend their fight for others' right to self-determination.

Sami, another member of my queer family who has tumbleweeded around the country and rolling-stoned her way from the development sector to academia to advertising, feels that the revolutionary potential of queer comes from our ability to fall in love with 'just anyone'—and it is in the living out of that love (or lust) that we unlearn and learn how to be around different people. 'Language, food, money, and how we're around these things, it's all socio-cultural, isn't it? So, in a way, we can shed the worst of our learnt behaviours, our savarnaness, our myopia, our selves. But it's really difficult to be open to doing this.'

'See, I like to make some decisions: *Chawal kaisa rahega, dal kaunsa chalega* [the way the rice is cooked, or which lentil we will buy], how I want my kitchen to look. But, among the four of us, Aamir ends up taking charge of the kitchen, figuring out what we'll eat, which vegetables to buy. I pay the rent. I know that there is an inequality in our monetary situation, but I don't want this inequality to creep into our relationships. I get very annoyed when Aamir spends his money and not mine. But at the same time, I also get why he does it. I'm worried that I will behave like my father, the way he behaved around money, and decisions, which I hated when I was growing up. That's my biggest fear,' Vaga says, explaining the complicated nature of decision-making when different privileges and entitlements intersect in a queer household.

'I also check myself. When is it okay for me to tell Vaga how to spend his money? Recently, he wanted to buy a television, and I asked him not to because it isn't needed,' Aamir says. (He has a point. A large white screen hangs in the room on which all four of them watch films from a projector.)

'Look, I understand that there is a right way to do queer or poly and everyone should earn and contribute and that's what we think "equal" looks like. But not all of us earn the same, or can work the same hours. And if no one questions having a single earning member in a biological family, why does it suddenly turn into an issue in a queer family?' Vaga asks.

How do you deal with the different earning capacities though, I ask all four of them in the room.

'We joke about it all the time,' Vaga replies.

Four years ago, Vaga and I were swatting away at a family of mice that had entered our Delhi home during the pandemic. My partner and I had broken up, and V had yet to meet any of his poly family members. He cooked, I cleaned the dishes and my partner's former partner, J, managed the house. In the anxious days of the pandemic, my partner's absence did little to affect my presence in that home. Neither of us expected the other to exit the family, because this family was bigger than us.

Early on in our relationship, L and I had agreed that our partnership was not to be the basis of the relationships we develop with the people common to our lives. Her friends do not automatically become mine and vice versa, and if we wanted to create separate relationships with each other's friends/queer family, we needed to have independent equations with them. We both agreed that primacy does not automatically adhere to the sexual partner, though we've been brought up to believe it does. Queerness entailed challenging norms that uphold the all-powerful Great Indian Family: based in caste and community, tied by blood, protected by personal laws. Our chosen family, on the other hand, centered around friendships, anti-majoritarian politics and relationships that had no name. It was, by comparison, frail and precarious. It needed ferocious support and intentional relating.

'The problem is that this sounds really cool and performative and Instagram reel-worthy,' L says. 'But this is the toughest part of our lives. You have to understand, this is survival. Until such time as we don't have it as easy as everyone else, it is survival.' L is nearly fifty, and she came out as a lesbian in the 1990s, when a journalist wrote a piece about her being assaulted in the women's compartment of a local Mumbai train for being masculine presenting. When she went on a news show in the late 1990s to talk about LGBT rights—'I did it because I knew there will be other lesbians watching and I wanted them to see that they were not alone'—she wore a cap and sunglasses to protect her identity. An audience member asked her if she would like to watch a blue film with him, and the others laughed at the insipid joke made by a middle-aged man, directed at a twenty-year-old, telecast on national television.

I understand her discomfort. In *Desi Queers*, [Hurst and Co Ltd., 2025] the authors talk about the allure of creating heroic queer pasts, where 'deviant and defiant actors' became 'heralds of queer possibilities being lived out in the present, fighting the good (progressive) fight'.

'But what happens when the allure of these pasts is pierced by events or incidents that produce undesirable knowledge?' Jennifer V. Evans, in *The Queer Art of History: Queer Kinship After Fascism*, [Duke University Press, 2023] writes about the 'messiness of commemorative practices' and asks, what happens when 'we invoke an identity politics that foregrounds identity but leaves the politics behind?'

For activists like L and J, whose lives predate so much of contemporary language (J, for instance, was responsible for coming up with at least some of the first literature on sexuality in Hindi through an NGO she founded), their politics and lives have already been the subject of intense scrutiny and judgement by friends, allies, co-litigants and detractors. A friend who visited often, called their dinner parties casteist, another published private conversations, yet another questioned them on their domestic help of many years living in their home.

At the same time, joining this queer family, with its relative material benefits and savarna privileges, implied that our politics were aligned. To be fair, for most part it was. But did we agree on everything? No.

The Me Too movement was a case in point. J and L differed widely on even the broad strokes of the arguments—L felt it was vital to believe the victim no questions asked, even when there was anonymity or when accusations were made through whisper networks. L had worked in a newsroom for much of the early 2000s up until 2015, and knew exactly how male bosses operated, as though they were running a boys' club. J and I shared some points of similarity in that blind belief in an accusation belied the feminist legacy of setting up systems to address sexual harassment. J's assertion was that women could lie too, and to presume that they wouldn't was unfair and essentialist. I, too, railed against systems, especially those that are meant to protect us, for failing miserably. But, the social media trials that enabled too-swift reprisals made me intensely uncomfortable. It took months for me to formulate my thoughts on radical empathy which, according to me, was what was needed to queer the Me Too movement. To have radical empathy would mean that you recognise the systemic victimisation of the perpetrator, particularly when the accused belonged to marginalised identities like Dalit-Bahujan men or the LGBTQ community.

So, no, our politics did not tear us apart.

L met J, ten years her senior, at a protest march for the screening of *Fire* in New Delhi in 1998.[4] Within five years, they bought a house and since they did not have a recognisable legal relationship to get a home loan, the house papers only bore one name. L paid the monthly installments to the bank, while J put down part of the money upfront. Both of their birth families, however, only recognised their partnership to varying degrees and that too, over time. When they ended their relationship after a decade, they stayed apart for three months, and then got back to living together.

'Outside of our queer family, no one recognises us as a queer family. We have to validate ourselves far more than others validate us. This is bound to result in socially awkward situations like where we need to prove the significance of a relationship that has no name. We will be at odds in a normative work or educational space or even a gathering of friends, where we must justify our chosen family relationships,' L says. 'When our relationships end, no one closes ranks around the family. Who is invested in us staying together and remaining a family?'

When L and I ended our relationship, I too moved cities after some months, returning to my home city of choice—Mumbai. As it happened, my parents had got stuck in Mumbai during the pandemic and my decision to return coincided quite neatly with theirs to stay. I began to live with them after nearly two decades of living independently. One day, while discussing options for beds, my mother, all too aware of my heartbreak, said, 'There's no need to buy a queen bed. Just buy a single one.' That's tough love for you. Then again, my mother was never much of a supporter of my (bi)sexuality.

Queer was once a paralysing slur, theorist Judith Butler wrote. When we began to use the word for ourselves sometime in the late 1990s and early 2000s, we knew the risk we faced from our families, workplaces, the law, the state and police, our religious and caste-based communities.

The lexicon of identity itself has mushroomed. The Ambedkarite anti-caste critique of queer politics has pushed many of us who were part of an earlier formulation of LGBTQ rights to interrogate our alliances. South Asian academia has begun to examine gender and sexuality in the subcontinental context. And, in the face of receding state welfare and casteist push-back to constitutional entitlements, occupants of marginal locations have only grown more insistent. Legally, too, LGBTQ people have begun to seek inclusion in state-sanctioned institutions like the electoral roll and marriage laws.

No doubt, this has an impact on how we imagine the queer family today, though the idea of the chosen family has been around for centuries. One must only look towards the gharana system among the hijras to understand how varied familial formations not rooted in caste and birth can be. Modern-day queer and trans imitations are not rooted in history in the same way, but some central ideas of security, belonging and what Gaston Bachelard, the French philosopher, referred to as the space to 'daydream', can certainly also define the queer home.

Recently, L and I resumed our relationship as consensual non-monogamous partners. We continue to have conversations about what constitutes a queer family, albeit over notes on a Google sheet (we're both writers, we both love manifestos and we both find varying degrees of joy in having a digital relationship, too).

This is what we co-wrote recently:

> As compared to biological families, where blood, the umbilical cord, the pain of a vaginal birth lend validity and authority to the connection between different family members, such that one can step out any time one likes but one can never leave, a queer family is intentional, individually sought after and maintained. A bio family doesn't need members to be intentional about this choice. Queer families require individuals to have a greater degree of self-awareness, but they are also precarious.

This document remains between us, and we update it whenever we feel the need. One day, the algorithm-hungry Google or Meta will read it and use it to answer someone's ChatGPT questions. The love letter with a stick figure will stay in a well-preserved box, and Vaga will find ways to keep the dreams of his poly and queer families alive. Sami will finally write a book of poems or erotica and L and J will build a home big enough to accommodate all of us and many more.

Imagine that.

Notes

1. Katherine R. Allen, Sally A. Lloyd, April L. Few (eds.), 'Reclaiming feminist theory, method and praxis for family studies', *Handbook of Feminist Family Studies*, pp. 3–17, SAGE, 2009.
2. Ibid.
3. 'No Outlaws in the Gender Galaxy', K-PUCL report.
4. In 1998, women's groups held demonstrations when Deepa Mehta's film *Fire*, which depicted a lesbian relationship, was prevented by members of a right wing political organisation from being screened. J remembers seeing L step out of the line of protestors outside Delhi's Regal Cinema in Connaught Place to hand over a pamphlet to a passer-by with the comment, 'Aunty, aap bhi toh ho sakti ho,' ('Ma'am, you too could be a lesbian'), a bold and slightly vexing challenge.

ABOUT THE CONTRIBUTORS

Dhiren Borisa is a Dalit queer activist, an urban sexual geographer and an Associate Professor at Jindal Global Law School, O.P. Jindal Global University. His work explores how caste and queerness shape everyday urban life in India and beyond. He is interested in queer world-making, messy archives and the stories that cities carry in their margins.

Dr B. Kiran Nayak is a disability, equity and gender equality activist who is the founder and general secretary of Karnataka Vikalachetanara Samasthe and general secretary of Society for Trans men Action and Rights. He is a Banjara tribal trans man from Warangal, Telangana, living with 75 per cent polio-related disability and has been a wheelchair user since the age of three.

Sintu Bagui is a noted transgender rights activist, feminist leader, and community researcher based in West Bengal. A trailblazer at the intersection of gender, sexuality, and labour rights, Bagui advocates for the rights of transgender persons, sex workers, and their families. She co-founded the Kolkata Anandam for Equality and Justice (KAEJ) in 2019, and her work spans participatory research, policy advocacy, and cross-movement coalition building. In 2019, Bagui served as a judge at the Lok Adalat in Sheoraphuli. An author, speaker, and filmmaker, Bagui continues to shape discourse on trans rights through writing, public engagement, and community-led research.

Rabi Raj is based in Belpara, Odisha, where they are a primary school teacher, a Dalit and LGBTQIA+ rights activist and a poet.

Vijeta Kumar teaches Communicative English and Creative Writing at St Joseph's University, Bengaluru. She is currently working on a PhD on the works of writer Dawn Powell. She also writes about films, books and has an ongoing column at *The Third Eye* where she writes an annual love letter to the classroom. You can read more of her work at rumlolarum.com.

Vqueeram Aditya Sahai is a teacher who lives and loves in Delhi.

Siddarth S. Ganesh is an independent curator-archivist who works with epistemic systems, focusing on making knowledge accessible. They have a Master's degree in literature, linguistics and civilization studies from the Grenoble Alpes University, France. Their research on archival theory and ethics has been published in English and French.

Kenny Awomi is a model and LGBTQ+ advocate from Nagaland who has emerged as one of the most visible queer voices from the Northeast. Based in Delhi, she began her career in fashion and modelling, participating in ramp shows, fashion campaigns and independent modelling events while openly identifying as a transgender woman.

Dit Thoudam is an intersex person from Manipur, India. He did his graduation from NIT Manipur in Electronics and Communication Engineering and completed his MA in Sociology from IGNOU. He has been a fellow at Yuwahh,

UNICEF India, the YP Foundation, Sangath Bhopal and Intersex Asia. His work experience includes being a peer counsellor at ETA, a community-led organisation for trans men supported by SAATHII in Manipur, a project co-ordinator at Ya_All: The Youth Network, Manipur and, currently is the superintendent-in-charge at AURA Home for Transboy.

Dr Aijaz Ahmad Bund is a Kashmiri academic and LGBTQ+ rights activist. He is the founder of Sonzal Welfare Trust, an organisation working for the welfare, awareness and empowerment of marginalised communities, particularly LGBTQ+ individuals in Kashmir. Through his academic work and social activism, he advocates for inclusion, human rights and community support initiatives in the region.

Dr Aqsa Shaikh is among India's first transgender medical doctors. She is also a professor, and teaches community medicine at HIMSR, Delhi. She is a member of the national taskforce on Student Mental Health and Suicide Prevention, set up by the Supreme Court in March 2025. She has contributed a chapter to the book *Transforming Law: How Law Shapes Transgender Lives, Identity and Community in India*.

Aryan Somaiya is a psychotherapist, gender and sexuality educator and lived experience expert at Guftagu therapy. He is co-author of 'Trans Affirmative Mental Health Care Guidelines: Results of a mixed-method inquiry in three cities of India', Tata Institute of Social Sciences, Mumbai. He has co-authored papers for journals and also contributed a chapter to the *Encyclopedia of Radical Helping*, Thick Press, USA, 2024.

Dr Sameera Jahagirdar is a transgender woman and medical doctor whose understanding of healthcare was shaped as much by lived experience as by clinical training. Navigating the same systems she was taught to administer—first as a professional, then as a patient—she came to understand that the most transformative changes are built from vulnerability, not despite it. Currently based in England, her work sits at the intersection of medicine, identity and advocacy, driven by the conviction that the journey toward equitable care is ongoing and without borders.

Ammel Sharon is a historian at the National Law School of India University in Bengaluru, where she is also building the Law and Society Archives. Previously, she was the director of the Queer Archive for Memory, Reflection and Activism (QAMRA). Her interests include higher education, disciplinary knowledge, writing pedagogy, archival studies and gender.

Sharanya Ravi is a visual artist and illustrator based in Mumbai. She completed her BVA in painting from the Maharaja Sayajirao University, Vadodara, in 2025. In her practice, she blends her contemporary reality with fantasy and mythology, telling stories of brown-skinned characters that have agency to embrace, strut, pose and thrive.

Priya Dali is the creative director at Gaysi Family, an LGBTQIA+ community platform. A Forbes India '30 Under 30' honouree, she co-founded Are You Serious?, a creative studio working at the intersection of design, culture and social impact. She dreams of making queer children's books.

Payal Rathva is a transgender Warli artist based in Rajkot, Gujarat.

L. Ramakrishnan, Amit Prasad Bisoi, Biswa Bhusan Pattanayak, Khushi Pahuja, Randhoni Lairikyengbam, Sharmista Das and

Swetha Shri work for SAATHII, a sexual health and rights non-governmental organisation (NGO), in various capacities. Between them, they also work on a range of issues from HIV/STI counselling and building community leadership and networks of stakeholders to facilitate legal and medical aid for queer and trans individuals, seeking inclusions within social protections and livelihood domains. Rahmathullah, who also co-authored the piece, is a trans man and helps advance trans community welfare in Chennai.

Kavish Kaushik is a forty-nine-year-old proud trans man and community leader from Haryana who chose to begin his medical transition at the age of forty-four after decades of silently battling gender dysphoria. He founded the Vimanastha Haryana Trans Group working for the dignity, rights and visibility of transgender persons across Haryana and beyond.

Ronit Jha was born in Bihar's Sitamarhi, in 2001 and has a BA and an MA in History from Patna. He is among India's first trans man sub-inspectors. Since childhood, he dreamt of wearing the uniform and serving the nation. Through determination and hard work, he turned that dream into reality.

Amritananda Chakravorty is a lawyer based in New Delhi with extensive experience in LGBTI rights litigation and advocacy. She has degrees in Political Science (Hons.) from Lady Shri Ram College for Women and an LL.B. from Faculty of Law, University of Delhi. In 2017, she started her own practice and currently runs a law firm, Chakravorty, Samson and Munoth, with two other partners.

Vikram Phukan is a Mumbai-based theatre practitioner and writer working across performance, dramaturgy, pedagogy and curation. His writing has appeared in major Indian publications, and he teaches at Drama School Mumbai while curating theatre at Hubba. Through Theatre Jil Jil Ramāmani and collaborations with cultural organisations, he creates performance works and develops projects focused on contemporary and queer theatre in India.

Bonita Rajpurohit offered one of the breakout performances of 2024 in the acclaimed Dibakar Banerjee film, *Love Sex aur Dhoka 2* (also *LSD 2*). A mumblecore-influenced filmmaker, she wrote, directed, acted and edited the short film *IYKYK* (2024), which won the Best Emerging Indian Filmmaker award at the Kashish Pride Film Festival. Her second short film *We Can Hear the Same Music* was first runner-up in Best Film category of the 48-hour Filmmaking Challenge held at the 55th International Film Festival of India (IFFI).

Tashi Choedup is a trans feminine Buddhist monastic in Tibetan tradition. They are a social justice activist with seventeen years of engagement in the areas of farmer suicides, palliative care, domestic workers rights, interfaith dialogue and LGBTQIA+ rights. Their primary focus is towards integrating Buddhist contemplative practices with social justice action and practices. They are currently involved with Queer-Trans Wellness & Support Center in Hyderabad, India, which they co-founded with a friend.

Oviya V. is a demiromantic demisexual author of *Being AroAce*, a book about underrepresented identities such as aromantic asexuals. She is currently pursuing her undergraduate degree in astronomy in the USA.

Vasavi Kalluru (Vasu) is currently pursuing an MA in Social Work with a specialisation in mental health from Tata Institute of Social Sciences, Mumbai. They did their undergraduate degree in psychology with honors from the University of Delhi and they are deeply passionate about the mental health of marginalised communities. As a Dalit trans person in higher academia, their anti-caste feminist values heavily guide their work to understand human behaviour and the complexities of mental health issues

Ankur Tangade is a stand-up comedian and human rights activist from Beed, Maharashtra. With extensive experience in public speaking, performance and facilitating workshops on issues like women's safety and sexual wellness, she co-founded Blue Material, India's first Dalit-led comedy collective, in 2022. In 2025, she created and toured Da-Lit Queer, India's first DBA (Dalit, Bahujan, Adivasi) queer fest.

Prathyush Parasuraman is a culture writer, journalist and film critic. He writes 'Counter Culture', the fortnightly column for *Frontline* magazine. His debut book is the film monograph, *On Beauty: The Cinema of Sanjay Leela Bhansali*, and his queer short story, 'Two Bi Two', was published in a Bombay anthology, *The Only City*.

Shripad Sinnakaar is a writer from Mumbai, writing on slums, caste and migration. His works are published in *The White Review No. 33*, *Mousse Magazine*, *The Funambulist* and *Wasafiri*. Presently, he is mobilising language against the Dharavi redevelopment project in Mumbai.

Susan Dias, along with her partner Aditi Anand, was one of the petitioners in the same-sex marriage equality case that the Supreme Court heard in 2023. A chartered accountant by profession, Susan has also been closely involved with the movement for legalisation and development of the Indian indigenous flower-based Mahua spirit. She lives in Gurugram with her partner, their son and their dog.

ACKNOWLEDGEMENTS

It is a somewhat surreal thing to make a book—it only happens when everyone involved in it *wills* it to happen, and continues to do so, with grace and patience, over the course of its coming together. Our first thanks are reserved for the authors who agreed to be part of this anthology. When we began discussions in 2023, the idea was to capture something that we felt was truly unique about where we stood as a country. Our gender and sexual identities are deeply woven with other locations like our caste and class and regionality. Thus, there is no single, overarching experience of what it means to be queer. Yet, given that the movement that coalesced around a barbaric colonial law still remains fresh in our memories, there is certainly a feeling of an overarching connection, which joins our disparate experiences of the LGBTQIA+ identity soup.

But how much weight can 'queer' carry? Does queer have anything to say about the climate, about the poison in the air, about eighteen-hour bone-crunching workdays? About authoritarian politics and every kind of sectarianism? When missiles rain from the sky and one's breath is choked by gunfire, when the unbearable tragedy of war and genocide slips into the everyday, when violence is orgy and prejudice is politics—what, then, is even queer?

The two years or so we dreamt of and wrestled with this anthology have been wondrous and frustrating. It has stripped away our fantasy of control and humbled us about our limitations. We couldn't do an open-call, but we hope to be able to do one in the future. We are more alive to the possibilities and constraints of the languages we speak and the ones we don't, the tongues whose lilt is lost on us, the spaces and pin codes we move in and the ones we don't. Quality, that loaded word with reverberations of caste, class and location, both helped and hurt us. In commissioning, chasing—what is an editor if not a beat cop—and condensing, we fought about ideas, writers and diversity. We kicked ourselves for not thinking of this or that. We wondered what queer writing—or indeed, a queer writer—is, and collapsed under the weight that the English language brings with it.

If then this book sits in your hand today, it is because of the thirty-six-odd writers and illustrators who held 'queer' in their hands and helped it metamorphose into something living. Sure-footed writers of English jostled for space with authors whose delicious puns and twists resisted any mutilation, those who had never written before, but imagined the sky, and those who never thought of writing, but dreamt up the moon. Over many commissions, conversations, telephone calls, translations, recordings, clarifications, requests and trepidation, suddenly, one fine day, the manuscript emerged. It had leaked from between our fingers. It stood on the shoulders of the many writers, published and unpublished, who had come before us and broken ground. More will do so in the future. Some will fill the gaps we couldn't. Some will pry new openings we didn't even think of. Our only hope is that this book becomes a signpost for this moment in our histories. If it does so, it is because of the labour of the people who built something worth cherishing. If it doesn't, the failing is entirely our own.

Parmesh Shahani, an extraordinary thinker and even more extraordinary doer, caught our drift, helped us hone it and gave the initial impetus. V.K. Karthika often played the devil's advocate and, in every meeting, lived up to her well-earned renown as a visionary editor–publisher. The MoU between Godrej DEI and Westland Books, which aims to bring out books about queer India, has the potential to transform the way our society understands and accepts the other: this is what queer politics fundamentally entails. We are not just grateful, but excited to see what other books populate this imprint.

Sanghamitra and Sanjana showed us the grit it takes to work with journalists who try to stick to book deadlines in the face of several others. *Hindustan Times* editor Sukumar Ranganathan encouraged us and gave us the much-needed time and space to work on this book. Our colleagues and friends in an extraordinary newsroom always enriched our perspective and tummies.

For Dhrubo, one mother gave life and another made it worth living; friends—queer or otherwise—who held the hope of a different world in their palms; we built something against the cold, not a wall but a greenhouse, warm and overgrown. And Dr B.R. Ambedkar, who dreamt of a life of dignity when none thought it possible.

For Dhamini, the queer and bio families, friends, lovers, elders and children with whom one exists—in contravention to, as a product of, and occasionally, deeply in love with—thank you for holding me. The feminists who prised open the grip of heteropatriarchal control over our bodies, one white-knuckled fingertip at a time; the queers who were here before us and bore the brunt of hatred on theirs; the activists who, shaking with anger at our inhumanity, dried up their marrow seeking a more equitable world; the poets and singers who made it all bearable, and still do in dark times—I write because you existed, and still do.

And finally, for every piece of queer writing and book over the centuries; the anthologies and collections cobbled together in times more difficult with resources less abundant; the people who held stories inside them even when they didn't dare say it out loud; the mimeographed zines stapled by hand in the back rooms of borrowed spaces; the little magazines that travelled city to city in someone's bag because they were too dangerous to mail; the hours spent in police stations or shelters for a scrap of safety; the women who underlined passages in borrowed library books and left them on shelves for another to find; the diaries that were burned before they could be read; and the stories held inside a body in silence for decades, only to spout forth in an inland letter destined for an unmarked post box, hoping for a future better than their present. You made literature out of longing. Thank you.